A City Ch Jennings

Published by Mission Point Press
2554 Chandler Rd.
Traverse City, MI 49696
(231) 421-9513

www.MissionPointPress.com

ISBN: 978-1-954786-47-9
Library of Congress Control Number: 2021917054

Printed in the United States of America

THE FIRST CENTURY OF SERVICE

A City Church

Linna Place

Country Club Christian Church
1921 · 2021

MISSION POINT PRESS

To the people of Country Club Christian Church
and all of our neighbors in Kansas City.

Preface

Country Club Christian Church in Kansas City, Missouri, is honoring its 100th anniversary in 2021. This account has been written as part of the churchwide commemoration of that anniversary, but it is intended to be more than a celebratory narrative. The church is a member of the Disciples of Christ denomination, a movement, and now an institution, that has been shaped by and contributed to the people and events of the United States from its earliest days, for nearly two hundred years. The compelling issues, values, and events that have defined our country: the frontier, wars, race relations, social justice, immigration, political and social unrest, the impact of industrialization, our cultural legacy, and so much more, have been integral to making Country Club Christian Church what it is today.

The history of a church is in many ways a biography, a collective biography to be sure, but an account that follows a narrative arc that starts with a birth, moves through a sometimes turbulent period of development, to an eventual maturity that continues to experience growth and change. A church can be said to have a personality and character; it interacts with the larger systems of which it is a part. To view a church in this way places an emphasis on the whole rather than the parts — the many individuals that together comprise church. And those individuals who do receive attention in an account such as this are generally in visible positions of leadership and authority. An understandable strategy, of course; it would be impossible, and meaningless, to attempt to discuss individual members in a church the size of Country Club Christian, but there are costs. Names are omitted, but not through neglect or oversight. Country Club Christian is here, because people have been here always, offering their unstinting service and devotion to the church they love that would not exist without them.

So many individuals have contributed to the writing of this history, and to the best of my ability I will acknowledge them with gratitude. But this is above all a story that has been created by many people, named and unnamed. More than ten years ago a History Committee, under the direction of Craig Doty, took on the enormous task of organizing church files, records, and objects, now recorded in a master finding aid. This book could not have been written without that archive.

Reverend Joe Walker was assigned the task of staff liaison, and has been unstinting in his support, ideas and encouragement. *Emeritus* Minister Dr. George Gordon, who has an apparently limitless record and institutional memory of his decades at Country Club, gave many hours of time describing the people and events that shaped the church. Senior Minister Carla Aday has employed the church's history in sermon series during the Centennial Year, with the happy consequence of bringing in still more information and memories from those who heard them. Former *Kansas City Star* editor, Jim Fitzpatrick, conducted many interviews with members. They are recognized in the source list at the end. A number of individuals in addition to Reverend Aday, Reverend Walker, and Dr. Gordon, read and commented on sections of the book: Dr. Mike Graves, Kay Barnes, Tom Van Dyke, Dr. William Shoop, Jim Fitzpatrick, Lesley Holt, and Mary McClure. To each of them, warm thanks.

The writing and research for this book were made possible by a generous grant from the R.A. Long Foundation in Kansas City. Mr. Long was a major philanthropist and very active member of the Disciples of Christ denomination, and it was his life's dream to make Kansas City a center for the denomination's mission.

By the end of the 20th century, church leaders began to ask, "What does it mean to *be church* in this time and place?" The question has served as an overarching guide to the creation of long-term plans and goals. A large portion of this book has been written during the Covid pandemic that began in March of 2020 and continues to the present day. In that time "What does it mean to *be church*?" has become far more than a driver of strategic planning. It is the fundamental basis for continuing as a viable community of faith in ways that could not have been imagined just a year ago. "Behold, I make all things new," has been both a challenge and a promise, grounded in our understanding of the past as a guide to the future.

LFP
June 2021

Amy Guthrey

Table of Contents

Preface   Page vii

Foreword, by Reverend Carla Aday   Page xiii

Introduction   Page xv

Chapter 1: Disciples Origins: An American
Religious Movement   Page 1

Chapter 2: A City Church: The Growth
of an Urban Ministry   Page 15

Chapter 3: Brookside Days: Meeting in the
Upper Room   Page 20

Chapter 4: Stone by Stone: The New Church
on Ward Parkway   Page 33

Chapter 5: Church Women: From Church Parlor
to Church Board   Page 56

Chapter 6: Between Two Wars: The Church
Responds to Crime and Depression   Page 73

Chapter 7: A Time for War: At Home and in Uniform   Page 100

Chapter 8: Objects of Faith: The Visual Expressions
of Community and Belief   Page 117

Chapter 9: A Singing Congregation:
The Sounds of Worship   Page 128

Chapter 10: Faithful in a New World: Baby Boom,
Cold War, and Church Crisis   Page 133

Chapter 11: Activism: Civil Rights, Vietnam,
and Community Engagement   Page 152

Chapter 12: Century's End: Affirming the Past,
Envisioning the Future   Page 189

Chapter 13: To 'Be Church': Planning for the
Second Century   Page 209

Endnotes   Page 221

Sources and Works Cited   Page 233

Index   Page 241

Foreword

For the past thirty-three years, I have spent most of my days inside the walls of this church, and more importantly inside the folds of this community of faithful Disciples of Christ members called Country Club Christian Church. That means my own story overlaps with one third of the hundred-year history of this congregation. I served as an associate under three senior ministers I admired greatly: Brice, Cueni and Miles. And I enjoyed watching senior minister *emeritus* Lawrence Bash come up to church every week for worship after he retired, often with a book tucked under his arm that he thought the pastor might enjoy. While reading many drafts of this book, I developed an even deeper appreciation for the men whose portraits I have walked past for decades: Combs, who preached from day one; Grafton who led us through the painful WWII years; and Wyle whose short tenure left a lasting impact.

When we read the Bible, we are reading the stories of how our spiritual ancestors experienced God. In that vein, this book adds to the canon. It bears witness to how our forebearers experienced the divine and followed a call to love and serve in a particular social context and moment of history. Dr. Linna Place gives an honest account of our history that, like Scripture, occasionally exposes our flawed human vulnerabilities and culture-bound decisions that a later reading of the Gospel exposes as broken or not illuminated by the Spirit. But as with Scripture, the knowing of our own faith narrative invites us to examine how we too are vulnerable to missing the mark with God. History is a great teacher.

When I arrived in 1988, we still had charter members attending and their stories of our birth inspired and challenged. In this book, Dr. Place brings their names to life with compelling clarity. The members built and sustained the church with courage and conviction. We read this book, not only for information about our heritage, but so that we might know our own spiritual DNA. In the stories of our forebearers we may recognize ourselves. The goal of this book is to glimpse the God who has claimed us and now comes alive in us.

The First Century of Service

The church first gathered in homes in 1919, just as the global flu epidemic finished ravaging so much of Kansas City. They must have been eager to gather and start life over. Now, one hundred years later, we too have lived through a pandemic. Now it is our turn to rise up and invite our neighbors to love one another and extend hospitality and grace to the city, nation and world. It is our turn to become the body of Christ that will shape the future. With courage, hope and joy, we create the next chapter.

Reverend Carla Aday
Senior Minister
Country Club Christian Church

Introduction

In 1931, R. E. Robertson, a charter member of Country Club Christian Church in Kansas City, wrote his recollections of the early days of the church. His and several other memoirs provide an invaluable and rich portrait of the history of the church that began with a meeting at the home of Mr. and Mrs. Frank Gentry in the fall of 1919, called by Reverend Frank L. Bowen, a Disciples of Christ minister. Reverend Bowen had a plan.

~~~~

Frank Bowen was the official Disciples of Christ "missionary" to the greater Kansas City area and the director of the Kansas City Missionary Society in the early 20th century. His assignment was to evangelize, to identify locations for new missions that could develop into churches, and to provide leadership in the building of those churches. He had been raised in a Disciples family and church in Rock Island, Illinois. As a young man, he announced his commitment to the ministry and applied for a scholarship to attend seminary. Some years later, a writer to the *Christian Century* recalled the less than promising review of young Bowen's application by the scholarship committee. "He was well indorsed (sic) by the church at Rock Island, but the indorsers (sic) said frankly that, in their opinion, it was questionable whether the elements of a successful preacher were in him ... Finally, a committee member spoke up: 'Brethren, let's take the risk and give the boy a chance.' Then it was so voted."[1]

That lukewarm assessment was soon refuted by Bowen's energy and obvious ability. After an initial assignment in rural Illinois, he was sent to Kansas City in 1897, where he and his wife, Mary, spent many years. They were spectacularly successful in a calling that was regularly recognized by major religious publications of the time. It was a day-to-day, on-the-ground effort as they "went up and down the boulevards and streets of the city, searching out families, gathering them into Sunday schools, in tents, store buildings, homes until they were ready to organize and build churches."[2] After more than two decades in the city, Bowen looked back over their work that he recounted in a sermon, "The Message of Twenty-one Years in Kansas City":

> Thirty Christian churches stand where about half that number stood when I came here from Illinois. We have established twelve new churches besides keeping several of the older ones from going to pieces at times. We have raised $250,000 and added 5,000 members to our church rolls. Marriages and funerals I can't begin to estimate but they've come along by hosts. As my work has always been largely in new additions in the city, I can say that the people in those sections have all been progressive in working up new churches in their communities. And the co-operation of the older Churches with new ones has been admirable too. Of course, things haven't all been done without work, but just the same I'm ready for twenty-one more years of missionary duty here. [3]

While Missouri had been a fertile ground for Disciples' work from the beginning of the Restoration Movement, Kansas City had lagged far behind. Francis Marion Rains, a Disciples leader in the late 19th and early 20th centuries, reminisced in 1919: "What wonders have been wrought here in America! Only forty years ago we had one church in Kansas City, which was divided over the organ! We were a feeble folk all the way from the mouth of the Missouri River to its source."[4] In January, 1921, *The Christian Century* again recognized Bowen's work, stating that "Kansas City is probably the strongest city center of the Disciples denomination... [Bowen's] policy has been to organize a new church and stay with it himself until it was safely on its feet. This policy has been carried out by means of the active support of all the churches of the denomination in the city. Their official boards maintain a unified organization for the direction of city mission work." The article ended with the intriguing news that the Bowens had been called to Los Angeles, but they had not yet decided whether to accept, concluding that "it seems unlikely that he will consent to sever his relationship with the Kansas City churches where his work continues fruitful."[5] The Bowens stayed in Kansas City for more than forty years.

The topic of discussion for the November meeting was another Kansas City church. Bowen had identified the new Country Club District

Frank and Mary Bowen, Disciples of Christ Missionaries to Kansas City for more than forty years. Founders of many churches, including Country Club Christian. *Missouri Valley Special Collections, Kansas City Public Library, Kansas City, Missouri.*

being developed by J. C. Nichols as a promising location. Nichols, born in Olathe, Kansas in 1880, was making his reputation in the Kansas City area, not only as a builder but as a designer of communities. He intended these communities to maintain permanence and stability that was assured by the presence of schools, churches, and shops. He was strongly influenced in his visions of community by several early trips to Europe, concluding that "European cities taught me never to apologize for beauty in city planning."[6] He readily supported the Parks and Boulevard Movement that was a national phenomenon in the late 19th and early 20th centuries, and was particularly strong in Kansas City under the leadership of George E. Kessler, a protégé of the famed New York park designer Frederick Law Olmstead.

In addition to providing what Nichols often referred to as the "amenities" of residential communities, he sought to maintain tight control of all details of community creation, including property ownership through a code of deed restrictions or covenants. The covenants governed "how the land could be used, what types of buildings could be constructed on it, and to whom it could be sold."[7] The last point specifically targeted African-Americans and Jews, and in the racially segregated world of Kansas City, the term "restricted" was a well-understood code that defined residential areas for decades, long after they were ruled illegal by the courts.

Nichols believed that what surrounded residential areas was as important as what was established within them, contributing to their longevity and value. Downtown Kansas City was a significant distance in time and miles for people moving to the new subdivisions and he proposed carefully managed commercial sites, or "shopping centers," strategically placed to meet the day-to-day needs of residents.[8] The first of these was the Brookside Shops anchored at 63rd Street and Brookside Boulevard. Nichols bought part of the once vast Wornall Homestead in 1909, but World War I and attendant economic uncertainty delayed the start of construction until September 1919. He had astutely sold one of the Brookside lots to the City for the purpose of housing police and fire services — essential to neighborhood security and stability. The first major construction, the Brookside Building, was a multi-purpose structure with a large second floor that became known as Community Hall. Community Hall would soon be the site of social gatherings, dance classes, Masonic Lodge meetings, and the early gatherings of the new Country Club Christian Church.[9]

The Brookside Building, 1919, the original meeting place for the new church at 63rd and Brookside. *CCCC Archives*

Reverend Bowen brought together a group of Disciples men to provide leadership for the new church. They began to meet regularly at the Brookside Hotel, built in 1918 at the corner of 54th and Oak Streets, across from Second Presbyterian Church that had been finished in 1915. The Brookside Hotel was a residential facility that had recently become home to Langston Bacon and his wife, Martha, who had extended an invitation to the Bowens to hold their meetings there. The Bacons had been leading members of Independence Boulevard Christian Church in northeast Kansas City, where Langston had been chairman of the board, a position he would soon assume at Country Club Christian Church. "Judge" Bacon, as he was always addressed, was an attorney and Justice of the Peace as well as a successful businessman. Marjorie Cupp Jenkins, a charter member whose family joined when she was still a girl, recalled that some Sunday services were also held in the early days in the lounge of the Brookside Hotel. [10]

Brookside Hotel and Brookside Drive, Kansas City, Mo.

The Brookside Hotel, a residential building that was home to Langston Bacon, the first chair of the CCCC Board, and the regular board meeting place for several years. It has had many identities through the years and today is once again a luxury residence. *Missouri Valley Special Collections, Kansas City Public Library KCMO*

Throughout that first year of organizing under Bowen's guidance, the leadership committee canvassed the neighborhood, calling on residents who were Disciples. They found about sixty people who were enthusiastic about a new neighborhood church, and who promised to support it. By September 1920, Bowen was ready to move forward. The recently completed Brookside Community Hall, down the street from the Hotel, was, everyone concurred, a good place to meet, and the J. C. Nichols Company agreed to rent the Hall on Sundays. On October 17, 1920, those sixty individuals gathered together in the Hall; Country Club Christian Church was launched.

Some adjustments in the arrangements were necessary from the outset. The Hall was used for dances on Saturday nights and the floor was waxed for that purpose, with the unintended result that the slippery floor proved a nuisance if not outright hazard on Sunday mornings. There was the problem with the folding chairs that tended to collapse when the occupant adjusted position; a suspiciously high occurrence of these mishaps seemed to occur among the younger attendees. The Nichols Company finally agreed to lay a canvas flooring and as temperatures soared on the second floor, also provided two fans. [11] Above all, there was the "hubbub" as Marjorie Jenkins described it: one big room whose walls and center were lined with Sunday school classes, separated only by canvas hangings, "where all the teachers were talking at once." [12] None of these issues deterred worshippers whose numbers continued to increase.

Community Hall on the second floor of the Brookside Building: slippery floors, canvas dividers, an ever-expanding congregation that stretched the space. *The State Historical Society of Missouri Research Center-Kansas City*

CHAPTER 1

Disciples Origins: An American Religious Movement

The Bowens' designation as "City Missionaries" was an indication of the profound changes that had occurred within the religious movement that began on the American frontier. The foundations of Country Club Christian Church stood firmly on more than 100 years of growth, change, and commitment that began in the early 19th century, during a thirty-year period of religious revival that came to be known as the Second Great Awakening. Following the Revolution, established churches declined, losing control and influence, and many commentators fretted over the perceived loss of religious commitment in the new nation. It was a time of religious dissent and turmoil in an era that historian Alice Felt Tyler famously termed "Freedom's Ferment."

Although the East Coast and Old South experienced religious revivals and transition, the rapidly expanding frontier offered unique challenges and opportunities to spread God's message in new ways. The "ferment" produced new religious associations often distinctly American in character, including the Shakers, the Mormons, and a large loosely connected body of believers that was variously referred to as the Restoration or Reformation Movement. The Disciples of Christ is a product of that movement, gradually evolving over the course of the 19th century into a recognized denomination. But many events, crises, and challenges would need to occur before institutional identity was confirmed. "Was this small, obscure band of Christians a movement, a sect, a church, a cult, a society, an association, or a denomination? Were they reformers, restorationists, responsible pilgrims, wayfaring strangers, or simply a rebellious, dissenting fringe? They would be known by all those names and more." [13]

Four individuals were central to the formation of this singularly American expression of faith: Thomas Campbell, his son Alexander Campbell, Barton Stone, and Walter Scott. Thomas Campbell was born in Ireland in 1763 of Scottish descent. Unlike many of his future American contemporaries, Campbell had a formal university education followed by seminary. He moved from his Anglican origins to become a Presbyterian minister for the "Seceder" Presbyterian church, whose self-evident name described its estrangement from the Church of Scotland, establishing a pattern for Campbell of not being confined by orthodoxy or hierarchy when he disagreed. He had wearied of schism, dissension and sectarianism — "fraught with the awful consequences of distracting, disturbing and dividing the flock of the Lord's heritage and of sowing discord among the brethren." [14] He was considered frail in health and his physician told him his only chance was to emigrate to America, enjoying the benefits of a long ocean voyage on the way. He did so in 1807; apparently it was an appropriate remedy as he lived to be 91.

Campbell preceded his family — wife, son Alexander, and younger children, in order to establish a home for them, and at first things went well. He was warmly welcomed and assigned to a post in Pennsylvania. He was popular with those who attended his sermons but soon ran afoul of church leadership for, among other matters, serving "open communion" to those who were not members of the Presbyterian church. After more than a year of wrangling and disputing, and a complicated series of hearings where he was "rebuked and admonished," Campbell announced that he was withdrawing from the authority of the Presbyterian governance, and was promptly suspended. He continued to preach, and in the following year, 1809, he pulled together an association of like-minded individuals that called itself the Christian Association of Washington (Pennsylvania). It was to be an independent organization, welcoming members of diverse churches, but most emphatically not proclaiming itself as a church. In his address to the group, he concluded with what became the clarion call of the Movement: Where Scripture speaks, we speak; where Scripture is silent, we are silent. [15] That simple, direct statement would not always be easily interpreted or applied. He then prepared and delivered the 56-page *Declaration and Address* that argued for a return or restoration of "primitive Christianity" — that is, practicing the faith in the simple and basic way described in the New Testament.

Campbell's son, Alexander, and the rest of the family arrived in America as the *Declaration and Address* was being brought to press. Their journey had not been easy; they were shipwrecked shortly after departure and, safely rescued, had to spend some months in Glasgow. That proved a seminal time for young Alexander who, like his father, took up studies at the university and prepared for the ministry under the guidance of prominent clerics in the city.

Thanks to his father's childhood tutelage and the university experience, Alexander was superbly educated and would employ his learning and erudition throughout the rest of his life. There was little communication between Thomas and his family while they were separated, and he and Alexander had no way of knowing that they were undergoing similar experiences of doubt and questioning about the strictures of the Presbyterian church. At that time, in order to partake of communion, in a practice dating to John Calvin's days, an individual needed to pass an examination by church leaders and elders, who would then give a small token as indication of acceptance. The token was to be submitted at the communion table on Sacrament Day, usually an annual event. In the famous and oft-told account, Alexander, who had passed his examination, agonized until the very last moment, and then walked to the table, set the token down and walked out of the Presbyterian church, never to return.

An example of the type of communion token commonly used in Scots Presbyterian churches. *https://en.wikipedia.org/wiki/Communion_token*

The Campbells were re-united in America and 21-year-old Alexander read his father's *Declaration and Address* with enthusiasm. The family moved to Washington, Pennsylvania, where Alexander spent the next six months in rigorous study under his father's guidance, and then gave his first sermon on July 15, 1810. Alexander was not ordained, one of a number of issues that once again elicited the critical scrutiny of the Presbyterian Synod, with the inevitable result that the Campbells withdrew once and for all, and proceeded to form their own church based on the initial Christian Association of Washington.

Alexander soon became the recognized leader of the new church with his father's endorsement. From early days, through a long career, he espoused the essential tenets of the Movement: "the independence of the local congregation; weekly observance of the Lord's Supper; a plurality of elders; the denial of clerical privileges and dignities; the right and duty of laymen to have a part in the edification and discipline of the church; and a conception of faith as such a belief of testimony as any man is capable of by the application of natural intelligence to the facts supplied by Scripture."[16]

In 1801, some years before the arrival of the Campbells in America, what began as a typical frontier camp meeting at Cane Ridge, Kentucky exploded into one of the largest and most famous religious events in American history, reportedly attended by as many as 20,000 people. In addition to non-stop preaching and prayer, the Cane Ridge Revival (and others to follow) was the scene of ecstatic raptures and agonized repentance in the forms of singing, screaming, fainting, and bodily spasms. One of the leaders at Cane Ridge was Barton Stone, the only American-born of the four early leaders of the Restoration Movement. In later life, Stone pulled away from what he regarded as the emotional excesses of the Revival, but it had been an important moment in his life, particularly in regard to his views on slavery. Stone was also a Presbyterian minister who found himself in profound disagreement with the doctrines of that church. When he and other revivalists who shared his views were accused of heresy by the Kentucky Synod, they pulled away to form their own church, which they called simply "Christian," agreeing to follow only the Bible for guidance.[17] Of the four early leaders, he was the most opposed to civil institutions and he "urged his followers to turn their back on civil society altogether, abstaining from jury service, political elections, and office-seeking."[18]

Stone and Alexander Campbell met in 1824 while Campbell was

on a speaking tour in Kentucky. They were kindred spirits; in Stone's words, "Our views were one,"[19] although there were actually signifi-cant differences in both theological perspectives and their personalities. "Campbell was extroverted, aggressive, self-reliant, a dominating per-sonality; Stone's demeanor was self-effacing, gracious, modest, irenic [e.g., in favor of reconciling differing religious points of view], forbear-ing. Campbell enjoyed debates; Stone disliked them and declined every opportunity to do so."[20] And, perhaps the longest-lasting legacy, they differed in their choice of name for the Movement: Stone's followers pre-ferred "Christian" while the Campbellites called themselves "Disciples." The similarities, however, were more compelling than the differences and eventually the two movements merged in 1832, to be joined later by adherents of Walter Scott.

The "merger" was not an administrative act, but a gradual process dependent upon individual congregations and their leaders agreeing to unite.[21] Prior to that merger Campbell, in 1815, had approved an associa-tion with the Baptists that proved far less successful. He promptly started a periodical (his first) duly named the *Christian Baptist* that he used to express his always strong, and often pugnacious views. He announced that "I intend to continue in connection with this people so long as they permit me to say what I believe, to teach what I am assured of, and to cen-sure what is amiss in their views and practices."[22] His less than gracious reference to presumed brethren as *this people*, and clear intent to *censure their views* when he felt it necessary did not portend a warm relationship, and by the 1830s everyone seems to have recognized that the primary basis for affiliation, the shared practice of adult immersive baptism, was insufficient for the long-term.

Walter Scott, also a Presbyterian minister from Scotland, was the youngest of the four men. He read and was influenced by many of the same writers who had shaped the thinking of the Campbells. Not long after his immigration to America in 1818, he met Alexander Campbell. Scott brought much-needed organizational skills to the Movement. He was an able preacher who had the gift of presenting sometimes puzzling theological concepts in a clear, direct manner. He most famously created a "five-finger exercise" that ticked off the basic elements of belief: faith, repentance, baptism, remission of sins, and gift of the Holy Spirit. The "exercise" was a regular and very popular feature of his sermons, readily adopted by those who heard him.

Barton Stone and Thomas Campbell were the authors, respectively, of the two most significant statements in Disciples history: *The Last Will and Testament of the Springfield Presbytery* (1804), and the previously mentioned *Declaration and Address of the Christian Association of Washington* (1809). Despite considerable difference in length, the two documents laid out the basic assumptions that would inform and guide the Movement as well as be the basis for controversy. They share an emphasis on Christian unity and warn of the evils of schism and sectarianism; the authority of the laity and the importance of individual insight and rational apprehension of faith; the independence and self-governance of individual churches; reliance on Scripture (particularly the New Testament) as the one source of divine word; and rejections of specific creeds as a basis for admission into fellowship.

None of these principles was unique to the Movement nor, for that matter, to America. The well-educated Scottish preachers had read and been strongly influenced by, among others, the writings of John Locke, who argued that rational thought and religious belief were not incompatible. Locke also argued for Christian unity. The authority of the laity (based on the assumption that human beings could make reasoned decisions about faith) and the independence of individual congregations were concepts that found ready acceptance in the new democracy among Protestants and also Catholics, especially in the case of the immigrant groups of the later 19th century.

"Pioneers in the great religious reformation in the nineteenth century," a famous engraving depicting the four founders of what became the Disciples denomination. *Library of Congress, Prints and Photographs Division.*

There were many able leaders in the early years in addition to the four profiled here, but they arguably had the strongest voices. Of them Alexander Campbell assumed the greatest role: a larger-than-life figure who strode across the frontier exhorting, praying, preaching, baptizing, writing, and founding churches. Campbell made at least four trips to Missouri; the journey in 1852 was especially well-documented.[23] As always, he kept his followers informed of his travels through his second periodical, *The Millennial Harbinger.* One goal was to raise money for an endowed chair at Bethany College, which he had founded in 1840, in Virginia, today West Virginia. Missouri was settled early on by adherents of the Movement, many of whom came from Kentucky, Virginia, and the Carolinas, and Campbell, who resided in the South, had learned that he had better luck with fundraising in slave-holding states.

He began his Missouri travels in Hannibal in November, came across the entire state to St. Joseph, Liberty, Independence and on back east again through Arrow Rock, and Columbia, finally arriving in St. Louis, with many stops and visits along the way. He maintained a grueling schedule, preaching regularly and meeting with prominent religious and community leaders. He spoke at colleges, including several that were founded for female students, where he abjured them to always remember that "flattery is deceitful and beauty is vain, but a woman that fears the Lord shall be praised."[24]

Campbell had lunch with Disciples clergyman James Shannon, at that time the President of the University of Missouri, and a highly controversial figure and rabid pro-slavery advocate, who, by all accounts, gave new meaning to the term "fire-eater."[25] He also addressed the Missouri House of Representatives. Although he was often lavishly and very comfortably entertained by various hosts, there were episodes of frontier roughness as well: swollen rivers, ice cold winter temperatures, and one alarming journey in an open wagon driven by two men who "freely paid their respects to the frontier horn, well fitted with corn."[26] He returned home, after a journey of more than 2,800 miles, with more than $16,000 for the Bethany endowment.

A number of factors contributed to the rapid growth of the Restoration Movement, including the popularity of public debates, the widespread dissemination of periodicals, and the establishment of institutions of higher learning. All of these were nurtured by the intellectual and scholarly depth of the original founders. Public debates were a common feature of 19th century society, a source of entertainment and edification.

They focused on every imaginable topic ranging from secular to spiritual and provided an opportunity for people to come together, often from great distances, in a shared forum. Alexander Campbell, by virtue of intellect and temperament, particularly enjoyed debates and he excelled in his performances. He participated in at least five highly publicized events, none more famous than the Owen-Campbell match-up in 1829 in Cincinnati, when Campbell responded to a challenge from Robert Owen, a staunch non-believer who had founded the communal settlement at New Harmony, Indiana. The event was spread across two weeks, from April 13-21, in morning and afternoon sessions. Although wide ranging in focus, the primary purpose was to debate the truth of religion, Christianity in particular.

Among the large audience was Frances Trollope, an English visitor on tour in America (and the mother of Victorian novelist Anthony Trollope), whose *Domestic Manners of the Americans*, published in 1832, became and remains a classic account of life in the early Republic. Her lively description of the event described Campbell as being far more prepared for the debate than Owen, and it is clear that she was partial to Campbell, noting that "his person, voice, and manner [were] all greatly in his favor."[27] She observed that the debaters remained in good humor and regularly dined with one another. There are many detailed accounts of the debate;[28] to read them is not only to appreciate the education and erudition of the two participants, but also that of the audience who listened day after day to complex, often abstruse arguments.

The well-attended event was held in a large Methodist meeting house, capable of seating more than 1,000 people. Mrs. Trollope was struck by how well-dressed many of the attendees were, reflecting with evident surprise that matters were different in America from England; even working people dressed like the upper classes! While there was no official winner, Campbell had clearly triumphed and left with a greatly enhanced reputation. Mrs. Trollope was obviously captivated by the entire process, but could not refrain from something of a verbal sniff that "all this I think could have only happened in America. I am not quite sure that it was very desirable it should have happened anywhere."[29]

"The simplest, and probably the best way to trace the course of Disciples history is to study the editors and periodicals of the church."[30] Periodicals were another important means of evangelizing and communication within the Movement. In the 1820-1860 period alone, preachers and laymen produced over one hundred journals, magazines, and newsletters,

A lithograph of the Owens-Campbell debate in Kentucky in 1829.
The debate received widespread attention and a lengthy description
in *Domestic Manners of the Americans*, by Frances Trollope. Thomas
Campbell peers over the balcony watching his son Alexander and
Owens. *Original drawing by Auguste Hervieu. Library of Congress, Prints
and Photographs Division.*

and their literary output would remain prolific well into the 20th century.
"These publications were central to the rapid rise of the Movement, especially on the frontier where few congregations had the leadership of a
full-time pastor. Executed by the most influential editors and evangelists,
the periodicals provided guidance and leadership for the otherwise independent and unorganized series of congregations." Disciples historian
W.T. Moore added that the "Disciples of Christ do not have bishops, they
have editors." Historian Winfred E. Garrison concluded that the "editor's
chair has come nearer to being a throne of power than any other position
among the Disciples. Their newspapers served as arenas for free discussion among the brethren to settle theological issues, interpret scripture,
and promote the restoration of New Testament Christianity."[31] Alexander
Campbell, not surprisingly, published, edited and contributed to many of
them.

Colleges and seminaries were founded early in the Movement's history. Alexander Campbell established Bethany College in 1840. It originally admitted only men and its primary purpose was the training of clergy. Education was a priority for Campbell who declared that "With me education and formation of moral character are identical expressions."[32] By the outbreak of the Civil War, twenty-nine colleges had been established; six are still functioning: Bethany, Hiram, Columbia, Culver-Stockton, Chapman, and Butler University. Two of those institutions, Bethany and Butler, provided the voices for an angry debate over slavery and abolition. In 1855, fifteen years after the chartering of Campbell's Bethany College, a wealthy Disciple named Ovid Butler, along with others, founded North Western Christian University (so named because it was located in the Northwest Territories) in Indianapolis. Butler was a prominent abolitionist who declared in an 1863 book that "No one but God can own a man."[33] He and the other university founders made it clear that their institution would support an anti-slavery position.

Alexander Campbell was not pleased by competition; he had long argued that Bethany should be the educational institution for his followers. An exchange of open letters between Campbell and Butler appeared in the *Millennial Harbinger*, at first fairly civil in tone, but quickly escalating to smoke rising from the pages, particularly on Campbell's part. Butler's motives, he insisted, were "essentially local, sectional and selfish."[34] Responding collectively, the North Western Board replied that their school's location in a free state meant that the "students attending it would not be brought into contact with habits and manners that exist in populations where slavery exists." Bethany, of course, was in Virginia, a slave state, but Campbell promptly retorted that the college was in one of the *free* counties. Campbell, as the head of the school, issued an edict forbidding on-campus discussion of slavery and abolition.

One of the students openly defied the ban by giving an anti-slavery sermon at a neighboring church. He found support with other students, all of whom were promptly expelled from Bethany. They made their way to North Western where they were accepted — a breach of academic etiquette that held that schools would honor one another's disciplinary actions — and furthered the bitter dispute between Campbell and Butler. The two men had very different views of the purpose of education. Campbell believed higher education did not have a role in addressing social and political issues. Butler was convinced that it did. His views proved prescient and influenced not only higher education but also the stance of the evolving Disciples church in the next century. And it may be argued that he had the last word, for North Western Christian University was renamed Butler University not many years later.

There is an irony in the enthusiasm for debates, periodicals, and academic institutions among the early Disciples, for each provided a forum for discussion that could become dissent and disagreement in a movement grounded in an absolute commitment to unity. The leaders recognized the dilemma and at various times tried, never successfully in the long term, to avoid or suppress opportunities for divisiveness. Editors would forbid discussion of challenging topics such as slavery, and then rescind the ban. Schools tried to manage curriculum as well as campus dialogues, again with marginal success, as the Butler/Bethany episode illustrated. The same movement that argued that human reasoning and diverse opinions were to be valued struggled to affirm unity and brotherhood. And in the background, the drums of war had begun a steady beat.

Both Alexander Campbell and Barton Stone were slaveholders but similarities in their responses to that institution ended there. Stone was born into a genteel, slave-holding family in Maryland whose fortunes declined after the early death of his father. He inherited two slaves whom he freed as a matter of conscience and morality after his experience in the 1801 Cane Ridge Revival, as did many other participants who found slavery incompatible with Christian teaching. His anti-slavery views predated the Revival; he had been repelled by the abuse he had witnessed on his journey through the South as he moved west to Kentucky. He eventually left Kentucky for Jacksonville, Illinois, sickened by the institution and his own inability to further the cause of abolition. In old age, he moved to his daughter's home in Hannibal, Missouri. In *Ancestors,* William Maxwell's evocative memoir about his midwestern Disciples forebears, he writes about Stone's young grandsons who played with their neighbor and close friend, Samuel Clemens. Years later, writing as Mark Twain, Samuel recalled the childhood escapades with Stone's grandsons, and their somewhat cantankerous grandfather, immortalized in *Tom Sawyer* and *Huckleberry Finn.*[35]

Campbell's wife had inherited slaves from her father and by the laws of the time, they became her husband's property. He too freed his slaves, but only when they were in their twenties, arguing that earlier manumission would leave them unprepared for life in the world. His views on slavery were complex and, some would argue, conflicting and ambivalent. He and his father were avowedly anti-slavery, but Campbell did not support the abolition movement. Committed above all to Christian unity, he understood slavery and abolition to be profoundly divisive within the Movement. His extensive properties in Virginia included his home and Bethany College. He was concerned about the potentially hostile responses from fellow citizens if he was too adamant in his statements. Over the years he alternated between openly engaging the issue, particularly in his widely read periodical, *The Millennial Harbinger*, and imposing a policy of suppression when matters grew too heated. Scripture, he argued, certainly speaks of slavery, but it neither condemns nor supports it.

Scripture, of course, was used by nearly all who debated the slavery/ abolition issue, whichever side they were on, often using the same citation, such as Paul's Letter to Philemon. Campbell took the position that without explicit scriptural guidance slavery was a matter of "opinion" — specifically political opinion, and politics was outside the realm of church doctrine.[36] Citizens of a democracy were entitled to form and vote upon their own opinions derived from their God-given attributes of reason. In 1845 he launched a series of articles, with an opening essay by his father, that laid out "Our Position to American Slavery." He hoped that in his role as the highly respected leader of the Movement, his articles would close further divisive debate.[37] It was not to be.

After the war, the accepted interpretation by chroniclers of the Movement was that the Disciples, alone among mainstream Protestant groups, did not divide over slavery. Minister Moses Lard's summation was widely quoted for decades: "We can never divide,"[38] and Disciples historian J.W. Garrison declared that "Methodists, Baptists, and Presbyterians divided ... Disciples were nearly equal in numbers, North and South. They might easily have divided, but they did not."[39] The reality is considerably more nuanced. Methodists, Presbyterians, and Baptists had nationally institutionalized organizations. The loosely connected churches of the Restoration Movement, always fluid and characterized by diversity, did not, prompting one Disciples historian to conclude, with admirable brevity, that "one reason we didn't divide was that we didn't have anything to divide."[40]

The differences and dissensions that had been present in the Movement from the beginning, encouraged by a policy of openness and welcome to all without any creedal requirements, made rapid growth possible. Those differences were nurtured and reinforced during the Civil War. Despite the passionate pleas for neutrality and unity from the leaders, many adherents found themselves responding to the claims of other loyalties. The sons of both Campbell and Stone (who had died in 1844) wore Confederate uniforms. As a young man prior to the conflict James A. Garfield, devout Disciple and lay leader who would become the 20th President of the United States, argued that participation in politics was unchristian. But he increasingly became convinced that slavery was evil and must be ended, and he enlisted in the Union army, rising to the rank of major general during a distinguished time of service. Others struggled with their profound opposition to raising arms against their brothers. Unlike the peace churches (Amish, Mennonite, Brethren) the Movement had never made pacifism a matter of creed and membership. It was another personal decision, up to each individual to determine, and many chose to go into combat.

Alexander Campbell died in 1866, the last of the four original leaders of the Movement. His death and the watershed of the Civil War provide a clear demarcation between the first generation of the Restoration and those to follow. When schism finally did come, it was motivated by many circumstantial factors: sectionalism, urban/rural differences, and the industrial/agrarian dichotomy. The defeated and impoverished South remained largely agrarian and religiously conservative. The North became the locus of modernization, the sweeping juggernaut that wrought profound changes in virtually every aspect of life. Industrialism, urbanization, rapidly developing transportation and communication systems, the expansion of government, and incredible wealth for some — it was a new world. The rural and village safety nets that had protected the aged, the orphaned, the ill and disabled eroded and gradually disappeared. The burgeoning cities were slow to recognize and address those needs, but throughout the remainder of the 19th and early 20th centuries demand for social justice grew louder, and in the case of the Disciples, "their focus shifted from a divided Christendom to the needs of the world."[41]

The very diversity that had allowed the Movement to grow in pre-Civil War America was now the basis for division and sectarianism. By war's end, differences had coalesced into two broad streams: Christian Churches/Churches of Christ, and, by far the larger Christian Church (Disciples of Christ). Some argue that there were originally three branches, but contemporary scholars consider Christian Churches and Churches of Christ (there are a number of other similar names) to be loosely related as "independents." Despite the similarity of names, confusing to this day, there are circumstantial differences as well as significant theological/liturgical disagreements between them. Those differences influenced one another, forming the warp and weft of the character of individual churches and the Disciples denomination. In 1906, the U.S. Religious Census acknowledged what had been the *de-facto* situation for some time: the Disciples of Christ and the Churches of Christ were separate denominations. However, it would be many years before formal restructure confirmed that administratively.

Disciples were shaped by three growing trends: modernism in theology; ecumenical cooperation; and the concept of open membership. "Modernism" is a broad term that describes new approaches to Biblical interpretation, grounded in expertise in the languages that were the basis of the Bible (Greek and Hebrew), a belief that interpretation and understanding were ever-evolving rather than immutably fixed, and that sources beyond the Bible could inform and enrich spiritual understanding. All of this required a sophisticated level of instruction for clergy resulting in post-graduate programs at schools such as the University of Chicago, Yale, Princeton, Union Theological, and Harvard. By contrast, those who did not embrace these views, the Bible Colleges, continued to focus on undergraduate education. The often-acrimonious differences led to a "heresy trial" in 1917 at the College of the Bible in Kentucky, and while the professors who were accused of heresy in their teaching were cleared, the division within the Movement was deepened.

The push toward ecumenism was a direct rebuttal to those who continued to advocate for the original commitment to restoring primitive Christianity, rather than moving toward Christian unity. The arguments over what exactly constituted primitive Christianity had, according to the unity proponents, actually created division. Broader views of Biblical interpretation and cooperation at many levels among various religious organizations led, almost inevitably, to a policy of "open membership" on the part of Disciples churches. Open membership, in simplest terms, means that there are no requirements for joining the church. It was an old discussion dating to the earliest days of the Movement, and it too provoked bitter controversy. The conflict was never resolved, despite years of efforts to reconcile, including a major report submitted in 1948 calling for unity. From that point on, the two branches moved in different directions, culminating with formal separation and restructure in 1968. From here forward, our narrative will focus on the Disciples of Christ, the denominational identity of Country Club Christian Church. [42]

CHAPTER 2

A City Church: The Growth of an Urban Ministry

In his reflections on his time in Kansas City, Frank Bowen noted that he had always worked with city churches, a clarification that would not have the same significance today as it did then. Country Club Christian Church was one of the new generation of "city churches" that started appearing in the late 19th century in response to rapid urbanization. These churches took on the character of their urban surroundings: substantial buildings designed by architects, with multi-purpose facilities intended to meet wide-ranging needs among the congregation and the community. City churches often provoked criticism if not outright scorn from rural and small-town counterparts, as well as some Disciples leaders. The Movement had always embraced the agrarian ideal, the conception of America as the new Eden, in language that equated morality and purity with rural life. Cities, the critics declared, were centers of crime and moral corruption. As usual, the discussion was carried on in print in articles that expressed alarm with such titles as "The Problems of the Cities," and "Why Does Crime Increase?" Organs and other instrumental music, formally educated ministers, choirs, and various "societies" for promulgation of the faith became standard elements of city churches, distancing them even further from their rural brethren. [43] Underlying all this was the economic reality that increasingly divided urban and rural churches and was the basis for passionate views on the merits and perils of wealth in God's work.

Those Disciples who advocated for urban ministries argued that cities were now the sites of pressing needs: more people, many without church affiliation, and social and economic issues that posed a "monstrous threat to Americanism, Protestantism, and capitalism."[44] An early response to these concerns was the organization of evangelistic City Mission Boards such as the one Frank Bowen led so effectively in Kansas City. The City Mission Boards were intended, initially at least, to purify urban centers through evangelization, but they soon became agents of change, acknowledging an industrializing and urbanizing world. Evangelism required substantial financial support as a Disciples leader stressed in 1893:

> If we have not foothold in the cities, they [young Disciples in the cities] are lost to us, and we can ill afford to lose them, for they are the chosen, the enterprising, the self-sacrificing. They are the men who will be able to build hospitals, endow colleges, and single handed do as much as our Missionary societies … .[45]

The tone of that comment is jarring 100 years later, but in the context of the times it reflected the high regard in which business and businessmen were held by many. In 1882, Civil War veteran, Baptist minister, and eventual founder of Temple University, Russell Conwell gave a lecture that he titled "Acres of Diamonds." He would repeat that lecture almost 6,000 times in the coming decades, and publish it in a book of the same title in 1890,[46] declaring that "I say then, that you ought to have money. If you can honestly attain unto riches … it is your Christian and godly duty to do so." Andrew Carnegie's 1889 article, "The Gospel of Wealth," provided a label for the argument that wealth could — and should — be used to promote the "general good."[47] In 1925, American advertising executive Bruce Fairchild Barton published *The Man Nobody Knows*. The best-seller portrayed Jesus as an outstanding executive and "the founder of modern business."[48]

George Hamilton Combs, the future pastor of Country Club Christian Church, often spoke of the need to include businessmen in the workings of the church, invoking their qualities of efficiency and professionalism. He included admiring portraits of Kansas City businessmen in his autobiography with a full chapter devoted to his friend and benefactor R.A.

Long that he titled "There Was a Rich Man." Unlike the rich man in Jesus' parable, Combs argued, Mr. Long had used his wealth for good and worthy purposes.

The esteem for business and its practices was by no means universal, however. Disciples joined others throughout the nation in condemning the greed of Big Business and the devastating problems experienced by the vulnerable working class. In the latter 19th century, "most Disciples moderates had no systematic philosophy of social reform ... "[49] but gradually the message of a Social Gospel claimed the attention of many, especially in the cities. J. H. Garrison, a leading Disciples' editor, declared in 1894 that "it is high time [that] the Church should come to the front as the champion of justice and equal rights among men."[50]

Concrete expression of the Social Gospel took many forms, including the creation of Institutional Churches, "probably the most important innovation to come out of the new social liberalism among Disciples."[51] The purpose of Institutional Churches was to provide community service, particularly to the poor and working class. Several Kansas City Disciples congregations embraced the idea. Central Christian Church, for example, had a food pantry, maintained a kindergarten, and sponsored an employment program. Future Kansas City pastor, Reverend Burris Jenkins, who at the time was completing graduate degrees at Harvard, wrote a major essay in 1895 that made a strong argument for Institutional Churches. "The Disciples," he declared "are adapted as few religious bodies are, to the methods of work employed by the Institutional Church."[52] Acknowledging that a definition was difficult, he posited four characteristics common to all Institutional Churches:

1. The physical church is open all day every day of the week.
2. A free pew system is in place; "Men who cannot pay for pews will not go where pews are paid for." (Startling as that point is, the fact that Jenkins mentioned it in his list indicates that the practice continued in some churches.)
3. Substantial staff: "plurality of workers."
4. Dedicated space for classes, "amusements": (e.g. gymnasiums), medical facilities, etc., depending on location and population needs.

The last point in particular provoked objection from those who opposed secular activities in sacred space — *billiards,* no less! Jenkins dismissed those concerns by asserting that "there is no difference between the secular and sacred."

Burris Jenkins returned to Kansas City, his hometown, in 1907 to assume the pulpit at Linwood Christian Church. When it was destroyed by fire in 1939, he oversaw the construction of a new building, designed by Frank Lloyd Wright, at 47th Street and Main, aptly renamed Community Christian Church. For thirty-eight years he was a leading progressive Disciple locally and nationally. He and George Combs were friends and colleagues and undoubtedly influenced one another's leadership and theology. Combs devoted several pages in his autobiography to his friend, including one wry anecdote about Jenkins' generous offer to Combs, as Country Club Christian Church was launched, to feel free to recruit from the Linwood congregation. Several years later Combs received a call from Jenkins telling him that he could stop recruiting now — Linwood was feeling the financial consequences! Combs duly stopped.

A further outcome of the city evangelism movement expressed through the Social Gospel was the recognition that programs were most effective when there was inter-institutional cooperation, another prickly issue for old-line Disciples, who, from early days had warned against participating in societies and associations outside the church. The Young Men's Christian Association (YMCA), for example, while overtly spiritual in purpose refused to acknowledge sectarian boundaries, and eventually welcomed not only men, but women and children and people of all faiths. Urban churches and their pastors worked closely with the "Y" as a way to share resources and strengthen outreach to the community.

The profile of the clergy in city churches was changing as well. Pastors of urban institutions and editors of major religious periodicals were increasingly individuals who, although born in rural areas, had acquired university educations and re-located to the cities — exactly the experience of George Hamilton Combs. [53] He arrived in Kansas City in 1893, at the high point of animated discussion about the role of the church in the city and he would have been well-versed in all the arguments flying back and forth. His first Kansas City pulpit was at Independence Boulevard Church, a church that eventually boasted a gymnasium, swimming pool, and multiple organs. Combs' experiences there prepared him to address perceptions of his new church on Ward Parkway by some as serving the wealthy elite, something he did immediately upon accepting the pastoral call from Country Club. In a lengthy interview with *The Kansas City Times* (which noted that the church was simply being *referred* to as the Country Club Christian Church, since a permanent name had not been selected), Combs declared that he knew nothing or next to nothing about its constituency or its plans. My conviction is that its success and the measure of its growth will be determined solely by the measure of service it shall render the community. If the church meets a real need, it will prosper … And I am talking of religious need. This church will be concerned only with a ministry to the real religious needs of the community. It's going to be a church and not a club … The Country Club district is no different from any other district save in a mere outward and physical way. The people who live out there are just folk. They need religion as much as the North Side … I have not thought of building up a rich man's church. In the sight of Jesus there are no rich and no poor.[54]

The awkward term "Institutional Church" soon faded into disuse, but it created a model for implementing the Social Gospel and placing the church at the heart of the community, setting the path for faith and practice in the coming century.

A 1926 montage of Kansas City Disciples of Christ churches. CCCC is at the top of the second column on the left. *Missouri Valley Special Collections, Kansas City Public Library, Kansas City, Missouri.*

CHAPTER 3

Brookside Days: Meeting in the Upper Room

The first meeting in the Brookside Community Hall in October 1920 did not include a service. Bowen asked for commitments of support and thirty-six individuals gave their verbal pledge. He assessed interest and solicited ideas for developing the church, and set about organizing for the coming months. Reverend Bowen would lead the services the first three months. Sunday school classes were planned, an offering was requested for supplies to be ready by the following Sunday, and a follow-up meeting was scheduled for later in the week. Bowen also announced that he had access to 200 song books; these were duly purchased. Talk turned to the all-important matter of finding a permanent minister. At that point, one of those present, Robert Stone, spoke up. He and his family were "Combsites," he announced; if Dr. Combs could be persuaded to take the pastorate, they could be counted on. [55]

George Hamilton Combs had recently retired as the senior minister of Independence Boulevard Church in northeast Kansas City. During his twenty-seven years there he had acquired a national reputation as minister, author, and public speaker. He and his wife Martha were living comfortably in a country home they had built on Woods Chapel Road in eastern Jackson County. There he planned to garden, read, write, and venture out for the occasional guest sermon. His retirement had been a difficult and painful decision, but he had returned from volunteer service in Europe during World War I broken in spirit and body, and realized that he could not continue his former schedule. His departure received widespread attention in periodicals and newspapers.

Combs was born in Campbellsburg, Kentucky in 1864, one year before the end of the Civil War. He spent the first eight years of his life with his parents on his grandfather's 1,000-acre plantation where the newly freed slaves continued to work and live as they had always done. Their children, who addressed him as "Mr. George," were his playmates. He was a product of his time and locale, and his autobiography conveys the attitudes and worldview of the mid-nineteenth century South. When he was eight, his parents bought a small farm of their own and young George's daily routine became a much more serious matter of hard-working rural life in which he was fully engaged. While he was not particularly nostalgic for those days, he retained a love of gardening throughout his life.

In scenes reminiscent of young Harry Truman and Abraham Lincoln, Combs described his discovery of books at an early age, and he became a voracious reader. Having abandoned his boyhood ambition to be a stage-coach driver, he decided that his passion for reading supported by his rural schooling ("Two and a half miles I walked ... cross-country, over fields sometimes muddy, sometimes snow-covered ... ")[56] was preparation for his goal to be a lawyer and politician, both of which would allow him to practice his true passion: oratory. Those plans took an abrupt turn one day when he was twelve, spending time in the kitchen with his mother. Pulling a pan of biscuits from the oven she turned to him and said, "Son, I want you to be a minister." His family had Disciples roots, and the Bible was a mainstay of his early reading, but he had never considered a vocation in the church. However, he responded without hesitation, convinced that he had a call. He progressed through a series of higher education institutions: Home College (where he met the president's pretty daughter, Martha, soon to be his wife), Fairmount College, Kentucky University (now Transylvania), concluding with a doctorate from Wooster University in Ohio.

After several years as a transient country preacher with multiple churches, he received a call from a church in Shelbyville, Kentucky. He, Martha, and six-month old Pryor readily accepted, and moved to the picturesque community where they fully expected to spend their lives. Shelbyville was an appealing vacation area, especially to Kansas Citians with Kentucky roots. Dr. Combs was unaware of a visitor in the congregation one Sunday morning, but not long after a letter arrived asking him to consider assuming the pulpit at a Kansas City church. He said yes, although the conditions of the new position were not particularly appealing. As he recalled nearly fifty years later, "To this day, I am still in the dark as to the motivation of that response ... though never have I regretted it."[57] The church that he referred to as the "little church around the corner" was a fledgling congregation that became, under his leadership, the Independence Boulevard Christian Church, a flagship of the Disciples denomination. He achieved national prominence in his twenty-seven years at Independence Boulevard and was revered by his congregation.

In late March, 1912, editors of *Collier's, The National Weekly*, a popular periodical, posed a question: "Are Churches Failing?" To answer that question, they presented a series of profiles of six of "the most prominent preachers in America": a rabbi, a Catholic Priest, and four Protestant ministers. The clergymen were drawn from representative cities in which they had "wide popular acceptance."[58] George Hamilton Combs, of Independence Boulevard Christian Church, with a membership of 3,000, was one of the six. The essay that appeared on April 13, 1912, is remarkable both for its portrait of Dr. Combs as well as for its breathless and dramatic literary style. It begins with a description of the pastor as a man of "leaflike frailness" with "large brown eyes that burn with lustrous fire. He has the face of the poet." But what follows is a portrait of a consummate orator in full command of his powers. The focus of the essay is on the delivery of a Sunday sermon based on the text from Exodus 14:14, "Go forward." With gestures, long strides across the wide pulpit platform, alternating his volume of delivery from barely a whisper to an "electric thunder crashing" exhortation, and perfectly controlled timing of his utterances, he urged his congregation to avoid "standpattism," a widely used term in the early 1900s, usually with derisive intent. "Now, 'Standpattism' may or may not characterize an admirable political temper," he declared, "but certain it is that in its wider reaches it makes a sorry appeal. Standpattism is unnatural. Nature's way is the way of motion."[59]

The Brookside group organized a committee to undertake the minister search, and quickly decided to approach Dr. Combs.[60] There are several versions of how they met with him: at his home in the country, or a dinner at the City Club, a men's social club then located at the corner of Twelfth and Wyandotte Streets. Perhaps both; he agreed to look into the matter, and after some hesitation, he said yes, and that he would assume the pastorate on January 1, 1921. He described his goals in his autobiography: "I didn't want, I repeat, a great church. I wanted a little church, with all the dear intimacies of a family, of which I should be a part."[61] He also informed them that he would not expect a salary initially as he had been provided a stipend by R.A. Long at the time of his retirement. Long was the chief benefactor of Independence Boulevard Church and a close friend of Combs.

George Hamilton Combs, the first Senior Minister who served the new Church for 21 years. *CCCC Archives*

The extent and complexity of the relationship between Country Club Christian Church and Independence Boulevard Church resembles that of a large family reunion where everybody understands that they are connected but are at something of a loss to recall exactly how. The obvious link, of course, is George Hamilton Combs who served both congregations as senior pastor for a combined total of forty-seven years. Likewise, the lay leadership of Langston Bacon in each church also provided connection and continuity. Another name that would have been well-known not only to Kansas City and Missouri Disciples but nationally as well was R.A. Long, a wealthy lumberman who was a founder and leading benefactor of Independence Boulevard Christian Church. He purchased a Disciples periodical, *The Christian-Evangelist*, and its parent publishing company in 1909; the publishing house was renamed Bethany Press and then Chalice Press, its current name, and remained the primary base for Disciples publishing throughout the 20th century.[62]

R.A. Long, patron and benefactor of Independence Boulevard Church and George Hamilton Combs. Long was a major lay leader in the Disciples of Christ denomination for many decades. *Missouri Valley Special Collections, Kansas City Public Library, Kansas City, Missouri.* **His daughter, Loula Long Combs, driving a heavy harness pair with her dogs at an Ak-Sar-Ben (Nebraska) stock event in the 1930s.** *Omaha World Herald/AKSARBEN Stock Show*

Long was a founding member and key funder of the Disciples National City Christian Church in Washington, D.C., a member of important Disciples boards and committees locally and nationally, and a regular attendee at their many meetings across the country. His personal loyalty always remained with Independence Boulevard, but his stature in the denomination cast a far broader influence that affected many other Disciples congregations. In 1917, his daughter Loula, renowned horsewoman and founder of the American Royal, married her childhood friend, Robert Pryor Combs, the son of her pastor.

In addition to these individuals, there was another factor linking the two congregations, one that *The Kansas City Star* identified in an article about Combs' retirement from Independence Boulevard that described changes occurring within that church:

As the years passed there came a change, almost imperceptible at first; the mountain was leaving Mahomet. The leaders in manifold activities of the church were departing. The trend of population was out south and as time went by the pull on the congregation grew stronger. As he looked over his audience each Sunday Doctor Combs missed a face here and there. Sometimes they would reappear at wide intervals, but their strength was lost to the church. [63]

Early members confirmed *The Star's* account in their own memoirs. The family of Charles Waldron, the grandson of Langston Bacon, was among the "exodus of members from Independence Boulevard Church who moved to the Country Club District." They initially attended Second Presbyterian before the Christian church was organized. [64] Sybil Sweet Woodbury recalled living on Gladstone Boulevard across the street from the Combs family when he was the pastor at Independence Boulevard. "We were all active in that church … after my marriage to Frank H. Woodbury, Jr., we moved out to the south part of town, as did so many of

Independence Boulevard Church, the mother church of CCCC located in northeast Kansas City. It was built in two phases: 1904-1905 and 1909-1910. Its sanctuary is built in the auditorium style popular in the late 19th and early 20th century. *Missouri Valley Special Collections, Kansas City Public Library, Kansas City, Missouri.*

our friends." They promptly joined the new congregation that was meeting in Community Hall. [65]

The relationship between the Country Club and Independence Boulevard churches has continued through the years to the present day. The northeast neighborhood experienced the familiar arc of change common to many urban core settings. Independence Boulevard Church remains a locus of stability, community outreach and support, and Country Club members are actively involved in projects such as the Micah Ministry and Northeast Community services. The "Combsites" and other Disciples were moving south. Frank Bowen, who knew and could probably greet by name most of the Disciples in the city, would have been aware of the population shift. There was work to be done, but there was also possibility and promise.

George Combs preached his first sermon, "Our Program," in the second floor Community Hall on Sunday, January 2, 1921. The sermon title plus the questionnaire appended to the back of the morning bulletin provided a clear message from the new minister: we have work to do and it starts now!

The Questionnaire
In starting a new work where we are all more or less strangers to each other it is important to know who are experienced in church work and what their experience consists of. Will you kindly, therefore answer the following questions and hand to one of the ushers?

The questionnaire concluded with an inquiry that became a signature of Combs and the church in the years to come:

Do you know of any one in this community not now attending Church who might be interested in coming here? If so, please write name here and hand to the pastor. [66]

"Hand to the pastor" (not an usher). There was to be no question about who was in charge of building the membership. A four-part sermon series followed, intended to deal with what were described as "Country Club problems." The first sermon posed the intriguing question, "Is the

Country Club District Pagan?" No record survives to explain how he answered that question.

Attendance flourished in spite of what was probably the shared opinion of many of the attendees as expressed by one man who became a faithful member: "If any one had said a year previously that he would drive eleven miles each way every Sunday and sit through a Sunday School hour in the edge of a corn field, [I] would have called him crazy."[67] There were soon three hundred-plus congregants who were, in Dr. Combs' frustrated words, "worshipping in a hall! It wouldn't do. We must build."[68]

With a new pastor in the pulpit, church leaders worked to create a formal institutional organization. A Church Board, chaired by Langston Bacon, was approved by the congregation on February 27, 1921. There are no official records of how the men were selected for the board. Most likely, it was a fairly informal process that brought together individuals originally tapped by Frank Bowen along with others. The first official meeting of the board, consisting of 28 men and Dr. Combs, who always played an active role, met on March 2. Virgil McDaniel, the treasurer, reported that the church treasury held $855.53. Dr. Combs stressed the importance of finding a site for the church and to commence building as soon as possible.

The board convened a special meeting a few weeks later on March 23 to decide on a number of matters. It was agreed that Dr. Combs was to be paid an annual salary of $4,500. The chair of the Special Building Site committee reported on two possible building sites for the new church: one at 61st and Ward Parkway, and a second one also on Ward Parkway just south of 59th Street. Dr. Combs said that the board should be further increased by appointment of "eligible and efficient" men, and the board also decided to propose three men to the congregation as the first elders. It was at this meeting that the necessity of covering the slippery Community Hall floor with canvas was discussed. J. C. Nichols' agent told the responsible board member that the cost would be $350, half of which the Church was expected to assume. The Church representative countered with a $100 commitment, which the Nichols Company accepted. A small matter, but the first of many that indicated that Church leaders would be firm, and frugal, in their dealings with the realtor.

At the April 4th meeting the Building Committee again discussed several possible locations, indicating a preference for the 61st and Ward Parkway lot. Members agreed to invite J. C. Nichols to a special meeting one week hence. The board also decided to purchase New Testaments to be given to received members upon baptism, a practice that continues to this day with presentation of the full Bible. The special meeting on Sunday afternoon, April 10th, with 34 members present, convened at Community Hall where J. C. Nichols provided a history of the Country Club district and his optimistic predictions for the future. The group then adjourned to 61st and Ward Parkway. There, on a cool Spring afternoon, members of the board approved the selection of that site for the new church and moved that their recommendation be presented to the full congregation the following Sunday.

The April 16, 1921, edition of the local newspaper published the usual Saturday announcements of that week's service schedules and sermon topics; the Country Club Christian entry included an additional item: "IMPORTANT NOTICE — The site committee will report on the proposed location for the new church. Every member should be present." [69] At the close of the service on Sunday morning, April 17th, the motion to approve the purchase of the lot at 61st Street and Ward Parkway was unanimously approved by the congregation. The purchase cost was $24,000.

The empty field that was soon to be a construction site was part of the Wornall Homestead. The pastoral setting belied its history. Wornall Road to the east followed the tracks of the Santa Fe Trail that in turn had been the path for the Osage tribe. The Battle of Westport, the largest Civil War battle west of the Mississippi, was fought just a few blocks away. Howard Monnett, an early member of the church, recalled collecting war relics on the grounds and at nearby Loose Park as a boy. Marjorie Jenkins' parents built a home on the north side of West 61st Street near Summit in 1917. Their view was "beautiful pasture land where we could see cows grazing." But one morning in April, the view abruptly changed; army tents now stood where cows had been the day before. The Third Regiment was training before being sent to the front lines in Europe. Marjorie had vivid memories of Camp Nichols, as it was called:

> It was like having a box seat to all that went on in the neighborhood. Every day we could watch the soldiers drill and practice other war maneuvers. On the crest of the hill to the west, we could see long lines of soldiers waiting to go into a large mess tent to be served. Taps told us when to go to bed at night, the bugle call awakened us in the morning. The camp of course was under wartime discipline, being patrolled on all four sides by sentrys

[sic]. The perimeter of the camp formed a square starting at the corner of Sixty First Street and Ward Parkway,
then a dirt road south on Ward Parkway to about what
is now Meyer Boulevard, east across pasture land to
Pennsylvania, north to Sixty First Street, then west, back
to Ward Parkway. [70]

Only later did she realize that the young men she watched with such
interest were among the first Americans to be deployed to the blood-
soaked fields of France, where they fought in the ten-month-long Battle
of Verdun. The cost was horrific; 1,100 of the 1,700 soldiers of the "Old
Third" did not return home. [71] After their departure, J. C. Nichols designated the land for use as Victory Gardens until war's end, and then briefly
converted it to a golf course.

**Before there was a church: Tents for Camp Nichols Army training site during
WWI, later a vacant lot that was purchased for the new church.** *Missouri Valley
Special Collections, Kansas City Public Library, Kansas City, Missouri.*

Matters moved quickly. Ideas became proposals and proposals were
shaped into plans. In later years, Dr. Combs would reflect that "It was
never thought of as a mission. To neighborhood eyes and to city eyes, it
was, from its very beginning, a 'going concern.'" [72]

The board held both regular and special meetings in May to work out the details of the purchase. Nichols had informed the Building Site committee that neighbors adjacent to the proposed building had raised unspecified objections to the project, but that he, Nichols, was confident that those objections could be addressed. Dr. Combs, undeterred, told the board to continue personal calls to members, soliciting subscriptions that would be paid in five installments over several years. At another meeting the board agreed that a basement, sufficient to support the planned super-structure, should be built as soon as funding was assured, an estimated $60,000. The first unit would, long-term, be planned as the Sunday school wing. By May 19th, $32,000 had been raised, an amount that rose to $45,000 by early June.

At that same May meeting the board took the rare step of denying a request from Dr. Combs. "Dr. Combs stated that we had been assessed $1000 by the Inter-Church World Movement, and in order to get the matter before the Board, moved that this apportionment be accepted and paid as soon as the money is available." Despite the spare tone of the minutes, it is clear that this was an awkward moment for the group. At first, they decided to table the motion for later discussion, but then finally agreed to a motion that Chairman Bacon write a letter to the Inter-Church group, declining to accept the assessment. The action is significant on several levels. George Combs normally led the way in church decisions, and bringing this matter before the board may have been a calculated effort on his part to assure that any response went beyond just his voice.

The Inter-Church World Movement was a Protestant ecumenical organization, founded in 1918 in response to the war.[73] Its purpose was to unite inter-denominational resources to address social conditions and human needs, a message that would have fully resonated with Combs. Some of the most eloquent passages in his autobiography describe conversations with fellow clergy as they sat by the campfires in France. "Such high hopes I had cherished 'over there' of world betterment, of a new interdenominational order, of a purified, revived and united church." It was not to be. "When I got home, did I find this dream on its way to bud? Far from it; its very seed was frozen."[74] The Inter-Church World Movement was already floundering and would soon fold. The board's gently measured response spoke to their understanding of their minister as well as the needs of the church.

At the conclusion of the Sunday service on July 17th, Judge Bacon informed the congregation that it was time to appoint trustees to provide

Ground Breaking - April 1921 - Looking south

So much space, so much to build. Ground-breaking day, August 1, 1921.

"This, children, is for you," Dr. Combs hands the shovel to the children attending the ground-breaking ceremony, August 1, 1921. *CCCC Archives*

oversight to church business. Members unanimously approved F. G. Robinson, O. V. Nelson, and T. S. Ridge. The administrative structure was now in place. Negotiations with the J. C. Nichols Company continued through the summer, clearly supported by several of the businessmen on the board, including Junius B. Irving, the president of Irving-Pitt Manufacturing, the producer of three-ring binders. Irving would become a close confidante of Combs, who dedicated his autobiography to him.

Board minutes soon recorded regular presentations from "Mr. Root." Walter Clarke Root and his partner, George Siemens, were successful architects in Kansas City, the creators of a wide range of buildings that included private homes, academic structures, office buildings, and churches. Root was the younger brother of John Wellborn Root who, with his partner Daniel Burnham, presided over the famed architectural firm of Burnham and Root in Chicago. Walter had gone to work for the firm and was sent to Kansas City in 1886 to supervise several of their projects under construction there. He realized that the city offered exceptional possibilities for a young architect wanting to establish his own career beyond the shadow of his brother, and he remained there the rest of his life. [75]

At the July 19th meeting, Root said that the basement, first, and second floors could be constructed for $50,000 if a temporary roof was used initially. The board agreed to ask contractor John Neal, a church member, to assume responsibility for construction. Neal accepted, and would charge 5 percent of cost, not to exceed $50,000. Groundbreaking was August 1, 1921. When Dr. Combs was asked to turn the first spade he turned to the children standing close by and said, "Children, this church is for you. YOU throw out the first shovelful." [76] Frank Bowen offered a prayer and the group sang "Praise God From Whom All Blessings Flow."

CHAPTER 4

Stone by Stone: The New Church on Ward Parkway

"Mr. Nugent moved that we build a Gothic style Church."

Mr. Henry Nugent's motion to the board on July 19, 1921, duly seconded and approved, was made in response to Walter Root's request that the board decide on a style for the new structure. The choice of a Gothic influence aligned the church on Ward Parkway with a trend across the country as new suburban churches embraced Gothic architectural design. Some, mostly in larger cities, were stately testaments to high cathedral style, but typically they reflected the comfortably dignified appearance of small city and village churches in England.

The physical structure referred to as "church" is far more than an arrangement of walls, floors, doors, and windows. The building is a symbol and a product of religious practice and belief, as well as a historical artifact. Social, cultural, and economic forces shape church structures as surely as the hammers and tools used to construct them.[77] Church historian Jean Halgren Kilde characterizes church architecture as "a text through which we gain access to the thoughts of the creators."[78] Church architecture — evangelical Protestant church architecture, specifically — evolved through several stages in the second half of the 19th and early 20th centuries. After the Civil War, many urban churches adapted (with minimal changes) theatre and auditorium design plans, recreating the old-time revival setting with upholstery and lighting. Banked rows of individual seats curved toward a platform or "stage" that held the pulpit and behind which sat a choir and the "pipe fence" of the increasingly important organ.

There were variations to the plan, but the emphasis was on engagement between minister and congregation — the "audience." Kilde argues that architecture promoted changes in the service itself that now contained "two critical worship components: the sermon ... and musical performance," where previously the sermon was the main focus. "In addition, the huge sweep of amphitheater seating indicated that the audience itself would take on a larger role in worship."[79] George Combs' first Kansas City pulpit, Independence Boulevard Christian Church, was built in this style.

Other changes in both architecture and practice reflected the profound impact of modernization, a transformative process that went far beyond factories and trains. The emerging middle-class redefined family life according to norms that have come to be identified as the "Cult of Domesticity."[80] Proponents argued that the family home should be a haven from the harsh external world. It was a sacred place, presided over by Mother, a woman charged with raising her children to be pious and responsible citizens. The sacred identity of home was confirmed by the ecclesiastically influenced furnishings and décor stylistically referred to as Gothic Revival. Expectations for daily prayers and Bible study, behavioral codes for dress, alcohol and tobacco consumption all contributed to the sanctified home. This was an ideal, of course, not shared nor experienced by all, but it dominated popular culture and became a source of aspiration for many. It was an ideal that strongly influenced Protestant churches in the years between the Civil War and World War I.

Church-going families began to speak of their "church home" as domestic functions associated with the family home were now also performed in church: church dinners, small groups needing comfortable space that boasted carpets and fireplaces in rooms that were referred to as parlors. Many of these functions were the purview of women; church was considered a safe and appropriate setting for genteel women to gather and work outside the home. Church dinners required kitchens (usually in the basement) and even dedicated social space for presentations of those dinners.

Addressing the needs of the family meant all members of the family and that included formal religious education for children based on an established curriculum and conducted in classrooms within the church. Public education in the late 19th century evolved from one and two rooms of mixed age pupils to age-differentiated classrooms; so too Sunday school classes were also organized by age and, often, gender. The old adage that form follows function applied to the change in church architecture as well. As the functions of church life expanded, so did the architectural adaptations that supported those functions, including that quintessential need of modern life, storage space. Closets for choir robes, filing cabinets for music, cupboards for dining service and liturgical pieces, shelves for baptismal towels, and on and on. "From Sunday schools to drill rooms to gymnasiums, evangelicals recast church architecture to accommodate functions never dreamed of a century earlier."[81]

The second wave of architectural styling, the late Gothic Revival favored by the Country Club Christian Church board, also signaled changes in ecclesiastical practice and liturgy. Theatre-type floor plans were superseded by elongated naves lined with pews in straight rows on either side of an aisle intended for processions. The aisle ended in an apse, the altar area. Some churches followed the cruciform pattern with transepts jutting out on either side of the aisle, while stained glass windows provided visual and meditative focus. The clearest departure from the earlier amphitheater style was the implementation of the "split chancel" that created a geometrically balanced presentation of Protestantism's key symbols: the Bible, the table, the pulpit, and the cross. "Balance among these symbols was achieved by placing the cross on the far wall at the back of the chancel, centering the table in the chancel on the longitudinal axis but several feet out from the wall, placing the lectern holding the Bible on one side of the axis, and positioning the pulpit on the other."[82] This is the pattern of the worship space in Country Club Christian Church. Style and space changed, but it sometimes took a while for vocabulary to catch up. Both Walter Root as well as church members continued to refer to that worship space as the "auditorium" rather than the nave, or today's more commonly used term, the "sanctuary" that became the standard usage with the arrival of Warren Grafton, the second pastor.

Gothic architectural design supported liturgical changes that evolved throughout the late 19th and early 20th century in what has come to be known as the Liturgical Movement. The long aisle enabled stately processionals and recessionals. An order of worship that included responsive prayer and sacramental rituals that were framed by the liturgical calendar were intended to more fully include worshippers in sacred dialogue. Clergy and choir wore robes; the altar was decorated according to the religious season. Many of the practices and rituals were shared among various denominations, contributing to ecumenism and a sense of unity. In his retirement, Dr. Combs reflected on those changes, many of which had occurred during his time in the ministry:

> in my preacher's span, one of the most significant changes in our churches ... is the change to liturgy, with its observance of days (Palm Sunday, Good Friday, Easter), its vested clerics, choirs, processionals, recessionals, and its call for the construction of sanctuaries best suited for that type of worship. There's little left nowadays to distinguish between the services held in the Baptist, Methodist, Presbyterian, Congregational, and Disciples churches and those held in the Episcopal church. [83]

At the same July 19th meeting when the Gothic style was approved, the board also hired Mrs. Esther Darnall as church soloist for a salary of $1,000 per year, as well as a new pianist for $10 an hour. Paid professional musicians were regular features of large urban churches in the early 20th century, reflecting a variety of influences: the theatrical arrangement of many church floor plans, an enthusiasm for the aesthetic in religious services, as well as an acknowledged effort to draw in more attendees. [84] Mrs. Darnall, a contralto, was a well-established performer in Kansas City, and was employed as Supervisor of Music in the Kansas City Public Schools. She had grown up next to the Combs family during his tenure at Independence Boulevard, and she would remain at Country Club for many years. From the start, she insisted on certain standards. At the September board meeting, the chair of the House Committee reported that the musicians were complaining about the piano being used in Community Hall. Mrs. Darnall had located a piano that could be rented for $15 a month, rental fee to be applied to purchase of the new piano. Chairman Bacon suggested that they get the current piano tuned; his suggestions were not usually ignored. At the October meeting, the issue was raised again; it was reported that Mrs. Darnall had found the piano she wanted at J.W. Jenkins for a rental fee of $12.50 per month, applied to final purchase, and the heretofore silent "ladies of the church" had agreed to pay the rental and possibly furnish the funds for purchase. The motion to approve was promptly passed without further discussion.

A City Church

Esther Darnall, the first music director at CCCC, who oversaw the development of a rich music tradition for 23 years. *Missouri Valley Special Collections, Kansas City Public Library, Kansas City, Missouri.*

Another matter was presented at that same October meeting:

> Mr. Gentry moved that 25% of the current expense income of the Church be devoted to missionary purposes. The motion was seconded. After discussion of this motion, Mr. Wilson offered a substitute motion, that we subscribe $400.00 for the current year to missionary work. The motion was seconded and carried on a rising vote of 12 to 5.

The dry language of board minutes obscures the significance of the issue at the base of this motion. From early days, Disciples had argued over how, or even whether, to support "missions" — both domestic and international. In blunt terms, the question was what do we support? Should our budget be primarily dedicated to a particular church/congregation; do we have obligations beyond that and if so, to what extent? It was a conversation that would be raised every time there was a capital campaign, a drive for a new updated organ, or a more aesthetically appealing baptistry, and it was a conversation that could become heated, with solid arguments on both sides. That it occurred so early in Country

37

Club's history at a time when most of the energy was directed towards a new building indicates its significance and theological implications that would carry through coming generations.

Construction was slowed by heavy autumn rains, and at a special October meeting, members learned that construction costs would be $60,000, rather than the previously announced $50,000. Serious discussion followed:

> The question confronting the meeting was whether to proceed with the building as far as the $45,000 already pledged would cover; or whether to attempt to raise the $15,000 deficit and proceed as per our original plans.

> After discussion, Mr. Dickey moved that we proceed with the building as originally contemplated — putting on a tile roof, the building complete with exception of the top story — and that the Finance Committee be authorized to go in debt for the necessary amount to complete the work as early as possible.

The discussion continued — should the money be raised from subscription (internal) before approaching other sources; should the subscription be extended to the public? The board agreed to bring the matter to the congregation the following Sunday, requesting a 50 percent increase in subscription from those who had already committed, and a first-time subscription from those who had not. The congregation approved the proposal that Sunday.

The last board meeting of 1921 on December 5th considered a number of items, most of them related to the construction. The walls had been completed to the second floor by November 14. Weather permitting, the stonework would be completed within a week to ten days. If all went well, the congregation hoped to move in sometime toward the end of January. One final item on the agenda returned to the discussion of "mission" giving raised in the October meeting. Frank Gentry, who had initially brought up the issue of dedicated donations, presented an alternative method for achieving that goal: "Mr. Gentry moved that we adopt the Duplex Envelopes for contributions, thereby allowing all who desire, to contribute a definite sum to missions as well as to current expenses." Gentry was referring to a financial management system described in a best-selling 1920 handbook,

A Guide to Church Finance, by Reverend Samuel Stein, a Lutheran pastor. Church financial practices had often been unsystematic and unreliable. The practice of pew rents, formerly a regular source of income, was disappearing, and churches began to look to business practices to achieve efficiency and predictability. Stein's book stressed an annual budget, an every-member canvass (a term George Combs would use regularly), and an envelope system of giving he called the Weekly Duplex Envelope System. [85] Some Disciples organizations had adopted the system in the past decade, providing enthusiastic reports on its efficacy:

> [The Duplex envelope] is perhaps the best system known to us so far. Duplex envelopes and weekly offerings mean that our money be spent in two directions and that it be done each week. There are two parts to this envelope: one part for ourselves and one part for others that we may duplicate ourselves … If your religion is not worth duplicating, don't use the Duplex envelope; but if you think the brand would look well on someone else, then duplicate it. [86]

"System," "brand," "duplicating," — the language of business had gone to church.

After Mr. Gentry made his motion, Mr. McDaniel stated that the envelopes for 1922, not of the duplex type, had already been ordered and were on hand. An extended discussion, with several different motions being offered, followed. There was clearly agreement that some mechanism for funding mission projects be implemented. The final approved motion read accordingly:

> A EVERY MEMBER CANVAS[S] be made on Sunday Dec. 18th, and that subscription cards be printed, providing a space for subscriptions to the current expenses, and subscription for missions; that a budget be authorized of $14,000.00, $12,000.00 of which be devoted to current expenses, and everything above $12,000.00 subscribed, not in excess of $2,000 to be given to missions, and that the Board request Dr. Combs to deliver a missionary sermon, making a special appeal for missionary subscriptions, sometime during the year.

It was probably the first time that a negotiated compromise position had been required of the board, after a year of consensus and frequently unanimous votes on such matters as the choice of a minister, and the purchase of a building site. The Duplex envelope system was eventually adopted, and the company made a weekly appearance in *The Christian* with a discreet advertisement called a "Homilope" — a short spiritual homily followed by company information.

While the construction of the new church dominated most discussion throughout 1921, by year's end the rhythms of church life and management had established themselves — often mundane, sometimes very urgent. Several key board members died, leaving leadership voids that needed to be carefully filled. Even as a very young organization, there were responsibilities to be met or refused in the larger constellation of city and national institutions, a process that demanded that members arrive at a sense of identity and purpose.

The year 1922 began with one clear objective: to move into the new building as soon as possible. As with many building projects, the occupancy date kept being pushed back; Sunday services in the Community Hall and board meetings at the Brookside Hotel continued as usual. By February, membership had increased to 450. In the same month, the church started a Boy Scout troop, Troop 84, that became an important element in youth ministry and education.

In April, the board posted a sign in front of the church building site "with the approval of Mr. J. C. Nichols" announcing the forthcoming church services and programs. Chairman Bacon informed the board that the building would be ready for occupancy by Easter Sunday, April 16, but after some discussion the group decided to hold Dedication Sunday on May 7th. In later years, it was widely assumed that J. C. Nichols was a founding member of Country Club Christian, but church records and rosters do not support this. His funeral in 1950, attended by hundreds and led by Reverend Warren Grafton, did take place in the church, the first of many occasions that it served the wider community beyond the parameters of the membership.

Worshippers in the new building might have been forgiven for wondering if it was a significant improvement over Community Hall. R. E. Robertson provided a full, if understated, description:

> The first unit of our new building was merely the shell
> of our north wing consisting of a large assembly room

Almost finished — the original North Wing or Educational Building, that
housed all services in the early years. The top image shows an unusual
figure of a woman on a work site; the tiny figure in the middle image is a
man cleaning the windows — glazed in those days; and the bottom image
reminds us that autos were still not the usual means of transportation for
most members. *CCCC Archives*

and kitchen in the basement ... and a large room on the first floor. The second floor was not completed and the third floor not built until later, the whole of this part of the building above the floor being somewhat like a big barn loft, with no means of access until some months later. The noise and confusion in the one big room, with so many classes during the Sunday School hours, was extremely trying upon both teachers and classes. [87]

The "one big room" employed canvas dividers to section off the Sunday School classes, reducing visual if not verbal distractions. The canvas curtains were pulled back for the morning church service. [88] Trying circumstances gave birth to creativity, and soon some of the men of the church cut a hole in the ceiling, built a temporary staircase to the upper level, and used beaver board to create a small meeting place, heated with a gas stove. [89] The baptistry was located in the northeast corner of the basement, "a large baptistry with a double trap door to enclose it at floor level." It was apparently large enough that the second child to be baptized proceeded to swim in it to the "amusement and consternation" of Dr. Combs. [90] Initially there was also a small gymnasium in the basement for the general purposes of shuffleboard and basketball parties, and socializing, but it was done away with because the children kept hurting themselves on the rock walls. It was converted to the Pine Room, regularly referred to in church records as a meeting place for various groups. Church announcements in the local papers always noted its convenient location at the end of the Sunset Hill Car Line, an advantage in the days before widespread use of automobiles.

With the successful and rapid transition from rented public hall to their own building, the board turned its energies to formalizing institutional structure. This included a coherent plan of financial planning and administration, the development of a professional and specialized staff, and hiring outside consultants. The April minutes refer to a "General Sweeney" in connection with the May dedication services, and the context suggests that he had been agreed upon as a speaker at the previous March meeting. Institutional religion, like other vocations such as medicine, education, and law became more professionalized in the early years of the twentieth century. Specialized training, acknowledged by the conferring of credentials and professional associations that set standards for their members, were consequences of the modernization process. So too was increasing specialization within the vocations and the role of outside experts who could be called upon to assist in a variety of tasks essential to institutional growth and success. These experts served as consultants, although the term would not be in general use until after World War II. General Sweeney was one of at least three such experts hired by the church in its early years. It is clear from the minutes and his autobiography that Dr. Combs was enthusiastic about tapping the expertise of individuals who could assist, particularly in the areas of fundraising and membership growth.

Unfortunately, the March 1922 board minutes are missing, an unusual lapse in the normally meticulously kept records. If the process of the decision behind engaging Z.T. Sweeney is not known, the motivations for his selection are abundantly clear. Zachary Taylor Sweeney was a prominent Disciples clergyman. He was born in Kentucky in 1849 and by 1871 had assumed the pastorate of Tabernacle Church of Christ in Columbus, Indiana where he would remain, with several leaves of absence, until his retirement in 1896 as pastor *emeritus*. Under his leadership, the Columbus church grew to be one of the largest in the denomination at that time.[91] One of his leaves of absence was granted when President William Henry Harrison appointed him Consul-General to Constantinople in 1889. Earlier that year Butler University in Indianapolis awarded him a doctorate and named him chancellor. His duties, not intended to intrude on those of the university president, were to "increase the endowment and add additional chairs of instruction," both of which further refined his skills for the church dedication presentations.[92] He was addressed by the honorifics of "Dr." and "General" henceforth.

Sweeney was older than Combs, an age gap that straddled the Civil War, making him theologically more aligned with the early generation of Disciples rather than those who grew up after the war. He opposed open membership and supported the group that brought heresy charges against the faculty in the Kentucky seminary. But in other ways, he was a thoroughly modern clergyman. His profile was similar to many of the successful Disciples leaders of the time: renown as an orator, an active writer, and regular contributor to the journals. He was encouraged by many to enter politics in which he was passionately interested, but believed that would dishonor his ministerial vocation! From early days, he proved to be a skilled fundraiser. He led his first church dedication in 1871 at the age of 22 and, time permitting, continued to do so throughout his ministerial career. Upon retirement, he became even more active; his biographer notes that by 1904, eighteen years before the Country Club service, he had led one hundred sixty-six dedications.[93] Church dedications at this time were, essentially, fundraising events, sometimes lasting for days; " ... generally an outside speaker was secured to give a fiery and challenging dedicatory address and then make an appeal for cash and pledges to finish paying for the building." The presentations tended to be lengthy, several hours at least, requiring an energetic and dynamic speaker. After Sweeney's first youthful effort, a commentator for the *Christian Standard* observed that "If anyone can get money from an audience and at the same time make them feel good over it, he can do it."[94] Apparently, he never lost his touch. He was phenomenally successful, raising more than a million dollars in the process of dedicating more than three hundred churches.[95]

In addition to the Sunday morning service, Sweeney was scheduled for the full week following with a commitment for daily evening services. Dr. Combs was eager for him to meet with the men of the church, to provide advice on fundraising. The Publicity Committee was in full operation: invitations to the dedicatory service were sent to all members and prospective members; announcement cards were sent to every resident of the Country Club district; *The Star* would print a four-inch announcement in the Saturday paper, as well as run a major news article about the new church. Board minutes from that period do not record the financial records associated with building the church and the pledges or "subscriptions" made by members to support the construction, so we do not have an exact way to determine the success of Sweeney's week in Kansas City. It is safe to conclude that things went very well ensuring the ongoing expansion of both the physical building and its membership. General Sweeney was paid $250 for his services that week.

The descriptions of the next dedication visit, which eventually occurred in 1926, are much fuller and quite effusive. We don't have his birth date, but George Snively's career spanned the same general time as Sweeney's. He worked with his father in various business settings, providing him useful background for his later work as a dedication specialist. He had several pastorates, but by the early 1900s seems to have moved full-time to the role of "general evangelist," and became one of the "most efficient men in the 'dedication of new churches.'"[96] Snively's name was first proposed to the board at a special meeting in December 1923 by Chairman Bacon, for the purpose of obtaining pledges from the membership to complete the present building and possibly raise additional funds to finish the main auditorium. Bacon's report was not accepted, a rare rebuff that generated "considerable discussion," a regularly used phrase in the minutes that can be read as code for "there was animated disagreement." A motion was passed to send Snively a telegram informing him that for the moment the board had decided on other ways to raise the funds. Langston Bacon reacted promptly; four days later a special meeting was held, with a guest: Reverend Burris Jenkins, the pastor of Linwood Church. Jenkins championed Snively, who had conducted a similar campaign at their church and he commented that "Mr. Snively was not only successful in obtaining subscriptions, but that he had done a great deal of spiritual good to the congregation." Once again, "considerable discussion" ensued, but this time the invitation to engage Snively was carried with unanimous approval.

Snively's name does not appear again until almost two years later in November 1925, when the board agreed to invite him to be the dedication speaker the following January upon completion of the "auditorium." There had been considerable back and forth debate about whether to complete the building in sections, or to commit to finishing the entire structure and have one dedication that was scheduled for January 17th, 1926. Snively arrived in Kansas City by January 5th to meet with church members at a dinner.

The exact process of the campaign is not spelled out; he may have worked behind the scenes until the 17th, to assure pledges that could be announced publicly at the Dedication Service per Marjorie Jenkins' description below. Whether or not he preached at the Dedication Service is unknown. Reverend Snively fulfilled all expectations, and Langston Bacon must have taken some satisfaction in introducing the following resolution into the February 7th minutes:

> Resolved, that the Official Board of the Country Club Christian Church, very highly appreciates the untiring efforts of Brother George L. Snively, by which we raised, one hundred forty-two thousand (142,000.00) Dollars to meet the obligations of the congregation for the completion of its Church home.

The resolution went on to express appreciation to Brother Combs who "very greatly contributed to Brother Snively's success" and to Brother Clay Peters "for his prompt assistance in enabling Brethren Snively and Combs to make their successful canvass of the membership."

Marjorie Cupp Jenkins remembered the fundraising campaign well. Her account differs slightly from the board record as to dates, but provides a lively portrait of the Sunday service. In the comments below, the reference to the "Chairman" refers to Snively who conducted that part of the service:

> [The] week before the dedication service a financial campaign to raise money was put on right there in the sanctuary. The Chairman stood on the rostrum and asked for pledges for the new addition. Starting with $10,000, how many would pledge that amount? Those who wanted to would stand up, give their name right before the entire congregation. Then a smaller amount would be asked for — and continued down to $29 pledges. Can you imagine people today being willing to stand in place before all the members and do that? I can't! [97]

Sweeney and Snively were heirs to the 19th century evangelist tent meeting tradition. The third individual who provided guidance to the new church was a younger man who would become a Disciples leader at a national level, and is the only one of the three to be recognized by Dr. Combs in his autobiography. Jesse Bader's focus was on membership development rather than fundraising, and he created strategies that proved enduring for many years to come.

> In all the twenty years of my ministry at that church, we had not a single "revival." Folk were brought into its membership and activities, not through preacher evangelists from without, but through lay evangelism from within. For the technique of this evangelism, we were indebted to Dr. Jesse Bader, who, in our beginning days, was with us in a visitation campaign and showed us how it should be done. [98]

Bader, who was born in 1886, served in several pulpits, including the Jackson Avenue Christian Church in Kansas City beginning in 1920. Like Combs, he had volunteered with the YMCA and served in France during World War I. His wife was also an ordained minister and he is credited for his advocacy for the role of women in the church. He was deeply committed to Christian unity and ecumenism and would soon find larger forums for his work, serving at various times in leadership positions for the United Christian Missionary Society, and the Federal Council of Churches of Christ in America, and most notably as founder of the World Convention of the Churches of Christ in 1930, an international organization intended to promote communication among churches emerging from the Stone-Campbell Movement. He was also the founder of World Communion Sunday, still celebrated on the first Sunday of October.

Bader's maxim "each one win one" underscored his philosophy of lay or "visitation evangelism" embraced by Dr. Combs and Country Club Christian Church. In February 1924, the local Council of Churches planned to have all churches in the city hold two weeks of evangelistic services prior to Easter. The board approved Dr. Combs request that Jesse Bader be called to conduct Country Club Christian's participation, devoting the first week to personal work among members, and the second to evangelistic service in the church. Bader guided the new church in the development of a protocol for recruiting members. The "visitation campaign" began in spring with Easter Sunday as the goal for welcoming new members. The "prospect list," started earlier in the year, was the basis of a major recruitment effort launched two weeks before Easter. The workers:

> mostly men, with only slight sprinklings of women assembled at church. To get our men out, or rather a commanding number of them, we gave them a complimentary dinner — and the dinner was always good. At 6:30 the dinner. After the dinner, instructions to the workers. Then they paired off, always going out in two to call on their prospects ... Each team averaged about three calls per evening. Calls completed, they came back to the church to make their reports. Returning to the church the same night, and presenting their reports in writing, I regard as a very important feature of the program. [99]

Given their association and the likelihood of friendship between the two ministers, Bader may have continued to provide advice and support in the years to come. Despite his acknowledged oratorical skills, Combs insisted that "Preacher feet are of far more importance than pulpit wings. Eloquent perorations may swirl for a while ... Echoes of knocks on the door will linger far longer." "I brought feet — feet that were to go, no matter how fatigued, up and down — literally up and down every single street of the Country Club district. They carried me to the home of every member of the church; they carried me to homes of prospects. A bell ringer was I." [100]

The lavish praise for George Snively at the conclusion of his dedication campaign contrasts sharply with the silence following Z.T. Sweeney's work two years earlier, but the difference may be a function of changes in record keeping rather than disappointment with Sweeney's efforts. Finances were a source of discussion and concern at almost every board meeting and were undoubtedly at the base of the initial refusal to approve hiring George Snively in 1923. The treasurer of the church resigned abruptly in January 1924, citing his heavy load at work. The minutes are generally discreet, but in June of 1924 things came to a head when the Finance Committee, under the leadership of Junius Irving, issued a "somewhat exhaustive analysis of our financial situation." The report noted that out of 713 members, 257, "or nearly 35 percent of our membership record no financial support." It goes on to say that an anticipated deficit for the year must be made up by those 257 who are not contributing. Most telling, the report continued: "Your Committee has found the present system of keeping our records inadequate." The report did not mince words:

> Your Committee finds that no small number of our members seem absolutely unwilling to contribute to the church. Some of them have been approached repeatedly without results. We consider such cases a waste of effort and a useless expense.

> We propose in the future, after making due effort and after satisfying ourselves that their lack of support is due to indifference rather than lack of ability to permanently remove their sheets from our files and turn them over to the elders for such action as they may see fit to take.

> It is our belief that in cases of misfortune and inability to pay, every care should be exercised to save the unfortunate from embarrassment, but those who can pay and will not should at least be placed in a list by themselves.

> Every member of this church adds to overhead and we
> can well dispense with those whose only interest is to
> improve their social standing and have a church handy
> for weddings and funerals.

The full report was read at the July 1924 board meeting, precipitating "considerable discussion," and prompting the secretary *pro tem* to add an irregular personal observation that one of the principle items referring to "the indifferent, inactive and non-contributing members, contained the most comprehensive bit of constructive sense that has been advocated in the past fifty years." The discussion continued with a motion that the report be published in full and distributed to all members. Cooler, or at least more cautious heads prevailed, suggesting that "discretion be used in issuing the report." Mr. Irving "acquiesced" agreeing that the report should be somewhat modified and issued in the form of a letter. He did, however, submit over 150 names to the board, that divided them into groups of five and planned to make calls within the next week to ten days. And at the November meeting he again called particular attention to "a group of members of the Church who failed to contribute to any of the funds, or to share any of the Church expenses. These accounts are to be segregated and handed to the Board of Control to deal with as they consider best." "Board of Control" is a term lost in the mists of the past. Its role is unknown, but can perhaps be surmised within the context of this entry.

Things seem to have settled down, and it is apparent that at least some reforms of fiscal management were put in place. In March 1925 the Sunday morning pew bulletin included a full financial report of all the funds managed by the church. Then, more than a year later in April 1926, a special meeting of the Building Committee was called to consider some disturbing news. The building thus far had cost more than $50,000 over the funds that had been raised, and "we were grossly in error in our estimates of the cost and of the amount of money needed to pay all our obligations." Further, some records had still not been turned over to the Business Manager, other records were "not in proper shape to make a good financial analysis," and they had "not established proof of the funds we have handled." It was necessary to have an outside audit, to be paid for by Junius Irving and O. V. Wilson. The audit was completed by June, but there is no record of its content. The board did not meet in July and August. Obviously, the building was completed on time, and, as we will see, the debts were eventually paid. Subsequent Financial committee reports are crisp and positive, revealing a command of the church's resources.

The financial tempest, distressing though it was, was relatively short lived, and it brought to light a number of issues that were not unique to Country Club Christian. The pitfalls of volunteer management, no matter how well-intentioned, became abundantly clear. By 1926 the church counted more than 1,000 members. An organization of that size required full-time professional staff beyond one senior minister.

The first addition to the staff arrived in 1924, when Paul Rains was hired as the director of Religious Education. The position had been first proposed to the board in December 1923, at "the suggestion of the Sunday School teachers and workers," and the initial job description also included the duties of financial secretary and business manager of the church, a breadth of responsibility that revealed, at the very least, a lack of understanding of the role of religious education in a major church. Religious education as a profession was quite new; Disciples institutions such as Eureka College and Drake University were among the first to offer courses in religious education, a field that grew beyond Sunday morning classes to include church camps and missionary education.[101] Standardized curriculums customized for different age groups were soon the norm. A 1922 newspaper announcement for Country Club Christian Sunday services described the Bible school at 9:30 as, "A thoroughly graded school with classes for all ages. A good place to bring your children."[102] A committee to recruit an education director was organized and, contrary to most committees, it included two women — Mrs. Combs and Mrs. Meriwether. Although there were several male teachers in the early days, Sunday school work, particularly for children and teens, tended to fall into the women's domain, possibly explaining further the relative lack of understanding on the part of the board for what the position really entailed. Just a month later in January 1924, the committee read excerpts from a two-page letter from Paul Rains, saying he would be interested in accepting the position of director. He had paid a visit to the city in mid-December; the letter is a polished statement of his expectations and hope for the position, that includes a tactful but firm "no" to the proposed fiscal responsibilities: "it has been my experience that my work will be seriously hampered in other lines, and the church itself is the loser, if it is expected that this [fiscal] detail should be done by me or if I am personally responsible for the raising of the budget of the church." The board agreed to hire him, noting that it was "not practical to get a man to act in all the capacities of Director of Education, Financial Secretary and Business Manager." His title was to be director of religious education, at a salary of $3,000 per year plus an automobile allowance.

Paul Boyd Rains was the son of Francis Marion Rains, a prominent Disciples leader who for twenty-six years had served as secretary of the Foreign Christian Missionary Society. F. M. Rains was also one of the leading "dedicators" of the period, earning high praise from none other than George Snively who recalled: "In this realm [his ministry as a dedicator of churches] he was for a quarter of a century the unrivaled premier." [103] Paul Rains started working for the American Christian Missionary Society in 1917, and his name appeared a number of times in Disciples periodicals in announcements of his work throughout Nebraska and Iowa where he was variously referred to as district superintendent and secretary of the Northwest Bible School District. His name appears in the 1918 *Annual Register* of the University of Chicago, where he is listed as a student in The English Theological Seminary, a program designed for individuals already in the field who could not enroll full-time in a residential academic program. They were required to spend a summer on campus and complete the remainder of the degree through correspondence courses. The *Register* also indicates that he had done undergraduate work at Transylvania, a Disciples university.

Rains, who was in his late twenties at the time he accepted the Country Club post, was serving as director of Christian education at First Christian Church in Hutchinson, Kansas. He quickly settled into his new role and appears as an active presence in church records from then on. He came to be well-recognized in the larger community as well. A few months before Rains' arrival, in October 1923, Dr. Combs and two other board members had attended a meeting of ministers and Sunday school workers of churches in the district to discuss weekday religious instruction for children in the public schools. The plan was to provide release time, during the school day one or two days a week, to attend such classes in churches close to the school. The Board of Education had endorsed the plan; Country Club Christian would be expected to provide about $150 toward the program. Weekday religious education was not an entirely new concept, but it received a significant push starting in 1914 with a proposal by the superintendent of schools in Gary, Indiana.

When Paul Rains arrived at the beginning of the new year, the plan had been adopted. In September 1924, he reported to the board that 240 children were enrolled for the year, and the cost would now be $340, payable in four installments. By the start of the school year in September 1925, nine schools in the Kansas City district were participating with a total of 1,210 children enrolled. The five Country Club district churches had organized The Country Club Board of Week Day Religious Instruction with Rains as chairman. In addition to Country Club Christian, the group included Second Presbyterian, Wornall Road Baptist, Country Club Methodist, and St. Andrew's Episcopal, and students were drawn from Bryant and Border Star schools. With their parents' written permission, they attended classes at St. Andrew's and Country Club Methodist Monday and Wednesday afternoons after dismissal at 3:15. As surprising as the program seems to present day observers, there were thousands of such schools across the country. [104] In his detailed report, Rains argued that

> There is no present day movement fraught with more possibilities for Christian character building than the current movement which places religious instruction side by side with the secular instruction of the public schools on week days … Our responsibility is not only to teach young folks to 'make a living,' but to make a life. Skill without character is worse than ignorance. Skill plus character leads through the highways of success, happiness and abundant living. God has pointed the way, can we do less than help our children to find it? [105]

Paul Rains resigned in June 1927 after nearly three and one-half years of service to begin a career in educational publishing. It was an amicable parting, but met by the deepest regret on the part of the church workers and members. The board would not fill his position for more than a year after a long search, with predictable consequences for the Religious Education program. At one point, the Business Manager had to reimburse the Sunday school teachers, who were paid in those days, out of his own pocket, because matters had become so disorganized. They were simply unable to find an individual of Rains' caliber.

In December 1925, the Finance Committee made its annual report, and included several recommendations, one of which was to secure the services of a full-time Business Manager who would maintain an office in the building. The job description was robust: "general supervision of

A growing Sunday school, gathered in front of the church in 1929.

all church property; to act as clerk of the Board; to receive all funds, including the building fund; to make all collections on pledges to various funds; to maintain an accounting system satisfactory to this Board and the Finance Committee; to render to this Board from time to time comprehensive reports and statements as may be required of him; and perform such other duties as may be assigned to him by the Board or which could be broadly construed as within the province of a general manager." The very fact that the committee was in a position to articulate the Manager's duties underscored the growth that had occurred as well as the expertise of those creating the position. Their unanimous recommendation was that Charles Rouse be hired for the position. It was an obvious and very wise choice.

Charlie Rouse was a Charter member, whose daughter Katherine was the first child baptized in the new building. He had served on the board from the beginning. He appears everywhere in the minutes, assuming a wide variety of roles and responsibilities. He was highly regarded by all, as R. E. Robertson recalled: "our able and efficient Business Manager, who has the faculty of doing twenty things at once for as many impatient people, and managing to keep smiling through it all ... "[106] The committee recommendation concluded by noting that they had interviewed Mr. Rouse who said that he would accept the position at a salary of $3,000 per year, a lesser amount than his current income. "The services of such a man would greatly facilitate our work and would prove a source of profit rather than an added expense."

In five years, Country Club Christian Church had grown from a small gathering of sixty or so people in a rented second-floor hall to a congregation of more than a thousand who assembled weekly in their own building. There were now three full-time professional staff members supported by many part-time and volunteer workers. In 1925, Ella Clark Loose, widow of Kansas City philanthropist and businessman Jacob Loose had gifted the church with a full set of chimes that rang across the neighborhood. A well-managed board had regularized finances and established oversight of all church functions. The introductory issue of *The Country Club Christian*, a weekly newsletter, was published on September 3, 1926. Board minutes suggest a newsletter of the same name had appeared previously, but 1926 marked the beginning of it being the primary means of communication for the church. It was directed to all members with the expectation that they pay a subscription fee and was also supported by paid advertisements. *The Christian* provides a broad and detailed picture of the life of the church.

Progress and growth had been steady, but there were challenges as well, particularly for Dr. Combs. Martha Stapp Combs died on Saturday evening, October 11, 1924, having been operated on earlier for appendicitis. Stunned members of the board gathered at church the next morning. They cancelled the regular worship service, but decided to hold communion with song and prayer as "an added tribute of our deep feeling" to be presided over by Paul Rains, the newly hired director of religious education. As the wife of the minister, Mrs. Combs had been an active presence in the church from the beginning. She had charge of the high school girls Sunday school class, and Marjorie Cupp Jenkins, her former student, remembered her fondly as a woman of "queenly presence" who was partial to large hats. She was one of the very few women to be appointed to several board committees, and she had served as an early president of the Women's Council. In his memoir, George Combs mourned that "she had not lived to see the building, into which she had put so much of her heart, wholly completed ... And it was hard for me to go on alone."[107] Three years later in the summer of 1927, he married Gladys Gwynne, the church organist, at a simple ceremony in the Pentwater, Michigan, vacation home of church members Mr. and Mrs. Fontaine Meriwether.

In sermons and writings and above all leadership of his congregations Combs was a determined optimist, undoubtedly at times to the exasperation of those charged with raising funds and filling pews. Always, he assured others, there would be a way. But shadows were present as well: the dark depths of the depression that engulfed him upon his return from the war; chronic and sometimes debilitating health problems; the divorces and consequent loss of custody of their young children of two of his three sons in a day when that was not commonplace, certainly not in a preacher's family; and the early deaths of one of those sons and his beloved Martha.

CHAPTER 5

Church Women:
From Church Parlor
to Church Board

Prior to *The Christian,* we must rely on the minutes of the board for the church's story, a rich account of the early years, but an account almost exclusively by and about one cohort of the church — the men. Only men held the positions of trustee, elder, deacon, and usher, and, of course, minister. A very few women, usually including Mrs. Combs, were appointed as members, never chairs, of board committees that were thought to benefit from a woman's perspective, like Sunday school, baptismal, and prayer meeting. Typical of the few references to women in the early board minutes is the peremptory October 4, 1926, entry: "The matter of pulpit flowers was brought up for discussion and it was moved by Moore and 2nd by Wilson to turn this phrase [sic] of the work over to the ladies. Carried." Presumably the ladies agreed to the assignment. Another entry notes the request by the Women's Council for permission to use the church parlor for a major presentation they were sponsoring — by Dr. Combs! Permission was granted, and the ladies sent a gracious thank-you to the board.

Omission from the record, however, is not evidence of lack of participation and service to the church. Notwithstanding the formidable Mrs. Darnall, who had so successfully enlisted the support of the ladies of the church in her campaign for a new piano, women had traditionally been barred from leadership in church services and governance. But they were there and they performed a wide variety of essential functions.

The evolving role of women in the church was closely integrated with changing definitions of "womanhood" in American society. Whatever the definition, women's identity from the early 19th century on was grounded in their perceived moral authority, a perception that would both constrain them, but ultimately lead to their claim of leadership in the larger society. Participation in church work that, in industrializing America, moved beyond church walls, was an extension of their moral power, and "their belief in their moral superiority to men also empowered them to attempt to right the wrongs, especially alcoholism and prostitution, inflicted on society by sinful men." [108] Although women continued to face huge obstacles to gainful employment beyond domestic roles, the Civil War and the Industrial Revolution had provided opportunities heretofore unrealized, as would both World Wars. Office work, previously assigned to men, was one arena into which women quickly moved — at much lower salaries. About the same time that Charles Rouse was hired the minutes note that the church should hire a "female stenographer."

In her lively account of the origins of the CCCC Women's Council, Nettie Wharton begins by asking: "And what of the ladies — God bless them — were they satisfied to drop into the quiet demure position occupied by their respected grandmothers? Not so anyone could notice it!" [109] The women organized that first January while still meeting in Brookside:

> They immediately began to clamor for something to do,
> and as they were women of long experience in church
> work, they knew that only in union was there strength,
> and they planned to organize a council at once; there
> being at that time just 100 women on the church roll.

"Women of long experience" — therein lies the key to understanding the development and progress of Disciples women as they found their voices in the institution they loved. It was experience derived not only from years of church work, but also from membership in women's clubs and organizations, and participation, often as leaders, in many of the major social issues campaigns that flourished from the post-Civil War years on. They acquired invaluable skills as organizers, communicators, and fundraisers, recognizing that "only in union was there strength;" they learned how to network and create hierarchies with clear lines of command.

The very qualities of empathy, nurture, and moral rectitude that some argued were most suitably expressed in the domestic sphere motivated many women in the 19th and early 20th centuries to become actively involved in the reform movements that sought to address the consequences of the industrial revolution. Women founded organizations such as the Red Cross and the YWCA. They were leaders in campaigns for prison reform, child welfare, humane mental health treatment, immigration settlement, temperance, labor laws, and so much more. One of the more colorful, if not especially beloved, Disciples women in the temperance movement was Carrie Nation, the hatchet-wielding nemesis of saloon keepers. Her visit to Kansas City in April 1901, earned mention in the *New York Times* with a report of her arrest and consequent appearance before a magistrate who imposed the unusually large fine of $500 to be collected if she and her hatchet did not immediately board the next street car out of town, never to return. She departed fifteen minutes later. [110]

The Club Woman Movement contributed further to enabling women to establish focus and identity within supportive groups. Clubs existed prior to the Civil War but expanded dramatically in the latter half of the 19th century. Although they remained segregated, both White and African-American women found meaning and shared purpose in their clubs. Disenfranchised women gathered on a regular basis for purposes of study and education, social action, promotion of arts and culture, and friendship. Local clubs often belonged to larger regional and national associations that held conferences and maintained communication among members. In a comprehensive history and survey of women's clubs published in 1898, Jennie Croly had this to say:

> The Club, from the beginning, accomplished two purposes. It provided a means for the acquisition of knowledge, the training of power; and the working of a spirit of human solidarity, a comprehension of the continuity of life: its universal character and interdependence. It is not too much to say that this aspect changed the whole point of view of the woman who came under its influence. Her ideals were elevated, her trust in eternal goodness and its purpose strengthened, and her own possibilities as a social and intellectual force brought out and gradually molded into form. [111]

Women's clubs were highly effective participants in Home Front operations during World War I, and as a consequence garnered support for suffrage that would finally be confirmed by the 19th Amendment in 1920. The Alternate Tuesday Club (ATC) in Kansas City, for example, suspended its study program for the duration of the war to focus on activities ranging from knitting garments for soldiers, working at Red Cross stations, raising funds for military hospitals and displaced children, and creating supply kits for the armed forces.

Like other activities that seemed to pull women out of the domestic sphere, clubs came under attack. Mrs. Croly includes a comment from a member of '81 Club, another Kansas City group (named for the year it was organized), who briskly responded to predictions of a "wrecked home life" as a result of women's participation in such organizations:

> I would like to bear witness that our homes are still well ordered, our children fed, clothed, and educated with the same interest and care as in the times gone by when the only approved assembly for women was the church sewing society. [112]

Many of the 100 women who were early members of the church were almost certainly members of local women's clubs and participants in the social reform movement.

The third stream of influence was women's work within the Disciples organization itself. Typically, Disciples leaders did not speak in a unified voice about women's roles within the church. Alexander Campbell had always advocated for female education, grounded in his conviction that women needed to be prepared to lead the "school of the home" as they educated their children. Campbell's son-in-law, William Pendleton, argued that women had the right to lead worship in "private" but not in public forums. All of these discussions were reinforced by dueling citations from Scripture, usually from one individual — the Apostle Paul.

In her chronicle of Disciples women, Debra Hull notes that "almost simultaneously, in a sixteen-year period following the Civil War, congregational women's organizations joined to form national women's organizations in all the major Protestant denominations." [113] Disciples women organized the Christian Women's Board of Missions (CWBM) at the national Christian Missionary Convention held in Cincinnati in 1874. Isaac Errett, the well-regarded Disciples clergyman and editor of the *Christian Standard*, had supported women's enhanced place in the church and he introduced this resolution:

> That this Convention extend to the Christian Women's Board of Missions their recognition and hearty approval, assured that it opens a legitimate field of activity and usefulness, in which Christian women may be active and successful cooperants of ours in the great work of sending the gospel into all the world. We pledge ourselves to help these women who propose to labor with us in the Lord. [114]

The resolution passed unanimously, but despite the generosity of spirit behind it, the us/them distinction in language makes clear who is in charge. Not all at the convention shared Errett's enthusiasm. Francis Rains recalled that in addition to discussion about the use of the organ in public worship (always a contentious issue), there were those who opposed women talking in public. As Caroline Neville Pearre (the founder of CWBM) spoke from the lectern that year, an acquaintance sat next to Rains, clearly disgruntled. "What are we coming to? See that woman talking here before all this assembly, when Paul positively prohibits such a practice?" That individual, at least, underwent a change of heart, and according to Francis Rains had later "urged many sisters to talk in public." [115] The CWBM "became the first woman's board to do both home and foreign work, to employ both men and women, to manage their own business, to choose their fields of service, to own property, and to raise and administer their own funds." [116]

Missions, both domestic and international, became a prime focus for Disciples women in the fifty years following the 1874 convention. Mission work addressed the causes that already claimed women's interests: children, family life, improvement of living conditions, and advancement of women's rights. There were practical issues as well; male missionaries had little success in countries where cultural norms restricted the relationships between women and men. And, to date, funding for missions was scarce. The leaders of the CWBM proved able fundraisers and soon supported a number of female missionaries who served in four identified areas: the American West, Jamaica, the freed slaves in the South, and Asia (especially India and China). Some, like Sarah Lue Bostick, were women of color; she served forty years in Arkansas, ministering to former slaves.

Loretta Long, in her profile of Disciples women concluded:

> Women made their presence felt in missions in a way
> never contemplated. Often their fundraising efforts
> outstripped those of the [male-dominated] American
> Christian Missionary Society and established women as
> the premier financial managers of the churches. [117]

Disciples women in Missouri responded to the call to service by organizing a state-based program to support a Sunday school evangelist. Mary Crowe Bryant of Ashley, Missouri approached the Ninth District convention with a proposal that was promptly approved, and she was named president of women's missionary work in Missouri. She in turn submitted resolutions to the state board to the effect that "the Sisters of the Christian Churches represented in the meeting shall organize a society to the State Sunday School Aid Society, for the purpose of best promoting the interest of that cause in the State of Missouri." Ever mindful of the possible reaction, the resolution closed with "P.S. Finally, Resolved, that these resolutions are neither to be laughed at or voted down." [118] The state organization joined the national group that had emerged in the 1874 convention. In 1879, at the Missouri state convention, Maria Jameson, representing the Christian Women's Board of Missions, appeared at the podium, the first time a woman had addressed the group. A young woman who was present that day recalled that "you could have heard a pin drop ... . The spell was broken when Brother J. J. Wyatt, the most popular preacher in all northwest Missouri, said audibly, 'I am for Sister Jameson now and for the women's work all the time hereafter.' That settled it for Missouri!" [119] The Missouri group took the lead in recruiting younger women, in order to ensure continuity in the coming years.

In 1876, six Disciples women gathered in the basement of their St. Louis church to pray about ways they could respond to the needs of the poor and neglected. As residents of a large city, they had become keenly aware of the suffering and distress experienced by so many. The result was the National Benevolent Association (originally called The Benevolent Association of the Christian Church), founded in 1877 and still an important agency of the denomination today. The history of the NBA is one of response to the changing demands of the modernizing world, beginning first with orphanages for children forsaken by industrialization, and continuing through time to care for the aged, and mentally and emotionally disabled. In their eloquent words, "We conceived as our sole purpose the task of helping the helpless — to give a home to the homeless, to provide care for the sick and comfort for the distressed." [120]

One early member recalled that there was no comparable organization in any other church; "we were pioneers in this work." [121] A number of the founders, however, had participated in the temperance movement and the highly organized Women's Christian Temperance Union and were well-versed in social action. The more serious challenges came from men in the denomination and even women who had established roles within the institutional churches. Unlike the Women's Board of Christian Missions, the NBA founders did not see themselves as "women organizing women to do women's work." From the first, they envisioned a national and denominational agency.

Their first facility was an orphanage in St. Louis that moved to ever-larger quarters in the coming years. The NBA was not initially recognized as an official agency of the denomination, and its leaders had to engage in aggressive fundraising that did not compete with those agencies that had received accepted denominational status. In 1893, they designated Easter Sunday as a nationwide day to collect Sunday school offerings for the orphanage, a strategy that was promptly criticized since Easter was viewed as a "Catholic" holiday. [122] Many years later, the editor of the NBA publication recalled the efforts of the founder, Sarah Matilda Hart Younkin (who would become the first ordained female Disciple minister in Missouri in 1895):

> [She] nagged the chairmen of conventions in her efforts
> to get five minutes, or even three minutes, to say some-
> thing about Benevolence … . She would hang around the
> foot of the steps to the platform, waiting for a chance to
> make a dash for it if some scheduled speaker was a bit
> late or if there should be some slight crevice in the pro-
> gram into which she could slip. [123]

The goals of the NBA aligned with the Social Gospel and the Progressive Movement of the early 20th century, placing the NBA "at the forefront of a growing child welfare movement." [124] The authors of a valuable history of the NBA suggest that the women founders brought 20th century corporate understanding to their project, using vocabulary such as management, organization, efficiency, expertise and scientific methods. [125] Eventually, in 1899, the NBA was accepted as an agency of the denomination, but victory brought a bitter consequence. In 1901, the NBA hired George Snively (who would later lead a dedication campaign for Country Club Christian) to be its first general secretary. Snively was openly supportive of women as leaders, but the first step had been taken. In a 1917 letter, former President Fannie Ayers wrote:

> About that time Brother Mohorter [Snively's successor] decided that the Benevolent Association had gotten to be too big for the women to control; that it needed a businessman at the head of it, and by maneuvering that would have done credit to Tammany Hall they succeeded in having elected a man as president and as first vice-president, also as treasurer and himself as general secretary. So instead of a Board of women as it had been for almost twenty years, the Officers now are five men and two women. [126]

In the early 20th century, the NBA sought to expand its ministry through the development of social service agencies including hospitals. R.A. Long, Kansas City businessman, philanthropist, and leading Disciples layman who was at the time First Vice President of the NBA, proposed a hospital for Kansas City that would be characterized as a National Christian Church hospital, designed to serve the needy. *The Kansas City Star* announced the project with enthusiasm in several articles: "The Christian Church is in a flourishing condition in Kansas City and its vicinity, and the enterprises now announced will be a fitting expression of that condition. They will also be a conspicuously fine example of the general work of the National Benevolent Association of the Christian Church." [127] Long's dream was to make Kansas City the national headquarters for the Disciples denomination, and *The Star* noted that the hospital site would expand to include multiple buildings providing a variety of social services. "All of these institutions," the article concluded, "will be under the general supervision of the National Benevolent Association, but their practical management will be entirely local." [128]

From the beginning ownership and governance of the hospital seemed muddled, at least in the reports of newspapers and journals. At various times, the NBA, the Christian Hospital Association (specific to the Kansas City hospital), and the collective Christian Church in Kansas City were each identified as being in charge. As late as 1917, an article in *The Christian Philanthropist* (the NBA journal) addressed the matter:

> [The Christian Church Hospital in Kansas City] is temporarily under a local board of managers in Kansas City. A committee composed of men from the local board of the hospital and the president of the National Benevolent Association is now at work on a plan by which it is proposed to make the Christian Church Hospital an integral part of the National Benevolent Association. [129]

The same article continued its predictions: "Already a magnificent institution, it is destined through the wonderful energy, enthusiasm and vision of the Kansas City Disciples to become one of the greatest hospitals in the world." [130] Although it was never actually owned by the NBA, they identified it as one of its "twelve great institutions" in the country. [131] It was always considered a Disciples institution, and it was where Martha Combs died in 1924.

Christian Hospital, Kansas City, Mo.

Christian Church Hospital on West Paseo. It was intended to be part of a large Kansas City Disciples campus, but succumbed to economic and administrative issues. *Missouri Valley Special Collections, Kansas City Public Library, Kansas City, Missouri.*

Long offered a challenge grant of $200,000 if Disciples could raise an additional $150,000 to create an endowment. A major, and very successful fundraiser for 500 people where "women from various churches ... volunteered their aid in serving the dinner," was held at Independence Boulevard Church in January, 1911, where the Christian Church (Disciples of Christ) Hospital Association was officially announced. The association purchased the entire block on the east side of Paseo between 26th and 27th Streets in 1913. R.A. Long hired Henry Hoit, a well-known architect in Kansas City who had designed most of the buildings associated with the Long family, to create plans for the new hospital. Kansas City Christian Church Hospital was dedicated in April 1915 and opened to patients in April 1916.

The hospital was one of many sectarian hospitals (seven in Kansas City alone) built in the late 19th and early 20th centuries, a consequence of increasing professionalization in medicine and the expanding institutional structure of religion. As the primary donor, Long was in a position to make policy in keeping with Disciples tenets: the facilities and the benevolence should be provided without reference to creed or nationality, and one third of the beds should be dedicated to charity patients. In both respects, Christian Church Hospital differed from many other private hospitals of the day. It is not known whether this policy applied to racial minorities. Douglass Hospital was established in Kansas City, Kansas in 1909 by local African-American churches, and General Hospital No. 2, opened in 1930 with considerable fanfare to serve Kansas City's Black community, confirming that segregation applied as firmly to health care as to all other aspects of life.[132] Christian Church Hospital was initially successful, attracting positive attention from the local press, and building a residence for the nurses who had been boarding in private homes.

Kansas City Christian Hospital closed just ten years later in 1926, unlike the other denominational hospitals in the city that continued to grow throughout the century. *The Christian Philanthropist* noted bluntly in an October 1918 article that "hospital work is difficult in the last degree under normal conditions, but under war conditions it is almost impossible," with drug supplies, nurses and doctors all being claimed for the war effort.[133] Matters seemed to improve in the post-war years, but in January, 1925, the hospital superintendent resigned, marking the beginning of a rapid decline catalogued by front page headlines such as "Hospital's Fate in Doubt." The government made overtures to lease the hospital as a veteran's facility, and Kansas City Disciples were galvanized to protect the institution. At a large city-wide meeting they proposed creating a new board of trustees and a full reorganization of the hospital; a later meeting attended by "the boards and women's societies of the Christian churches of Kansas City" continued the discussion. The indefatigable Frank Bowen made an appeal. But it was too late. A strong article in *The Star* referred to "stunted growth" and "financial embarrassment." It quoted "A man very close to the hospital" as saying: "The management of the hospital in the hands of an independent board of trustees early alienated the strongest sources of support ... A closed staff of physicians was placed in charge of the hospital ... Various churches lost friendly contact."

In the first few years of Country Club Christian Church's existence, its board was approached several times by the hospital requesting support. A special meeting of the board was called in September 1925 to "consider the state of the Christian Church Hospital." After "much discussion" one board member was instructed to inform the hospital board that "we could not as a church help in any way ... on account of our building programme" and to "express our regrets." A 1926 *Star* article specifically noted that "funds were not forthcoming due, it was said, to heavy building expenses being incurred by one of the three Christian churches counted on as the main financial support." [134] Just two months later in November "the financial difficulties of the Christian Church Hospital" were again brought to the board; they decided to put the matter on hold "indefinitely."

The minutes are silent about the content of the discussions that were undoubtedly strained. The church supported other Disciples institutions in the city, some of them in dire straits. A number of Country Club Christian parishioners were personal friends of Long; members of the board as well as the larger congregation had been part of the early fundraising campaign to finance the hospital, and several, including Langston Bacon, had been on the original Christian Church Hospital Association Board. Their refusal to fund the hospital suggests concerns beyond just financial considerations.

The hospital was conveyed to the war veteran's bureau after a court case ruled that the lease was binding, and it was dedicated as a veteran's hospital July 31, 1926. In the years to come, it would serve as a psychiatric hospital and then finally sink into urban decrepitude. Today, it serves as a remodeled senior living facility and is listed on the National Historic Register as a building of significance.

Understanding the saga of Christian Church Hospital is often confusing and certainly subject to some speculation, but also instructive as an illustration of changing perceptions of the denomination's and individual congregations' roles in serving those in need. It highlights the rapidly expanding role as well as expectations of Country Club Christian Church as a leader in the Disciples denomination and Kansas City at large. The early decades of the 20th century was a time of transition from an industrializing economy to one that was increasingly service-oriented. Those who developed institutions such as hospitals, old-age homes, and orphanages often applied the methods and vocabulary of corporate development that had worked so effectively building railroads and heavy industry. The irony, of course, was that the needs being addressed by social service institutions were often the direct consequence of upheaval and human cost created by industrialization. Over time, other organizational models and professional development would be created that recognized that human beings are not machines.

Transitioning to appropriate institutional models was a challenge that most early social service organizations faced. In addition, Christian Church Hospital had succumbed to tensions between local and national authority as well as apparent mismanagement. The NBA president campaigned for hospital funds for more than five years, and R.A. Long was the NBA first vice-president — but the hospital was not, in fact, owned by the NBA, although almost always was listed as an NBA organization. To some extent, this underscored a very old debate dating back to the early history of the Disciples, who had been so concerned about external "societies" and organizations. Three years later, in his weekly column in *The Christian*, Dr. Combs mused on the challenges of cooperative enterprises, observing that conditions in the "golden days" of such work were quite different: the city was smaller, and there were only a few churches, permitting closer communication. In the succeeding decades large building expansions had focused individual churches on their own indebtedness over external outreach, and a divergence of theology and practices had broadened the distance among the churches. Perhaps more in hope than conviction, he concluded:

> Nor should differences in the past evaluation of certain joint enterprises be suffered to hinder this cooperative work. For example, our churches may not have been of one mind as to the importance of the Christian Hospital, but those past differences should not be permitted to block the way to the largest cooperation in the evangelization of our city.

The leaders of Country Club Christian Church would assuredly be influenced in future social service commitments by the disappointing experience of Christian Church Hospital.

The women who organized Country Club Christian's Women's Council had taken significant steps beyond the constraints experienced by their mothers and grandmothers. More women remained unmarried, and more chose careers beyond teaching and domestically related work. Their years of experience in well-organized clubs and social movements had provided them with invaluable skills. By 1928, the church would proudly announce an evening class for business and professional women who could not readily participate in daytime programs. The launch of *The Christian* provided women members a weekly forum to document their numerous activities. But the early decades of the 20th century were a time characterized by one chronicler of Disciples women as a loss of autonomy.

> The second decade of the twentieth century saw most women's organizations subsumed under denominational umbrellas and stripped of their operational independence. Influenced by the rise of big business in the larger culture and the societal prejudices concerning women, churchmen determined to remove women from positions of leadership and place their activities under more direct male oversight. [135]

The notices in *The Christian* duly recorded the regular meetings of the Women's Council and the circles in which many women participated. Considerably more language was devoted to the seemingly endless dinners prepared by the Women's Council: weekly Thursday evening meals, plus many special occasions that could bring in up to 500 people. Again, the record is quiet, not due to lack of participation, but who was making the report. Recalling the early days of recruiting new members, Dr. Combs' recollection of "only slight sprinklings of women" in these campaigns was given a decidedly different interpretation by Mrs. Wharton:

> A general church meeting was called for Wednesday night, January 26th [1921], at the Brookside Hotel, at which a membership canvass was launched by the men. They asked if the women could help in this, and our worthy President assured the dear brothers that we were

willing to charge upon the community with card and pencil and ready tongue.

As usual, the women did the housework, that is they called at every house in the district, ascertaining the religious preference, if any, numbers of children, and in many instances, family affairs, they were eager to relate; the data thus obtained being used for our own records as well as serving the men in their part of the work. [136]

Country Club Christian women might have questioned at times how their senior pastor viewed them and their role in the church. In his weekly front-page column in *The Christian,* November 27, 1926, George Combs fulminated about American democracy and the state of the home, placing the problems of each firmly in womens' lap:

Yes, we shall never have the democracy we might have until every man and woman shall have become a politician …

This need should especially be recognized by women. To most of us women's advent into politics has been a distinct disappointment. We had high hopes upon her coming into the rights and privileges of the voter …. We had felt that a great moral uplift would be had and that at least, government would be the cleaner because of women's enfranchisement. But nothing of the kind — as yet.

It is not subject to controversy that, as a rule, men pay less regard to home affairs than they one time did … Now this is serious enough but along with man's growing detachment, is the lessening consideration by the woman of firesides and roof trees and babies. The new woman does not fit snugly into the old scheme. Many women even though married, are obsessed with the notion of economic independence and feel that they must go out from the home to help earn the living. If not driven out by economic urge they are leaving the home for the "broadening" of they know not what.

Combs' readers would have recognized the term "New Woman" in use since the late 19th century to describe, in varying degrees, women who claimed the rights to economic and social independence and to work on an equal footing with men to improve society. Silena Moore Holman (1850-1915), a devout member of the Churches of Christ in Tennessee, was an unlikely New Woman, but became a powerful voice on behalf of her sisters. The Churches of Christ constituted the more conservative branch of the Stone-Campbell movement, and David Lipscomb, the editor of its journal *The Gospel Advocate,* did not hold back when writing about women's duties to be pious and submissive. Like so many before them in the Movement, Lipscomb and Mrs. Holman soon found themselves engaged in a vigorous debate that revealed the sharp minds of each of the proponents. In a number of articles, Silena posed challenging questions, such as "If women are to keep silent, then why are they permitted to sing in the worship?" At one point she concluded "My only endeavor has been to reconcile Paul with Paul, and himself with other inspired writers."[137]

Lipscomb's assertion, reiterated by Dr. Combs nearly forty years later, would be seriously tested nationally throughout the Roaring Twenties and the economic collapse of the Great Depression, as well as in Kansas City specifically by the corrupt and crime-ridden political machine of Thomas "Boss" Pendergast. Women responded; they organized, they voted, and they changed their world.[138] But without formal representation on the board, their activities could only be reported by third parties — usually Dr. Combs. They were invariably referred to in the collective as "the women" or less often "the ladies," a distinction from the carefully identified men's committees whose functions were usually explained. In February 1933, Dr. Combs sent a blunt directive to the head of one of the women's circles:

> I am enclosing a little note I wish you would read to your circle. I am curious to see what the women of the council, working through each circle, can do in putting over commandingly this programme. Pretty much everything depends upon the degree in which you, the leader, will put yourself into this special effort. Please see that the secretary who shall keep these weekly records is well known, so that your circle members will know to whom to report.

Although the "programme" is not identified, it was probably the annual spring recruitment for new members, referred to in the April board minutes: "Dr. Combs stated the women were following up our new members and agreed with Judge Stone in expecting the men to cultivate our new members at the time they joined with us." In his same report he also noted that "The women had the best Good Friday Service in the history of the church," without explanatory comment. By the end of 1933, the lowest point of the Great Depression and a year when the church experienced declining income, layoffs, and salary reductions, Dr. Combs' perspective was beginning to change. At the January 1934 board meeting, all the usual committee reports were presented. At the end of the review, Combs pointed out that the report of the Women's Council had been "overlooked" — whether one had been submitted and was ignored, or only he was privy to its contents is unclear. "Our ladies raised $5000.00 in 1933 and did not have to reduce their budget from the year before and are out after the same for 1934." And to emphasize his point, he continued that "he felt from time to time a representative of the [Women's] Council should be present at the Board meetings." "From time to time" was a small step, but it was in the right direction.

"The original Official Board of Country Club Christian Church was strictly patriarchal and permanent. Once elected to the Board you were on indefinitely. And there were no women." [139] At that time, the "Board" included officers and all the elders and deacons, but there are also references to a Board of Elders and a Board of Trustees. Dr. Combs made it very clear that he expected everyone to attend all board meetings. That he was routinely disappointed is clear from both attendance records and his regular comments within the minutes. Essentially the same individuals had been in place since the beginning, without any regular system for tenure, additions, or, if necessary, removals. As the years passed, board minutes reflected increasing concern with individuals who were not regular participants in meetings and the life of the church, but other than assigning a few elders to talk to the recalcitrant, there was no policy to address their behavior. Combs clearly saw the board members as the key recruiters for membership and "subscriptions" (pledges) and he regularly argued for a larger board to carry out those functions.

Board organization became a topic of discussion in the early 1930s, and in 1932 the board appointed a special committee "to devise a plan of appointing deacons, such as for one, two or three years of service, and also of eliminating them upon continued absence for insufficient reason."

The process quickly grew complex; deacons were to be appointed by a committee of five to seven individuals (elders, deacons, or laymen as they were still termed) appointed by the chairman of the board. After approval by the Board of Elders, the names of the proposed deacons would be submitted to the congregation for final approval. Further, the elders and deacons were to be divided into two groups (whose names would not be disclosed to the congregation at large): Group 1 would include the more active members, Group 2 those members not so fully engaged. All of this was to be managed and overseen by Charlie Rouse, the church clerk, a man of one title but endless duties. Dr. Combs was clearly buoyed by the plan and in the coming years he would issue regular sets of detailed job descriptions and expectations for both deacons and elders.

The early founders would have been bemused at the very least by the hierarchy and bureaucracy that constituted the operations of the 20th century church. While it is beyond the scope of this account to examine church governance in detail, the mind-numbing account above suggests the challenges that faced a large, affluent congregation in modern America when it came to determining who was in charge. The answer would change and evolve over the decades and would be shaped by a range of influences that included external social, political, and economic forces as well as the mission and purpose of the church and the denomination. The high regard for business and business practices in the early decades of the church motivated much of the organizational scheme, but that often ran aground against the practical reality of working with volunteers who, despite the determined language of various protocols, are very difficult to "eliminate."

In the vocabulary of church polity discussions, the Disciples are identified as a congregational denomination, meaning that individual churches are self-contained and self-governed and not subject to higher authorities such as bishops or synods. In the words of the 2017 *Design for the Christian Church (Disciples of Christ):* "Congregations constitute the primary expression of the community of faith within the Christian Church (Disciples of Christ)."[140] Today, the Disciples embrace a veritable alphabet soup of agencies and offices on a national level and consciously seek dialogue and exchange both within and outside the denomination. But the fundamental commitment to self-governance remains in place as does the concept of the "plurality of elders." That term has Biblical roots and for Disciples it refers to those elected individuals within a congregation who share in the church ministry and church leadership.

CHAPTER 6

Between Two Wars:
The Church Responds
to Crime and Depression

Country Club Christian Church's early development and growth occurred during some of the most tumultuous times in the country's history. The interwar years included the Roaring Twenties and the grim global Depression years of the 1930s that only ended with yet another World War. The 'Roaring Twenties,' often portrayed as a time of hedonism and moral lassitude were also a period of malaise and disillusionment, a consequence of the perceived failure of the high-minded goals of World War I. America, now a world leader, entered a period of isolationism and withdrawal.

Dress lengths grew shorter; Babe Ruth kept hitting home runs; the nation was riveted by the "Monkey Trial" where Clarence Darrow and an aging William Jennings Bryan debated evolution; the "talkies" provided an entertaining escape; Charles Lindbergh crossed the Atlantic by airplane and received a hero's welcome in Kansas City on August 17, 1927; and the automobile changed just about everything. Within the space of less than two years, the country passed two Constitutional Amendments that would dramatically affect people's lives. The 18th Amendment established Prohibition; it lasted until repeal in 1933. The 19th Amendment guaranteed women the right to vote, after decades of campaigning and growing ever more visible in public life.

Temperance movements had existed throughout the country's history and were often associated with mainline Protestantism. The Disciples generally supported temperance and Prohibition, convinced that alcohol was at the root of many social evils, a viewpoint that in turn influenced how they voted. As one chronicler concluded: "many Disciples tended to evaluate politics mainly in terms of their interest in the liquor issue."[141] The Temperance Movement (or Movements, as some argue) had a long and evolving history. In the early 19th century religious leaders tended to discuss the question exclusively from a Biblical perspective. This led to some rather tortured analyses that suggested, essentially, that the "wine" of the Bible was not the same as the wine of present day, i.e., less potent. Alexander Campbell, predictably, weighed in, supporting temperance but not temperance societies, arguing that the societies undercut the authority of churches, which should have sole responsibility for moral discipline.[142] And then, there was the question of *temperance* (moderate consumption) versus total *abstinence*, never entirely resolved although early Disciples leaders inclined to abstinence.

By the end of the 19th and beginning of the 20th centuries, the temperance discussion had taken on the language of the Social Gospel. Temperance organizations such as the Women's Christian Temperance Union and the Anti-Saloon League were "less reliant upon demonstrating explicit biblical support for its mandate," than the "culmination of a gradual movement away from moral suasion to legal means as the primary mode of achieving temperance."[143] Still to be resolved was the use of wine in communion. Disciples women were among the founders of the Women's Christian Temperance Union in 1874, and a number of them targeted the use of wine in communion. "From literally praying outside saloons to making speeches in church protesting communion while communion was being served, these Disciples Women fought fiercely for what they believed."[144]

Grape juice, specifically Welch's grape juice, was invented by a Methodist minister, Thomas Bramwell Welch, in 1869, for the purpose of removing alcohol from the communion service. It became generally popular when introduced at the Chicago World's Fair in 1893.[145] Wine was served at communion in the early years of Country Club's history, documented as an expense (modest) in the regular budget. It is not clear when grape juice was substituted for true wine, but that is the practice today. Disciples of Christ, unlike many mainline Protestant denominations, take communion weekly in accordance with the early Christian's practice of weekly meals together. It is one of the sacred rites in church practices, but it too has undergone changes, adapting to enhanced knowledge about health and sanitation, and recognition that alcoholism is a disease, not a moral lapse. Unlike wine, the dispensation of communion bread has prompted far less discussion: leavened or unleavened; whole loaf, individual pieces, or wafers; gluten or gluten-free?

Prohibition had a dark side, consequences that optimistic proponents did not fully anticipate: speakeasies, bootlegging, clubs that hosted gambling and prostitution (but also provided venues for the flourishing of that distinctively American music form, jazz), and the corrupt political machines that made it all possible. Kansas City was a "wide open town" in those years, under the firm control of "Boss" Tom Pendergast. It was sometimes referred to as Tom's Town, a city where the police and city government were simply extensions of Pendergast's vast empire. His was fully in place by 1925, but even before that events foretold the circumstances to come.

In June, 1923, W. Wallace Greene, a prominent Kansas City attorney, former State Senator in the Missouri House, and a member of Country Club Christian Church, was murdered in his home on W. 58th Street after he and his wife had returned from a moving picture show. The story dominated the news over the next 16 months, revealing the sordid Kansas City crime scene and providing a dispiriting picture of the police department. Dr. Combs led the funeral service, attended by more than 800 people with several hundred more left without seats. *The Star* documented his "impassioned appeal for a spirit of justice that will end the present crime wave. 'I can find no impropriety,' Combs stated, 'in standing beside the bier of my fallen friend and decrying the state of affairs of which he was a victim. There is no spirit of vengeance in the thought that urges every high-minded citizen to rise up against the menace that has taken Wallace Greene from us.'" [146] The church board took the unusual step of pledging $300 dollars to the reward fund.

Initially, investigators dismissed the possibility that the crime was anything other than a burglary gone badly wrong. By July 19th an arrest had been made. In the next few months in language that evokes a 1930s noir detective novel, *The Star*, usually on the front page, recounted the steps that led to the arrest and its consequences. The suspect was the proprietor of a "semi-saloon," a euphemism for a licensed soft drink business that illegally sold the hard stuff as well, located on 12th Street on the North Side "where some of the 'boys' have their hangouts ... soft drink parlors, shady houses, any place where the 'gang' happened to be." [147] He was unearthed by an undercover policeman who worked his way into the confidence of some of the 12th Street habitués. After his arrest, the suspect, a man named Richardson, signed a confession, but later recanted the confession, saying he had been subjected to the "third degree" with a rubber hose. That was vigorously denied by the police, one of whom said matter-of-factly, "there was no rubber hose used on Richardson. There was no need," begging the question of when there is a "need." [148]

The trial was conducted before a grand jury of twelve men; one of the Assistant Prosecutors was none other than George Hamilton Combs, Jr., a Kansas City attorney and active Democrat in Jackson County. Among a number of odd moves, the police at one point took Richardson to the Greene address and told him to re-enact the entire crime. He was quickly convicted and sentenced to life in prison despite the prosecution's request for the death penalty by hanging. The murder was never linked directly to the Pendergast machine, but the "underworld" so vividly described in news reports was clearly in the background. The boundaries between felons and police were fluid; Richardson was an ex-patrolman, and the undercover agent who was lionized for breaking the case and receiving much of the reward money was soon dismissed from the department for assaulting a local barber.

While his role in the Greene murder trial was relatively minor, George Hamilton Combs, Jr., at the age of twenty-six, was a rising star in Kansas City Democratic politics. In October 1925, he attracted the unwelcome and very public attention of Pendergast in what quickly turned into a shouting match on Walnut Street that also pulled in Joe Shannon (the leader of a Democratic faction that opposed Pendergast). Pendergast had taken umbrage at a reported verbal slight on the part of the younger Combs and made his ire clear to him and everyone else who had gathered on the sidewalk. In its front-page coverage, *The Star* reported that Pendergast was "rather flushed" and Combs was "pale."[149] As Combs, Jr. recounted twenty years later: "During this period I was informed that Mr. Pendergast was incensed over what he regarded as my personal attacks on him during the campaign. Aside from the reference to him as not big enough to dominate the party, I had made no such assault and felt badly about the misunderstanding because both of these Irishmen were the sort to command a good deal of affection (as well as respect!) and Tom had been generous to me in the past." They straightened matters out, and Pendergast ensured Combs Jr.'s nomination and election to Congress in 1926. [150] Young Combs was part of the generation that would eventually constitute the New Deal Democrats, who in the decades to come would address issues of race, poverty, social welfare, and government's increasing role in the lives of Americans. His father was a Southern Democrat of the old school and remained so throughout his life. The consequences to institutional religion were enormous and would take many years to be fully understood. [151]

The people and events of the Roaring Twenties and the Depression era to come filled the daily papers, radio broadcasts, and newsreels. But there is minimal mention of these matters in either *The Christian* or the board minutes. Both require a close reading to discern not only an awareness but a strong commitment to address the economic and social crises that were engulfing America and the world. A front-page article in *The Christian* in May 1930, spoke of "the bootlegging banditry of Chicago and Kansas City," and some years later in March 1935, the newsletter noted a "stirring talk on adverse civil and political conditions in Kansas City" presented to the Endeavor group (young adult class), but that kind of acknowledgment was relatively infrequent.

Sin, vice, and corruption have fueled the oratory of priests and prophets from time immemorial. Relatively few of Dr. Combs' sermons survive today; neither they nor his weekly columns in *The Christian* focus on the issues of the day and the crime that was drawing national attention to Kansas City. A few passing references to jazz (he didn't care for it) and Darwin occasionally appear but only in the context of other topics. And yet, to understand the significance of the times we need to heed the reminder that "men and women experience national and global events in intimate settings." [152] Country Club Christian Church was such a setting.

There are undoubtedly a number of explanations for what seem from today's perspective to be a mystifying lack of attention and concern. To some extent the lingering decorum and gentility of an earlier era still prevailed in mainstream Protestant services. Certain topics (brothels and saloons among them) were considered inappropriate for sermons and discussion, especially in mixed company. The assertion of early Movement leaders that politics was a matter of opinion, not church doctrine, continued to hold sway, and whether a Disciple or not, there was further assumption on the part of many that business and religion should keep their distance from one another. "With a few minor exceptions, the clergy in the past had rigorously observed the tradition that government was a monopoly of the businessman and their political stooges." [153]

In 1925, in his regular Sunday evening service, a Kansas City Disciples minister criticized the city's court system as corrupt and unfair. A furious local judge hauled the clergyman into his court the next morning and challenged the assumptions of the sermon. *The Star* provided front page coverage that, if nothing else, entertained the community for several days as attorneys and clerics expressed outrage. Frank Bowen called an "Indignation" meeting, and *The Star* proceeded to interview a number of local pastors, including George Combs, who stated, "I shall feel perfectly free at all times to discuss public questions not connected with partisan politics."[154] Alexander Campbell would have approved.

Pendergast, some argued, was good for business by creating jobs, a particularly strong argument with the onset of the Great Depression, and by attracting people to the city's lively social and cultural scene. And for some years, there seemed to be a tacit agreement to live and let live. Westbrook Pegler, the acerbic and often controversial New York columnist wrote of Kansas City in characteristic style:

> Here is a paradox for you. Tom Pendergast, the Democratic boss of Kansas City gives good, rotten government, and runs a good, rotten city whose conventional Americans of the home-loving, baby-having, 100 percent type live on terms of mutual toleration with wide open vice and gambling.
>
> But in spite of all this — and this is what drives the opposition wild — Mr. Pendergast runs a good town, with efficient public services and with comparatively little violent crime.[155]

As late as 1932, when serious challenges to the Pendergast machine were being posed by clergy, one Chamber of Commerce representative said, "It is all right for the churches to go on preaching the old-fashioned gospel and building up a moral laity, but when it comes to ministers fighting politics, I just can't follow them."

Perhaps not ministers, but an energetic rabbi had greater success. By the 1930s, Pendergast's critics were organizing under the leadership of Rabbi Samuel Mayerberg, the dynamic head of Temple B'nai Jehudah. Mayerberg had arrived in Kansas City in 1928. From the beginning, he was an outspoken advocate for social justice and good government. By 1932 he was targeting the corruption in Kansas City government and in May of that year he gave a speech to a group of club women, the Government

Study Club, that was received enthusiastically and reported in the paper. Club women, as they were always described, would provide the backbone for Mayerberg's anti-corruption campaign for years to come. One of them was Margaret J. Kemp, the wife of William Kemp, one of three Country Club members, along with Ilus Davis and Kay Barnes, to be elected mayor of Kansas City. Mrs. Kemp, like her husband, was a progressive who held many significant leadership positions in social justice causes. In 1950 she was named the chair of the governor's Midcentury White House Committee on Children and Youth; she worked closely with Rabbi Mayerberg, and he joined her on the committee.

As a Jew and a relatively recent arrival to the city, Rabbi Mayerberg was in what proved to be the advantageous position of not being deeply entrenched in the Kansas City establishment that had tolerated Pendergast for so long. He had something to say to the businessmen, including those in his own congregation, whom he found to be complacent in the face of increasingly overt corruption and organized crime:

> It won't be long before you real estate men and you insurance men will be visited by a man, supported by another, who stands a pace or two to the rear with hand in a coat pocket, and hear a proposition whereby your visitor would receive a certain portion of your income. [156]

"The Rabbi could not at one blow knock out the deep-rooted convention that the preacher's place was in the pulpit, far above the mundane concerns of men, but he did succeed in demolishing the popular notion that ministers have no talent for the political life." [157] He was a gifted public speaker who addressed a wide range of civic and political groups in his efforts to organize an anti-Pendergast coalition. He maintained a warm relationship with Country Club long after the Pendergast era including as a guest speaker at the Young Married People's class in October 1934 where he generated "swelled attendance"; and the leader of a series of lectures for youth groups in 1947.

Another group was the Ministerial Alliance of Greater Kansas City, an ecumenical although largely Protestant organization that assumed the role of moral watchdog in the community, opposing gambling and the construction of racetracks, inviting Hollywood executives to speak on the moral issues posed by movies, and so on. Although individual members were often people of status who had influence with their own congregations, the group as a whole did not seem to have had much real authority. George Combs never referred to his memberships and community affiliations, probably a result of personal predilection as well as the long-standing Disciples aversion to "associations," but a man of his stature would assuredly have belonged to the group.

The Country Club Board actively supported anti-racing efforts. Reports vary as to the extent of support provided to Mayerberg by the Alliance, best summed up by Mayerberg himself in a later memoir when he described the "ringing endorsement" and promises of aid that he received from the Alliance. "I regret, however, that only four [of the ministers] remained with me to the end."[158] By the time his campaign was in full force, the Depression had taken a major toll on area churches. Some barely survived or folded; others, like Country Club, remained viable but at a significant cost: budget and staff cuts and the consequent reductions in programming. The immediate needs of the congregation and established commitments were priorities that superseded any additional involvement.

Mayerberg was threatened by calls to his home and survived an assassination attempt; he left town for a few months, assuring everyone that he would be back. His temple board warned him to cease his efforts, to no avail. The St. Louis paper, in an admiring article about the Rabbi, concluded that "The machine, of course, is not worried ... The organization is entrenched to a degree that it is almost invulnerable."[159] But the gradual chipping away of the Machine's strength had begun, further aided by the unrelenting attacks by William Rockhill Nelson, the owner and publisher of *The Kansas City Star*. It would take some years, but Pendergast was finally brought down on income tax evasion charges in 1939 and incarcerated in the federal prison in Leavenworth, Kansas. When he was released, his health was broken, and the machine shattered.

Not many years later, Dr. Combs broke his silence about Pendergast, writing about him at some length in his memoir, where he expressed the compassion of a pastor and the humor of a born storyteller. He framed his memories in terms of the conflict between a "great newspaper, *The Kansas City Star*," and a "great political boss, Thomas J. Pendergast." About *The Star*, he acknowledged that it was difficult to write since "its publisher and three of its editors were members of my church ... and most of the time, through the years, I have marched under its banner." But it was also difficult to write about Pendergast because of "my sympathies that go out to an old man broken on the wheel of life." Despite "marching under *The Star's* banner," Combs revealed his own political leanings:

A City Church

The fighting Rabbi. Rabbi Samuel Mayerberg with U.S. District Attorney Maurice Milligan who successfully prosecuted Tom Pendergast. Mayerberg is holding Milligan's book, *Missouri Waltz,* **while being interviewed by WHB's John Thornberry.** *Donald Dwight Davis Papers (K0934) SHSMO-Kansas City.*

"politically, *The Star* declares itself independent, though to some of us Southern-born Democrats it has an irritating habit in national elections of nearly always supporting the Republican party" with the result that "tens of thousands of Democrats were horribly confused" despite their opposing political corruption. But he resumed the voice of the pastor by concluding:

> With no condoning of his wrongdoings, I can but recollect that he was brought up in a rough, tough school; that he but did, in the large, what thousands of others have done in the small; that though with greater acumen than that of most political bosses, he was less gifted than they in the art of self-exaltation; that his sins were found out, and theirs weren't. Rather, my scorn is for his erstwhile satellites, who bowed before him in his years of power,

81

but now, only in the dark, if at all, ring the bell of a ghost-haunted mansion on Ward Parkway where lives a broken old man alone. [160]

More recent assessments of the Pendergast years share Combs' nuanced interpretation, noting that "the economy and population boomed," and as a result "Kansas City and its people seemed to weather the Great Depression better than most other places." [161]

In October 1929, the stock market collapsed, marking the beginning of a decade-long economic crisis that would only end with the onset of World War II. Economic uncertainty had already taken hold throughout much of the world; the Depression became a worldwide experience. In a 1965 essay that remains a seminal statement about American religion in the Great Depression, Robert Handy offered some "interpretative guidelines" that are useful for understanding the impact of the crisis on Country Club Christian Church. He argued that there were really two depressions — one economic and the other religious. The two were, of course, closely intertwined, but they were in many ways two distinct phenomena. The religious depression pre-dated the economic and it eventually reshaped American Protestantism. It was characterized by a number of markers: a general spiritual and cultural malaise that resulted from the disillusionment that followed World War I; a dramatic shift (what some would call loosening) of cultural and social norms symbolized by the Roaring Twenties; and a decline in support of religious missions, both domestic and foreign. [162] When he resigned from Independence Boulevard Church, George Combs spoke for a generation when he explained that "he had come back from France seeing things religious with different eyes than when he went, and could not reconcile himself to continue in view of prevailing conditions." [163]

Handy, along with many others, makes a strong case for the concept of a "Protestant America," dating from the latter half of the 19th century, that was challenged by all these factors and collapsed under the weight of the economic calamity. Protestant America posited an "identification of Protestantism with America": Protestant values were American values; patriotism and citizenship were closely aligned with spiritual premises. [164] The perceived failure of these values, many concluded, was an indictment of the apparent failure of religion, specifically the Protestant faith. But in the end, religion, both institutional and spiritual, endured in new and sometimes unrecognizable manifestations by adapting to a dramatically changed society, leading observers to recognize " … the remarkable persistence of religious proclivities in a century many thought would see the triumph of secularism."[165]

The decline in missions, one of Handy's indicators of the religious depression, was a source of serious concern to Country Club Christian Church, which had actively supported a variety of domestic and foreign missions from the beginning. "Mission" — a term inextricably linked with evangelical Protestantism — was central to the Disciples tradition. Alexander Campbell had originally argued that the church performed the role of mission and anything outside the church diluted its authority. He gradually altered his views and by the end of the 19th century there was agreement, at least among what became the Disciples branch, that administratively distinct missionary programs, both domestic and foreign, were necessary.

In its broadest sense, mission conveyed the commitment to sharing the Christian message; in practice it took many forms, both at home and abroad. Frank Bowen was a "missionary" to the greater Kansas City area, a position that was both entrepreneurial and administrative. Country Club supported the Mexican Christian Institute at 2322 Mercier in a variety of ways, many of which fell under the heading of social services. Its identification as "Mexican" and its status as a mission, referred to as a "home-foreign" missionary project, spoke to perceptions of its members as somehow "other" despite the fact that Mexican-Americans had resided in Kansas City for generations. The Institute was supported largely through the Christian Women's Council and the Joint Board of Christian Churches of the City Missions Committee.

They gathered at the river. Photo sent to Country Club by the church-sponsored "Ozark Missionary" in the 1930s. *CCCC Archive*

During the 1920s and 1930s the church also contributed to the support of an Ozarks missionary who provided colorful letters to his sponsors that were often included in *The Christian*. His work fit the profile of earlier itinerant pastors who travelled from community to community, preaching, leading revivals, and above all saving souls who responded to the "call."

Home missions lost support well before the 1929 crash as attested to by the executive secretary of the Home Missions Council: "Almost all major denominations are now in a period of financial stringency in the conduct of mission work."[166] In January, 1930, Frank Bowen made an unusual plea to Kansas City Disciples that was printed in *The Christian*:

> This is but the second time, in all my work as City
> Missionary, covering a period of almost thirty-three
> years, that I have sent out an appeal like this one ...
> Most of our schools [i.e., Church schools] contribute to
> state and national work and I firmly believe that they will
> help City Missions now ... We are suggesting an amount
> which if given by the several schools will make it possi-
> ble through some other assistance to get out of debt and
> pay those we owe. Our fields in which we cooperate are
> General City Missions through myself, The West Side
> Church and our City Mexican work.

He was requesting $100 each from targeted churches, over and above the usual annual contribution and the record shows that Country Club complied.

Finally, there was a long history of Disciples missionaries who served overseas, often in circumstances of considerable hardship, danger, and persecution. Many of these individuals were sponsored by a Disciples missionary society; there had been a number of such organizations, sometimes at odds with one another, since the early 19th century. The history is complex and reveals changing views of the concept of mission as well as who should be in charge. At the annual convention in 1874, the American Christian Missionary Society, begun in 1849, sponsored a standing committee called the Christian Woman's Board of Missions, and a planning committee for a Foreign Christian Missionary Society (even-tually a stand-alone entity). By 1920, all the missionary organizations were united under one rubric, the United Christian Missionary Society (UCMS) with two divisions, foreign and domestic.[167]

The changes that occurred over a century within missionary work were far more than administrative. A gradual, often incremental transition from early strategies that employed language such as "heathens" and "superstitions" and were grounded in the old colonial and imperial equation of civilization, Americanization, and Christianity gave way to broader appreciation of the singular traditions and customs embraced by cultures around the world. The transition was formally acknowledged in 1959 by the UCMS, affirming "human dignity, freedom, and economic justice as legitimate concerns of Christian faith," and that "mission effort should intimately relate to the life of the people by assisting in the development of indigenous forms of worship, leadership, organization, and theology." [168]

Mission locations existed, or had been attempted, throughout the world. China, India, and Japan were particularly appealing to the mission impulse, combining the lure of the exotic and a determination to spread the Christian message. Disciples had been active in China since 1886, and R.A. Long had funded an educational building at a Japanese mission in the early 1900s. "Preaching" missionaries on their own were not always very successful. It was only when they were joined by medical professionals and teachers that Asian communities were more receptive to welcoming the outsiders. Pearl Buck, who had been raised in China as the daughter of missionaries, published her enormously successful novel, *The Good Earth*, in 1931. It contributed significantly to providing readers with a sympathetic and humane portrait of the Chinese, as did A. J. Cronin's novel, *The Keys of the Kingdom*, published at the start of the war in 1941. His account, covering many decades, of a humble missionary priest in China further expanded western views of Asia and provided a nuanced, often moving account of a missionary's life. [169]

Among those Disciples serving as missionaries abroad was a relatively small group termed "Living Links." These were individuals who, in addition to support from the national organizations, also had an affiliation with one or more specific congregations. Starting in the late 1920s, Country Club Christian Church sponsored a young woman named Margaret Lawrence as their Living Link to China. During that time, she gained the affection and support of the congregation who followed her activities closely. It was a challenging time for missions; financial support had begun to decline before the stock market crash and would continue a steady downward trend. Missionary work had traditionally attracted young healthy adults, the very group that had been so disaffected after the war, and the number of new recruits declined significantly throughout the 1920s. The 1929 meeting of the Foreign Missions Conference of North America reported that only 252 students had volunteered for foreign assignment in 1928, a significant decrease from 2700 in 1920. [170]

"Miss Margaret" was born in 1900 in Maryville, Missouri, the daughter of a Disciples minister who relocated to Illinois in 1903. [171] She completed her education at Hiram College and Drake University, both Disciples institutions, and then began her first assignment in China in 1925 or 1926 as a teacher. It was a time of almost overwhelming turbulence in that country: civil war, famine, corrupt and broken government, and increasingly aggressive actions by Japan. She returned to the United States in 1927 where she continued her education, including study at the Kennedy School of Missions in Connecticut, an affiliate of the Hartford Theological Seminary. The seminary, the first in the country to admit female students in 1889 was in the forefront of theological education. The Mission School, organized in 1911, was a direct response to a call for more rigorous training of those working in the mission field.

At the May 1929 board meeting, Dr. Combs proposed that Margaret Lawrence be considered as a Living Link missionary, as "he believed our church should put a missionary out in the field next year and wanted our committee to confer with her and see if arrangements could be made to have her represent our church." At the June meeting, apparently after some discussion with Miss Lawrence, the board moved to contact the United Christian Missionary Society indicating their willingness to be identified as a Living Link church to sponsor her on behalf of Country Club Christian. But in July, UCMS responded that the situation in China was still too unsettled to safely send her back to China (the implication being to send a *woman*), and the board responded that the church would wait until such time as Miss Lawrence could return. UCMS took the hint and the September 1929 *Christian* published a letter from the organization under the title "Would You Not Like to Help?" It is a masterpiece of persuasion:

> We have been facing a very difficult situation because it was necessary to make a very severe reduction in our budget ... and China had to come in for a large part of this reduction. We were uncertain for a while as to whether we could send Miss Margaret out.

In these days of transition in China when the Chinese are so much in the leadership, they are very sensitive about the expenditure of money and the way it goes into work. To have to discharge quite a large group of Chinese trained leaders, and at the same time send out a new missionary from America, who would need an extra budget and would undertake new work, has presented a grave situation for us. I am wondering if you people there could do something beyond the Living Link, because of this emergency.

Miss Margaret is a wonderful girl. She spent about ten years of her life getting ready for the mission field, then went to China, then was obliged to come home because of the Revolution, and has been giving two more years to training with great difficulty because of personal expense involved, and is now ready to go. Her heart is almost breaking because of the uncertainty. Your church is very fortunate in having so noble a young woman, who has already made her place in China; and whose heart is in China and its work with such tremendous enthusiasm and consecration.

It happens that one of our schools out there for girls is just now suffering for leadership ... and for this year we can no doubt slip Miss Margaret into this school, and thus the Chinese will feel that we have done the right thing.

The letter is significant for a number of reasons: a decision that only recently would have been in the church board's exclusive domain (i.e., to fund the Living Link) has been opened to the entire congregation via the newsletter; the UCMS has referred a key decision regarding one of its primary functions back to a local congregation; and, the UCMS has expanded governance in a foreign mission to include the local population, who are no longer merely the objects of missionary efforts. All three transitions were to some degree the immediate consequence of the Depression, but they were not short term. The commonality among the three is a move from centralized top-down authority to a more inclusive decision-making process, and they signaled a major paradigm shift in Disciples operations.

Matters moved briskly from that point on, documented by almost weekly entries in *The Christian*. Perhaps not surprisingly, it was the women of the church who took on much of the care of "Our Margaret," hearkening back to long ago days in the Disciples denomination when women had been the principal advocates for missionary work. By 1929, it was considered safe for her to return to China under the official sponsorship of the United Christian Missionary Society as the Living Link of Country Club Christian Church. She located in the city of Wuhu, on the Yangtze River in southeastern China. The church shared her letters and chronicled her activities, often through a column in *The Christian* titled "World Friendship Corner" that reported on international matters in general with a particular emphasis on China. When she wrote that she was learning the "new language," finding it difficult but not "impossible" as the old language had been, *The Christian* followed up with several columns devoted to the development of a written form of Mandarin, the "new" language. Margaret became fluent to the point that she mixed English and Mandarin in the same sentence, and by the end of her life she preferred to say the Lord's Prayer in Mandarin.

Another front-page column in *The Christian* addressed the question: "Why should America be so concerned about what happens in China?" The response was straightforward: "There are two vital reasons — the one social and political, in a way, selfish; the other, religious — therefore unselfish!" And still another column told readers what the missionary does: "When the missionary goes to any field, his first concern is to find the greatest need of the people." Those needs included medical assistance, alleviation of hunger, construction of clean sturdy homes, clothing — all to be gained through training of essential skills, not simply donations. "Of course, the end aim is to teach and preach the gospel of 'Jesus and his love' but the [the missionary] 'becomes all things to all men' — literally."

Challenging years lay ahead; Miss Margaret was in Shanghai in 1937 when the Japanese attacked, and her lengthy letter, published in *The Christian,* gave a graphic, at times horrifying description of what she described as a "real war." She escaped to Manila, and then returned to Wuhu only to experience the bombing there as well. She assisted in the hospital and continued to teach, but was finally forced to leave China in 1940. Returning to America, she continued her education at Yale Divinity

School, and returned once again to Free China in 1943, after a long arduous journey over the infamous "hump" in southeast Asia, avoiding the Japanese-occupied coastline in China. She returned to Wuhu at war's end but by the late 1940s she left China, fully engaged in civil war, for the now-welcoming Japan where she continued to teach. [172]

Margaret had to resign her official association with Country Club in 1952 when she returned to the States to assume a national position with the UCMS, but remained "Our Margaret." Long-term member Jay Wooldridge recalled that the children all learned a Chinese song to welcome Margaret on one of her regular visits to Country Club. [173] She retired in 1967 to Foxwood Springs, the Disciples continuing care facility in Raymore, Missouri. Margaret Lawrence died on February 25, 1984, at the age of 84. At her funeral at Country Club Christian Church, the congregation celebrated her life by singing "In Christ There is no East or West."

Margaret Lawrence's devotion to China was shared across the missionary spectrum in the late 19th and 20th centuries. In 1953 a book entitled *The Lost Churches of China* expressed the deep sense of regret and loss for a country that had been the object of so much attention by so many. As Robert Ellwood observed, "it was a hard setback to accept, almost as much for mainstream Protestants as for evangelical and Roman Catholic missionaries who had suffered so much, for China had long been a special preserve of the liberal vision of Missions, educational and democratizing as well as soul saving, inspired by the 'best' U.S. values." [174]

"Our Margaret." Margaret Lawrence, the beloved Living Link missionary sponsored by Country Club Christian Church for more than two decades.
CCCC Archive

One area in which Country Club's experience does not mirror changes that were occurring throughout Protestantism in the Depression years was a decline in Christian Education. Handy and others note particularly the impact of reduced church staff, including directors of religious education, and cutbacks in higher education programs that trained such individuals. From the beginning, Country Club prioritized educational programs and continued to do so throughout the Depression. The church had been fortuitous in its selection of directors of education; Paul Rains was succeeded, after a year-long search, by the equally capable L. B. Conrad, who stayed for more than seven years, leaving only to assume an associate minister position in another church. He was followed by David Owen, who moved seamlessly into the position, bringing still more skills to the education program. The directors possessed endless energy and administrative skills, and the personalities that inspired others to work with them. They were able to successfully manage their offices, even while the support of state and national education organizations eroded. During their tenures, the number of classes expanded as did enrollment. The 1931-1932 year, an otherwise grim period for church staffing, boasted 112 education staff and teachers.

Religious Education in the first half of the 20th century was highly structured; directors such as Rains and Conrad were overseen and assisted by designated board members and "superintendents" — respected church members actively involved in programming. School-age children took tests and were promoted to the next level when they had successfully completed standardized curriculum and maintained regular attendance. Religious Education vocabulary is today much the same as one hundred years ago, but with changed meanings. Today we usually associate the term Sunday school with children under the age of eighteen; then, all ages were expected to be enrolled in Sunday school, or more commonly, Bible school. Hence, references in *The Christian* to the "school" referred to the entire congregation.

In practice, the entire congregation was not necessarily engaged in Bible school, something that Dr. Combs commented on regularly with disapproval. Everyone was expected to attend church services after Sunday school, again a practice not always followed, especially in the case of the children. Country Club children were grouped together by age fairly early in the church's history, but the adult classes continued to be segregated by gender until after the war, with the exception of several groups such as the Married People's class, launched somewhat earlier.

Superintendents and teachers received stipends, another practice that succumbed to the exigencies of budget cuts.

Like many institutions, Country Club did not immediately feel the
impact of the October 1929 crash. The board minutes and *The Christian*
document the experiences of the church throughout the years of the
Great Depression. The minutes are primarily concerned with finances
and administration, while *The Christian* offers rich detail about the many
ways the people of the church faced and responded to the crisis.

There were optimistic plans for the 1930 budget proposed at almost
$49,000, but by 1935 the budget was cautiously set at $31,560 and there
was a carry-over of a $2,183 deficit from the previous year. Dr. Combs
remained determinedly positive. At the first meeting of 1931, the board
cut the year's budget by almost $7,000 after the Finance Committee con-
cluded it would be impossible to raise the funds for the originally proposed budget. Dr. Combs followed that discussion by remarking that the
new membership goal for the year should be 500, "after attaining which
the finances would take care of themselves." Later that year he informed
board members that if their businesses had "suffered no larger slump than
had the church they were indeed fortunate men." Their response is not
recorded. But as the year wore on, it was clear that serious, if not draco-
nian measures were necessary. The salaried music quartet was dismissed
in the spring and told their contract would not be renewed for the following year.

Debate continued for many months, until finally at the end of December
the board convened a special meeting. It prompted "considerable discussion." One of the proposals was that Mr. Conrad (director of religious
education) assume the role of choir director, since he had done that prior
to coming to Country Club, and that Mrs. Combs resume her position as
church organist, but without pay — in other words, eliminate the Music
Department. That generated vigorous dissent from those who pointed out
that Mr. Conrad was already over-extended, and Mrs. Darnall had loyal
support within the congregation as well as a contract that needed to be
honored. The final budget included Mrs. Darnall, at a 10 percent salary
reduction; the organist would be retained and their salary would also be
cut by 10 percent,, as would the salaries of Dr. Combs, Mr. Conrad, and
Mr. Rouse. Individual board members agreed to cover costs associated
with *The Christian* and the annual audit.

The low point of the Depression was 1933, when newly sworn in
President Franklin D. Roosevelt told the country that the only thing to

fear was fear itself. In September 1935, FDR sent a form letter to ministers, priests, and rabbis throughout the country asking for their "counsel and help." Dr. Combs used the following Sunday's sermon to respond to the request, titling his sermon "If a Preacher Were President — What?" Slowly, the economy began to improve and by 1935 small indicators were reported in the church minutes: contributions for missions were up slightly; the chair of the Music Committee pointed out that the choir would lose key members who no longer needed to count on their stipends. The church made a significant commitment by agreeing to purchase an "Acousticon" with four receivers to be installed in what was still referred to as the Auditorium for the benefit of the hearing impaired. The cost was $350, which could not be handled by the budget; the funds would need to be raised as a special contribution. A delighted parishioner sent a thank-you letter to the board after Sunday's service, saying that "I heard a complete service from the tiny voices of the Kiddie Choir until Dr. Combs' benediction. For the first time in 30 years, I did not miss a single expression." He also astutely noted that his three guests who accompanied him to the service had placed larger than usual offerings in the plate.

These modest positive steps were countered by other reminders of the concerns that were so pressing. Interest on the church debt was significantly overdue; unpaid pledges to the Building Fund amounted to about $29,000, and the chair of the committee said he did not think more than $2,000 of that was good. There were monthly overdrafts. Even a relatively simple expenditure — the purchase of additional communion implements — was debated, and the original proposal to buy four sets was reduced to two. The board issued a stern and somewhat exasperated resolution attempting to address the situation, noting that "the deficit has increased constantly with no apparent definite plan for meeting the emergency ... other religious and educational institutions have met this emergency successfully by reducing expenses to an amount that is covered by actual income received." The resolution concluded that "no obligations of any kind whatsoever be created that cannot be paid out of current income during the year."

There was no single explanation for the budgetary issues; these were hard times, and the budget had been reduced to bare bones. Some of the problems related to the apparent inability to enforce standard procedures for incurring, documenting, and receiving permission for expenses. The board members were primarily businessmen — what Dr. Combs referred to as "substantial men." But they were also parishioners, loyal to and caring about their church, and willing to help however they could. The music budget was a case in point. The Music Committee invariably ran over budget, often significantly; Mrs. Darnall's artistic sensibilities were not readily constrained by mere numbers. Just as invariably board member Mr. Nugent, who was in charge of the Music Committee, wrote a personal check to make up the difference. That helped, but it didn't actually square the bookkeeping, to say nothing of creating an untenable precedent. Charlie Rouse, and others, would write painfully courteous letters to the committee, explaining that they really needed to adhere to the budget, only to have to do so again the following year.

Mr. Nugent's generosity was by no means unique. By 1935 Langston Bacon and a number of the early members and leaders had died or could no longer participate. As the economic crisis deepened, the minutes acknowledged ruefully that those who had once been in a position to help were not there, and many active members were barely making ends meet. The long-term consequences, however, suggested considerable potential for leadership and management. The early charter members were singularly effective in launching and running the church. But the glacially slow process of creating a regular system of leadership rotation had resulted in a closed group who, for good or ill, seemed to have everything in hand. Despite Dr. Combs' insistence that more people be added to the board, elder and deacon rosters, the leaders remained in place, with little apparent opportunity for newcomers to assume those roles.

The Christian documents a record of steady efforts throughout the Depression era to provide for those in need. A December 1931 article invoked the tenets of the social gospel:

> With a growing appreciation of the social implications of the gospel of Christ our churches are taking an increasing interest in the care of fatherless and motherless little children, and their aged members left alone and in need in the decrepitude of old age. To answer the appeal of the worthy brother or sister in need and the cry of the helpless child is not optional; it is clearly **a divinely imposed duty.**

The Women's Council and associated circles were actively engaged in relief work: sewing clothes and blankets; collecting clothing, shoes, and food; and sponsoring and contributing financially to mission work as well as agencies serving children and the aged. The women were responsible for raising their own budget and did so by sponsoring fundraisers such as the annual Christmas bazaar and sales of the always popular cookbooks, as well as direct solicitation from members. Goodwill Industries placed announcements in *The Christian*, requesting donations and reminding readers to be sure they were actually giving their items to authentic Goodwill employees, not the imposters who were taking advantage of the times.

Regular pleas were printed in *The Christian*, especially at Thanksgiving and Christmas, from denominational agencies that served the orphaned and aged. Among the latter were elderly ministers who could no longer work and had no source of income. This had been an issue within the denomination for some time with efforts to protect pastors in dire need dating to 1895. What began as the Ministerial Relief Board was reorganized in 1928 as the Pension Fund of the Christian Church; the first payments were made in 1931. George Combs advocated strongly for the pension fund and Country Club's support of it, but it would be some time before coverage was widespread. During the Depression, the church "adopted" a retired minister who had been a long-time missionary in India. His son, a physician, presently served in India but had contemplated returning to America to care for his indigent parents until the church stepped in.

Much closer to home and distressing to many was the news in June 1935 that Frank Bowen was seriously ill. He had been the city evangelist for 40 years and was currently serving as pastor at Paseo Christian Church. The Joint Board of Christian Churches in Kansas City, which he had led, had been dissolved, still owing Reverend Bowen $1,000 in back pay. Paseo Church continued his salary of $2,200 a year, but could not continue to carry that amount. Board minutes concluded that "some relief must be given to this church immediately by the Christian Churches in greater Kansas City." Within weeks, Country Club and Independence Boulevard churches along with many other city churches had pledged $50 per month to relieve Bowen's situation, along with a commitment of $300 from the church mission fund.

Reverend Bowen died on March 30, 1938, at the age of 71 after a long and painful illness during which he continued to receive financial support and nursing care from Disciples. He and his wife and co-evangelist, Mary, had created and led one of the largest Disciples communities in the nation whose multiple institutions and programs served the community and beyond. His funeral service at First Christian was followed two weeks later by a memorial service held in conjunction with a meeting of twenty-seven area Disciples institutions, with an expected attendance of 500 people. Dr. Combs was one of the speakers. The board entered a resolution of thanks that included Mary, who continued to receive an allowance after her husband's death, and was also printed in *The Christian,* concluding that "We, each of us, owe him a debt of gratitude we can never pay and wish to make a record in the archives of our own church of this, our humble recognition of his splendid life and service here amongst us."

A number of the social service agencies (orphanages, old age homes) were part of the National Benevolent Association, which, like the UCMS suffered dramatic financial losses during the Depression. New Deal programs and their successors would gradually assume responsibility for services traditionally provided by religious institutions that had been overwhelmed by economic crisis, and that transition would be the basis of serious discussion among Disciples about their purpose and obligation in the world.

In March 1935, the board decided to invite Dr. Alexander Paul, for forty years a renowned missionary in China, to speak later in the spring for the purpose of renewing enthusiasm and raising money for mission work. His visit was announced in *The Christian* under the headline "The Irishman Who Wore His Hair in a Queue." The language in the article — "superstitions" and "yellow men" — was not unusual in discussions about foreign missions, but probably revealed more about the home population than Dr. Paul. His visit was billed as a fundraising event for missions and he exhorted his listeners to understand the significance of the cause:

> The orient offers a field for Christian teaching unparalleled in history. From the north, hordes of communists are sweeping down out of Russia with their insidious atheistical propaganda while at the same time we in our lethargy are year after year withdrawing Christian missionaries from the field ... Shall we do our part in the shaping of India, China, and Japan, and through them perhaps the entire world, to Christian ends, or shall communism and Godlessness triumph?

The political/military significance of the conflict between "atheistical communism" and "Christian democracy" would dominate religious

---

WHICH SHALL WIN— COMMUNISM OR CHRISTIANITY?

HALF THE WORLD'S POPULATION SWINGS IN THE BALANCE— IT IS FOR US TO DECIDE

Dr. Paul recently told us in his great missionary address how the walls of superstition and tradition are breaking down among India's 325 million people, among China's 400 million, among Japan's 100 million. Of these orientals who constitute half the inhabitants of the globe, eighty per cent are ignorant and illiterate but anxious to be taught.

WHO SHALL TEACH THEM?

THE HORDES OF COMMUNISTS SWEEPING DOWN FROM THE NORTH
or
THE APOSTLES OF CHRISTIANITY WHOM WE SEND TO REPRESENT US?

The first sow discord, promote war, create hopeless disaster. The second bring harmony, teach the ways of peace, create understanding, brotherhood, love. The former invade the orient in ever increasing numbers; of the latter—the missionaries we formerly sent out—only about half remain on the field because of lack of funds. Last year we held our own, withdrawing no missionaries; this year shall we not advance?

Cast your vote on the right side next Sunday—CHILDREN'S DAY— by being present in one of our classes with a generous offering to maintain our own Living Link in China and to help in the work around the world. Aid us in routing Communism. Join the militant forces to make Christ triumphant around the world!

Christianity vs. Communism. The stakes are high, as expressed in this strongly worded plea in *The Christian in 1935* to support Christian missionaries in Asia in their efforts to counteract communist influence. *CCCC Archives*

debate and would define and shape much of the 20th century. But as several months of board minutes document, Alexander Paul's proposed visit as well as other influences recall earlier discussions in the 1920s about the very mission of the church itself. In March 1935, the same month as the decision to invite Dr. Paul and the resolution regarding strict management of expenses, the Missionary Committee issued a two-page report to the board that offered a perspective on planning for the future. The document is significant for its spiritual argument as well as the fact that it was written in the midpoint of the Great Depression.

> By unanimous vote of the Committee, this report reiterates our conviction that the financial prosperity, substantial and persistent growth, and the spiritual welfare of the Country Club Christian Church are indissolubly interwoven with our interest in and service to our "brother" whoever and wherever he may be.

> We believe that the soul of the individual Christian who allows himself to become smug and self-satisfied, confining his interest and his service to his intimates and those of his own social stratum, will shrivel and die. We, likewise, believe in the inevitable death of that church which confines itself to its interests, to its own affairs [and] its own neighborhood.

> We feel throughout our church a decided lack of interest in the program of our Brotherhood at large ... would our membership be satisfied to know that less than three cents out of each dollar subscribed to our budget is expended for "others."

The document then outlines specific steps for better informing the congregation about missions, domestic and international, and ways to support them. The report, submitted as a resolution to the board was approved and served to guide the agenda in the coming months.

The multiple Disciples publications published during the Depression afford additional perspectives on how the denomination and its adherents were responding to events. In his examination of Disciples journalism during the Depression, William Paulsell noted that "because of the congregational polity of the Disciples there was no such thing as 'official' doctrine or position on social issues."[175] He examined four different periodicals that provide a range of viewpoints from conservative to liberal. *The Christian-Evangelist* was a publication of the St. Louis-based Christian Board of Publication, whose owner and president was R.A. Long. The publishing house continues today under the name of the Chalice Press. "To the extent that the Disciples had a voice it was that of *The Christian Evangelist*, clearly the publication of the moderate, cooperative wing of the brotherhood."[176] The *C-E* was referred to occasionally in *The Christian* and would have been the journal of choice for the church as indicated by subscription reminders.

The Christian Standard was a conservative publication that generally represented the views of the "independent" wing of the Stone-Campbell movement that had broken away from the Disciples some years before. *The Christian Standard* tended to invoke Old Testament judgment, pointing to the moral and spiritual lapses that had characterized the 1920s and equating stock market speculation with gambling. It took aim at the business models that had so intrigued the American public, undercutting the teachings of Christ and making them shallow, and concluded that "we can redeem society only when we have redeemed men." [177] At the liberal end of the spectrum was a publication called *The Christian*, an outgrowth of Burris Jenkins' Linwood Boulevard Christian Church newsletter that ceased publication in 1934. Jenkins argued that the Depression was at least in part the consequence of the isolationist stance assumed by the United States after World War I — that is, a failure to recognize our responsibility to the rest of the world, as well as the vengeful reparations imposed on the defeated. *The Christian-Evangelist* also cited moral failing, but emphasized the need to help those in need. It became, by and large, a supporter of New Deal reforms and social welfare. Paulsell concludes that Disciples (he is using the term broadly to include all factions of the Movement) "had very little to offer during the Depression in terms of religion ... this body was theologically unprepared for the Depression." [178]

Prior to the 1935 pledge drive, Combs wrote in the October 10 *Christian* that he was not going to "soft pedal" things: "All salaries have been twice reduced, expenses have been cut to the bone, economy has been not only preached but practiced, still there is that 'somewhat in arrears' which to a church of such financial resources as our own, is decidedly not complimentary." In his annual Christmas message, he acknowledged that "merriment is quite beyond the reach of many of us," and so he wished all a "Happy Christmas."

The church celebrated its fifteenth anniversary in January 1936, as a maturing organization that had an established administration and program of service. The church year had settled into a predictable rhythm: new membership drive culminating on Easter Sunday, Homecoming in September, pledge drives in November — all punctuated by the holy days of the liturgical seasons. Summer remained a slow time; *The Christian* took a hiatus as did board meetings. In 1938, the governing board organized a small executive committee, charged with the regular oversight of church management — a major step forward in streamlining and regularizing operations. Missionary outreach, domestic and foreign, was never abandoned, even when budget cuts were necessary. The church used local radio stations to provide information and presentations such as performances by the men's Glee Club. A program of monthly shut-in communion began in January 1938. Maintenance and upkeep issues, not surprising after fifteen years for a building used by 2,000 members, made demands on the budget. and the frustrated House Committee chairman finally issued an edict: "You raise the money and we will do the work." The boiler and heating system were a constant worry. Large portions of the plaster ceiling in what continued to be called the auditorium broke away suddenly, to the consternation of the people being seated below for a funeral.

Dr. Combs and Mr. Owen, the director of religion who now carried the title of associate minister, kept up a grueling schedule of personal calls — almost 500 in two months. And at the end of 1939 the Finance Committee singled out the Music Committee for, in the first time in years, having stayed within budget. Not all improvements were exclusive to the church; in 1939 the board sent a hearty endorsement to the Kansas City Board of Parks and the Works Progress Administration for a plan to finally grade and pave the "west roadway" of Ward Parkway between Meyer and Gregory Boulevards. Automobiles were using the east lane in both directions!

CHAPTER 7

A Time for War:
At Home and in Uniform

On September 1, 1939, Adolph Hitler ordered German troops to invade Poland, launching the Second World War. Unlike his muted commentary on previous alarming events, Dr. Combs responded immediately with verve and urgency through multiple columns in *The Christian,* quite different from his usual homilies promoting church attendance and meeting financial pledges. He forecast the economic boom that would soon occur, but cautioned against profiteering. He announced his annual series of talks to be presented at the Thursday evening dinners, when he would speak about "countries under the long shadows of war." He was passionate in his discussion of Japan, arguing, as had Margaret Lawrence in her letters to the church, that the U.S. must stop selling supplies to that country. And while remaining determinedly non-partisan, he wrote with fervent patriotism in praise of America. In a moving piece he recalled his own experience during World War I and how deeply it had damaged him. Returning to the old Disciples call for Christian unity, he argued that "the church is but a pale ghost in this world approach to Armageddon … largely because it is split up into denominational fragments and has neither sense enough nor grace enough to unite its forces." As months went by, Dr. Combs urged his parishioners to avoid being "ostriches" by writing to Congress, demanding that peace could only be preserved by military defense build-up. But he remained strongly opposed to direct involvement in Europe, reflecting the view of many clergymen in the pre-World War II years. [179]

In December 1940, George Hamilton Combs announced his plans to retire at the end of the following year. Throughout 1941, the church focused on two matters — bidding farewell to their beloved pastor and choosing his successor. His service was honored many times in the coming months and he took an active role, at least in the initial stages, of helping to identify his successor. In January, Combs wrote a five-page memorandum to the board, stating that "knowing this committee has no wide knowledge of our ministry at large, I felt that a little explanatory work on my part would at least give you a start in this undertaking." He did so by contacting a number of professionals within the denomination, asking for names of possible candidates, and elicited fourteen suggestions with comments. He concluded his memo by saying that "here my own part in the selection of my successor ends." He also explained that he and Mrs. Combs would continue their membership at Country Club; his named appeared on church literature as minister *emeritus* and he returned to the pulpit on numerous occasions.

One of the names on the Combs' list was Warren Grafton, the forty-year-old pastor of Walnut Hills Christian Church in Cincinnati, Ohio. The board agreed to call Reverend Grafton on July 2, to be offered a salary of $6,000 per year, a decision endorsed by the congregation on Sunday the 6th. Grafton was the son and grandson of Disciples ministers, and part of his childhood was spent in Kansas City when his father was senior minister at Jackson Avenue Church. He had degrees from Butler University and Union Theological Seminary, and he had already served appointments on a number of important Disciples committees. His wife Elizabeth came from a long line of distinguished Presbyterian clerics, and they were the parents of three young children.

On Sunday, December 28, 1941, George Hamilton Combs gave his final sermon to 1,000 members of Country Club Christian Church and stood for an hour afterwards to shake hands. Only three weeks before, Japanese bombers had attacked Pearl Harbor, bringing the United States into the war. The impact on the church was immediate; a new board committee was created under the aegis of the Department of Missions, called simply "Relative to Service Men." That was soon changed with the belated recognition that men and women were serving. The organist was drafted, and Mrs. Combs resumed her former role for most of the war. In November, missionary Dr. Alexander Paul returned to speak after spending a year as an "enemy alien" in China.

Shortly after Warren Grafton arrived in 1942, he announced plans for a new organizational model by creating a pastor's cabinet. It was approved by the Board of Elders, and then presented to the full board in June where, predictably, it generated "much discussion." The cabinet was to consist of eight departments, each headed by a chair who would be a board member. The departments included committees, each with their own chair. So, for example, the "Department of Worship" oversaw five committees: Communion, Ushers, Music, Baptism, and Attendance. The full cabinet would comprise seventeen members as well as the minister, associate minister, and business manager, who would have oversight responsibility for specific activities. The cabinet was to meet once a month including, unlike the board, during the summer, and then the head of each department would report at the board meetings. The new structure was essentially a recognition of the exponential growth of the church and the tasks associated with its management. It streamlined organization and afforded the senior minister a clear leadership role that was both administrative and spiritual. When the board reconvened in the Fall, the agenda for reports replicated the cabinet structure.

Gas rationing prompted a front-page discussion in *The Christian* that outlined carpooling, reduction of active church meeting days to Thursday and Sunday, and the creation of a Transportation Committee. Reverend Grafton concluded his comments by reminding readers that "the church of Jesus Christ existed before Henry Ford was born." Plans were made for dealing with food rationing (the Thursday evening dinners) and fuel rationing (limited times for when the church could be heated). Rationing was not the only war-time imposition; the church was not exempt from strict government rules limiting purchases of items made of materials that could be used by the military. In June 1944, Charlie Rouse submitted a priority form and detailed letter to the War Production Board in Washington, requesting permission to purchase an Addressograph machine for use in the church office. The machine then in use was twenty-five-years old and was not new when purchased, and repairs could no longer be made.

The Christian, mailed to all church members in the military, carried regular reports on those in service and their families, and the various circles and clubs provided support from the beginning. In 1944 alone, the Women's Council sewed 2,400 embarkation shirts for enlisted men, 110 hospital shirts, 40 convalescent men's robes, 98 baby garments, and 552 knitted garments. The council also organized a new circle just for the wives of men in the service. By War's end, 396 women and men from the church had joined all branches of the armed forces; ten would die while serving their country. On Sunday, June 14, 1942, appropriately Flag Day, the Church's Service Flag was rededicated. A blue star was added for each man and woman in the service; as time passed Gold Stars replaced

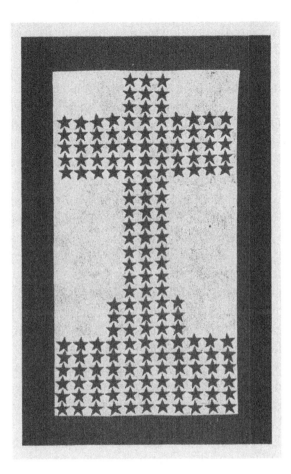

The CCCC Service Flag, dedicated on June 14th, 1942, that hung in the church foyer throughout WWII. The 5 x 8 foot flag was bordered in red; the blue stars, one for each member in uniform, were sewn on a white background. Ten of those stars were replaced by gold in honor of those who died. *CCCC Archives*

the blue — the first one in April 1943. The flag hung in the church foyer throughout the war.

The Service Flag Dedication figured in a letter Reverend Grafton sent at the end of May to all church members serving in the armed forces. Noting that "though I cannot see you and know you personally, I am conscious of you and of the service you are giving to our beloved land." He described the upcoming flag service where "prayers will be lifted, as they are on each Lord's day, for the triumph of the finest ideals in our Christian civilization and for your own safety during these days."

Grafton's concern was twofold: to provide ongoing communication and pastoral counsel to those in the service throughout the war, and to assure that they would return to a welcoming church that was prepared to meet their needs. To that end, in the fall of 1945 the minister proposed a new adult class for young married couples. They met for the first time on December 9, 1945, and decided on a name: Country Club Couples, or "Tri C's." They maintained a rotation of officers, but for thirty-three years there was only one lead teacher: Dr. Robert M. Myers, always addressed as "Dr. Bob." He was a physician and also an ordained minister who had planned to be a medical missionary, but those plans were cut short by the Depression and the inability of church organizations to support people in the field. The Tri C's maintained unusually thorough records of their membership and activities, and the multiple notebooks and scrapbooks are today an invaluable record of one contingent of what Tom Brokaw called the "Greatest Generation," those who had returned from the war, ready to start families, and build homes and businesses. They gathered each Sunday for a class that included prayer, hymns, and Dr. Bob's lesson. They socialized joyously: holiday parties, picnics, and family gatherings, and they celebrated successes and comforted one another in times of loss and distress.

When the class began, Dr. Bob announced "We have a responsibility far beyond the confines of this structure or of the area where we reside. People helping people must be one of our concerns."[180] They were vigorous fundraisers, having agreed early on that they would only support causes that were not already part of the church's regular philanthropy, thereby broadening the impact on the community. As the years went by, the notebooks included more and more obituaries. On Sunday morning August 27, 2017, the Tri C's held their last class, closing seventy-one years of service and fellowship. At the end of the 11:00 a.m. worship, a white oak tree was planted near the south entrance in their honor.

Another long-term consequence of wartime effort within the denomination was the creation of the Emergency Million Fund, the forerunner of the Week of Compassion that continues to this day "as the relief, refugee, and development mission fund" of the Disciples.[181] The fund began as emergency relief for missionaries still in the field, for retired ministers, and for Disciples serving as chaplains in the armed services. After the war, it expanded into far reaching global initiatives to assist with disaster relief, humanitarian aid, refugee resettlement, and much more. Country Club responded to the initial national challenge in 1942 with a pledge of $5,000; by 1943 more than $4,500 had been raised and would go beyond the $5,000 commitment, "giving hands and feet to our faith" in Reverend Grafton's words.

In the May 11, 1944, issue of *The Christian*, a small item on the last page posted an announcement that had also been made from the pulpit. For some weeks talk of the anticipated Allied invasion, referred to as D-Day, had been widespread:

> Our church will be open for prayers immediately following announcement of the invasion. Even though this may come during the night the sanctuary will be opened and an hour or so given to prayers on behalf of our boys in service. You are therefore invited to come directly to the church upon receipt of this news.

In the early hours of Tuesday morning, June 6, 1944, the doors of Country Club Christian Church were opened.

The invasion was a turning point of the war, or more correctly, the beginning of the end. It would be another long and brutal year, but a sense of hope and a determination to plan for the future took hold in the nation, the community, and the church. Change and growth at Country Club accelerated throughout 1944. The first ever director of women's activities arrived in January 1944. Mrs. O.S. Murphy (at all times addressed and referred to by her married name) was assigned a predictably broad portfolio of responsibilities as executive secretary of the Women's Council, parish visitor, and staff member of the minister's cabinet. Her tenure was sadly brief, cut short by illness and her resignation in October. But she had done such an outstanding job that a search for her replacement was soon underway. David Owen, the popular associate minister and director of education was hired by the Commission of the Christian Churches of Greater Kansas City to become its executive secretary, essentially the role held by Frank Bowen all those years ago. His position also was promptly filled.

Esther Darnall, the director of music since Brookside days, resigned in June. Dr. Combs wrote a moving tribute, remarking sadly that beyond a few others in the church he had known her longest and best. Within a few months, Melvin Gallagher became the first full-time minister of music. In addition to a considerably expanded roster of choirs he would also coach plays and pageants and form a choral reading group for unison reading of Scripture. Reverend Grafton was awarded a doctorate by TCU and the delighted congregation addressed him as "Dr." henceforth. The board agreed to take on two major financial projects: removal of the church debt targeting a $100,000 campaign goal, and support of the proposed new structure for the Woodland Avenue Christian Church, an African-American Disciples congregation in a sharply segregated city. It was by far the largest commitment from among the Kansas City Disciple churches. Woodland received regular mention in *The Christian* and board minutes, still referred to as the "Negro" or "our colored" church.

The church was long overdue for repair and maintenance, delayed by the Depression and war, and planning committees went to work. More exciting than an upgraded furnace was the announcement of three stained glass windows and new liturgical furnishings including a communion table, pulpit, and lectern. The original windows in the sanctuary were clear with a green tinted glaze. Two new windows were to be underwritten by the Atha and Daniel families, and the third was a memorial to Mr. and Mrs. Junius Irving from the board. By July 1945, the special committee in charge of the windows selected Charles J. Connick, an internationally known stained glass artist to design and build the windows. He also created the windows for Grace and Holy Trinity Cathedral, as well as other churches in the greater Kansas City area. The fabrication of the liturgical furnishings was done by American Sash and Door Company; the carving done by William Rensing, who did a number of church pieces throughout the Kansas City area. The liturgical furniture was donated by A.E. Mosier in memory of his wife, Margaret Ann. W.D. Wight, the architect/designer, monitored the entire process and had many conversations with church leaders expressing his frustration with the fact that the square pulpit would be placed against the existing curved wall of the chancel. At his tactful best, the board member in charge explained that while he of course agreed with the aesthetic conflict, it would be much too expensive to reconfigure the sanctuary wall.

The energy of that very busy 1944 was tempered at year's end by the German counter-offensive that became known as the Battle of the Bulge. Reverend Grafton wrote his weekly homily in *The Christian* in the form of a "Letter to G.I. Joe" in which he voiced concern that the church was growing lax in anticipation of a victorious end to the war. After four phone calls in a few days informing him of "our boys" who were injured, missing, or captured, he reflected in his homily that the war was indeed going to continue: "Then it was that I saw where the church must serve if she was to be worthy of living in an hour like this. It is as the Voice of Comfort and of Courage. Yours is the courage of action, and that calls for one type of faith. Ours is the courage of waiting, and that calls for faith of a different sort."

The waiting ended in part when President Truman announced Victory in Europe, V-E Day, early on the morning of Tuesday, May 8, 1945. As planned, the church was open for a service of Thanksgiving that evening, attended by 200 people. Reverend Grafton reflected the views of many when he said, "I wish I could get excited." His joy was muted by the knowledge that the war in the Pacific raged on and the toll, death, and carnage worldwide had been so great. But most profound was the realization that America was indeed the victor and that "puts the burden of tomorrow in our laps ... and the burden of the ultimate responsibility into the lap of the Church of Jesus Christ." On the evening of August 15th, 1945, the church chimes rang across the neighborhood for forty-five minutes prior to a service of thanks and celebration. Japan had surrendered; the war was over. But it was not "over" in the minds and spirits of many who had served.

> Capt. _____, who had been in the service for the past four years, returned home on New Year's night. Eighteen months of this time he was overseas. He served in France and Germany and has four battle stars.

That announcement (with his name redacted) was one of hundreds that appeared in *The Christian* from 1944 on. Its sparce language tells us very little. Four years in uniform — what had been interrupted: education, career, a new marriage? And eighteen months in the European theater with four battle stars acknowledging his participation in combat. What had he seen; what comrades had he lost; what memories refused to die? The demobilized veterans would return to a church that was changed in both personnel and appearance, but they themselves were also changed, often in ways that could not be easily discerned.

Dr. Grafton had focused on service men and women throughout the war and now he energetically prepared for their anticipated return. In June 1945 he organized a special Returning Service Personnel Committee that, he announced firmly, would in no way conflict with the mission of the

107

already existing Service Men's Committee. The purpose of the new committee would be to welcome and help re-integrate discharged veterans. The plan for carrying out those functions is a noteworthy document that reveals a sensitivity and awareness of potential issues for the returnees. Some were practical, such as how to look for employment. But attention was also given to possible emotional and psychological issues for men and women who had seen and experienced the unthinkable, and who were not expected or encouraged to talk about those experiences. "When we got out, you couldn't talk about things like that. You held it all in."[182] The veterans were expected to get a job, start a family, and get on with life. After all, they were the winners.

In recent years, several studies have examined WWII veterans' post war experience. Divorce, alcoholism, and suicide afflicted many and was the subject of numerous periodical articles in the first years after the war; the most popular post war movie, *The Best Years of Our Lives,* focused on three veterans' rocky return to civilian life. "Yet that discussion was short-lived, and cultural amnesia set in,"[183] as the positive view of the Greatest Generation became the accepted memory. In a memoir of his father's post-war struggles, Thomas Childers observed that "Today's comfortable assumption that 'the boys' returned home cheerful, contented, and well-adjusted, that no one suffered from serious emotional disorders, drank too much, or abused his wife or children, would have come as a surprise to contemporaries."[184]

In the fall of 1946, a little over a year after war's end, Dr. Grafton shared a letter with the Board of Elders that he had received from a church member who was clearly angry about the presence of alcohol at social functions sponsored by some of the Sunday school classes. Over the course of several months, the board conducted interviews with leaders of the various adult groups in the church, trying to determine practices and to suggest policy. One class in particular, the Seven C's, had been targeted in the letter. The Seven C's had been in existence for many years, organized specifically for members between the ages of eighteen and twenty-eight. In 1935 Dr. Combs had praised the group on the front page of *The Christian,* noting its success with a population that was typically difficult to "be reached and held by the church."

Alcohol was not the only issue, but it was the easiest to identify. As the various reports reveal, the group was perceived by many in the church as clubbish and self-contained, uninterested in the functions of the church or in considering themselves part of a larger unit beyond the class. Class participants were drawn from all over the city and many were not church members. Alpha N. "Pop" Brown, the popular leader of the class from its beginning, was a man older than the class members who held him in high esteem. He wrote a lengthy letter to the board in response to the inquiry. It provides a moving and eloquent portrait of the generation that went to war, and the response of at least some to their needs. It merits substantial quotation:

> This is the age group that, because of status and youth, almost 100 percent fought the war at the battle front.
>
> We must not overlook the fact that young women of the romantic and marriageable age as well as young men have been denied normal association with the opposite sex for periods varying from 1 to 5 years. This age group has suffered the frustration and abnormal psychological and social effects of a devastating war and is now going through a period of reconstructing their lives, without the "sobering responsibility of making a home, of wifehood, husbandhood and parenthood." These conditions do not exist in any other adult group of the church school. [In other classes whose men fought in the war] the wives remained at home and maintained church connections.
>
> The problems of reconstruction therefore are not superficial ones. They need a sympathetic approach to their readjustment problems; their pre-war friends are scattered; many of them are married; they want association with the opposite sex in normal contacts.
>
> Of course due allowance must be made for [a] changed world. Necessarily, therefore and in an effort to supply this aid, during the period of post war reconstruction, the major emphasis has been upon attendance at class and an attractive social program ... remembering always that the basic function of this group is to build the kingdom of God in the hearts of men.

Finally if we recognize that beneath the surface jollity, there is seriousness; that beyond the apparent flamboyance of youth striving for re-adjustment, there is an embarrassment of purpose; that the religious outlook of these young people who grew up during a period of economic depression and spent their early manhood in fighting a war and returned to a world of social unrest, cannot be the same religious outlook as those who grew up in the peaceful days before World War I, and that religion is not outwardly expressed by youth in the same way it is expressed by age; that maturity, and the normal experiences of normal life bring increased recognition of religious values; then, with sympathetic under-standing these young people can be led to a consciousness of the abiding presence of God working in the hearts of men.

Letter from Alpha N. "Pop" Brown to the Board
Leader/Teacher of the Seven C's class
December 12, 1946

This remarkable letter was incorporated in the elder's final report along with specific suggestions and recommendations, among which, to the chagrin of the elders, was the observation that the Seven C's class had never been included in the usual church assignments (all member canvassing, etc.) directed to the other adult classes. [185] Unlike all the other adult classes, news of their meetings was only occasionally included in the weekly class notes in *The Christian*. As a consequence, it was now understood, they did not feel part of the whole church. Participants on both sides of the issue acknowledged responsibility and the need to reform, as evidenced by this Seven C's announcement in the weekly notes in September 1948: "[The leader's] lesson was a discussion of the objective of the class and church and their connection and relationships. All activities should conform to the highest ideals of Jesus and be consistent with the objective of religious education."

There is no reliable way to determine the extent to which Country Club's careful plans for the returning servicemen and women succeeded, but the long-lived Tri C's class, created for the newly discharged, is one example of individuals who created a mutual bond of support, sharing, and love that met the expectations that Dr. Grafton set before his committee. The re-entry program was publicized in *The Christian*, providing the uniformed recipients early knowledge of the support that was being prepared for them. One of them wrote a response that was published in *The Christian* on November 15, 1945:

> Very few of the soldiers here are optimistic enough to expect a post war Utopia with a grateful world handing them the world on a silver platter. They are looking forward to, however, and planning on, a better world than the one they left behind. I certainly think your proposed committee system to help the returning veteran is an excellent step in the right direction. A sane, sensible approach to the soldier isn't looking for any reward other than some intelligently planned guidance. No serviceman, or woman, wants anything crammed down his or her throat, not does he expect to be considered a 'social problem' to be handled with kid gloves. Your committees … in my opinion are definitely in line with all that.

There was another dimension to the way war-time service influenced not only the veterans, but the nature of religious life in post war America, especially for mainline Protestantism. "There are no atheists in the foxhole" was the often-repeated axiom, but its meaning invites interpretation beyond terrified pleas to be saved. Young women and men found themselves thinking about questions of faith, of life's meaning, of the future. They mingled with others who had not been raised with their views and traditions, and at times were drawn to those practices. Sectarian divisions, again especially within Protestant groups, lost meaning. One was as likely to hear a Methodist chaplain speak as a Lutheran; Catholic and Jewish clergy, like their Protestant counterparts, served all military personnel. In his superb analysis of military personnel's interactions with religion during the war, Kevin Walters concludes:

> … that the challenges of wartime service provided the impetus and the opportunity to improvise religious practices, refine religious beliefs amid new challenges, and broaden religious understanding through interaction with those from other traditions … As soldiers and sailors formed bonds with those from other traditions, it

became more difficult to maintain previous assumptions rooted in suspicion and rumor about other faiths. [186]

Once home, many of these young veterans joined or re-joined churches where in the ensuing years they would become leaders. They tended to be more open to cooperation across religious lines, interested in ecumenism, and supportive of international missions.

Church growth in the post-war years continued to be influenced by all that had gone before and paralleled demographic changes throughout the country. Many families relocated after the war, moving great distances in response to economic disruption, housing shortage, and soaring inflation. *The Christian* carried long weekly notices bidding farewell to members moving out of town. But new arrivals to Kansas City took their place, bringing membership to 2,840 by fall 1946. Church members were part of the Baby Boom as well — the Tri C's class alone over a two-year period welcomed dozens of infants. Each new birth was heralded by the church

The war is over. The Tri C's Sunday school class picnic, shortly after the end of the war. *CCCC Archive*

chimes playing Brahms' "Lullaby." Dr. Grafton provided a word of caution when looking at the growing numbers, noting that the city's growth continued to expand rapidly to the southwest, and it was just a matter of time before new Disciples churches appeared to serve that population. He instituted annual planning retreats where church leaders deliberated spiritual and physical growth and commitment to external missions.

The war was over, only to be followed by international tensions, the re-positioning of former allies, and the introduction of a new term — the Cold War. The front page of a September 1948 *Christian* announcing the upcoming World Communion Sunday warned that "A Cold War Can't be Stopped by Lukewarm Christians." Dr. Grafton spoke of places with names like Buchenwald and Dachau, and he referred regularly to the appalling implications of the atomic bomb and what were certain to be its successors. But there was also a determination on the part of many to create a new and better world.

One response was "A Crusade for a Christian World," launched in 1946 and the basis for the previously mentioned Week of Compassion that is still part of the Disciples mission program. The Crusade was the largest program ever undertaken by the Disciples, and Country Club pledged a generous donation to be paid over a three-year period. The success, and also the challenges of the Crusade, re-awakened the old discussion about the need for centralized organization that would provide more effective services and reduce duplication within the denomination.[187] The Crusade was a Disciples project, but a second broad-ranging program was international and ecumenical: The World Council of Churches, begun in Amsterdam in 1948. Country Club greeted the World Council with enthusiasm, recognizing yet another opportunity for ecumenism and the Disciples' goal of Christian unity.

Immediately upon the war's conclusion, financial and material relief programs were put in place for the war-ravaged overseas countries. Dr. Grafton was insistent in his messages that the abundant consumer goods now available to Americans did not build a life of faith. The church adopted the denominational theme "With Christ We Build Anew," and the Easter offering in 1946 was dedicated to the Christian World Relief and Reconstruction Fund promoted by a "Post War Planning" message in the April 4, 1946, *Christian*.

The Crusade and organizations such as the World Council captured the attention of church members who were kept apprised of their activities in *The Christian*. But by far the main focus of interest in the final

POST-WAR PLANNING

I planned an ultra-modern home when priorities were lifted . . . .
But a Belgian woman whispered: "I have no home at all."

I dreamed of a country place for luxurious week-ends . . . . But
a Jewish lad kept saying: "I have no country."

I decided on a new cupboard right now . . . . But a child of China
cried out: "I have no cup."

I started to purchase a new kind of washing machine . . . . But a
Polish woman said softly: "I have nothing to wash."

I wanted a quick freezing unit for storing quantities of food . . . .
But across the waters came the cry: "I have no food."

I ordered a new car for the pleasure of my loved ones . . . . But
a war orphan murmured: "I have no loved ones."

These words of Mrs. Mayme Garner Miller appeared in a recent
issue of "World Call." Here is portrayed the needs that cry out to us
as we plan our offering for the Christian World Relief and Reconstruction Fund to be given on Easter Sunday. Let each of us prepare to
give sacrificially that the prayers of our Christian brethren may be
answered.

**A blunt reminder in *The Christian* that much of the post-war world was
experiencing very hard times.** *CCCC Archives*

years of the post-war era of renewal and building was the extensive modernization and renovation of the church funded by the "Onward Country
Club Christian Church" campaign. To have undertaken two ambitious
financial campaigns (Onward and the Crusade) simultaneously had been
an act of optimism and faith fueled by a rapidly accelerating economy
and an unprecedented growth in mainstream Protestantism.

The Practical Services Committee presented ever-longer reports to the
Minister's Cabinet and the board as it sought to address serious, very
expensive, and long-overdue building issues. Replacement of the almost
non-functional heating system was deferred for at least a year, while
the tower that had been struck by lightning just thirty minutes after the
conclusion of a service was repaired. As they planned to install the two
new stained-glass windows (increased to five since) church members in
charge of the project realized that the existing window casings were rotted
through and needed to be replaced. Stone work was quite literally falling
to the ground, so loose it was possible to push one's hand through a gap.
Charles Connick, the window designer, died unexpectedly in January

1946, but his workshop wrote a letter, published in *The Christian*, assuring the church that his completed designs would be executed "without faltering in the high ideals he always maintained ... in the spirit of a memorial to the man we believe to be the greatest modern master of color and light." The windows were dedicated on Sunday, May 4, 1947. The window over the altar was dedicated to George Hamilton Combs, paid for by parishioners. Combs delivered the sermon. [188]

As part of the 25th anniversary ceremonies, the church celebrated the liquidation of debt with a mortgage burning on January 10, 1946, followed by a rededication service on January 13. Just two years later, the congregation committed to raise $200,000 for the "Onward Christian Campaign." The campaign, to begin on December 1, 1947, was to fund the enlargement of teaching rooms, a youth recreation center to be open to all youth in the area, a new heating plant, expanded music space (the choir was currently rehearsing in the kitchen), "rehabilitation" of the organ, and a new chancel that would be dedicated as a memorial to the ten Country Club servicemen who died in the war. It would be appointed with the new liturgical furnishings: pulpit, lectern, and communion table.

The chancel was designed by the Kansas City architectural firm of Wight and Wight that, among many significant buildings in the area, had created the Nelson Art Gallery (the main building on the west side of the Nelson-Atkins Museum of Art), the Kansas City, Missouri City Hall, and the Jackson County Courthouse. The Wights were brothers, originally from Nova Scotia. [189] J. D. Wight was the designer of the new communion table, lectern, and pulpit, and undoubtedly was pleased by the opportunity to reconcile the rectangular features of the table to the remodeled chancel.

It was a major project, presented to the congregation in the November 20, 1947, issue of *The Christian*, with descriptions of "the mellow richness of polished wood ... the splendor of stained glass, and the exquisite detail of pierced carvings." Seventy feet of symbolic carving would ornament the choir stalls, reredos (the wall behind the altar) and chancel rail; the carvings would match the designs on the communion table, pulpit and lectern. Twenty-five yards of folded damask would hang behind the communion table. The sliding doors of the baptistry were to be decorated with a brass tree of life motif. A panel of sculptured plaster carvings of the four evangelists, Matthew, Mark, Luke, and John was to be placed above each of the two doors on either side of the chancel.

All of that, of course, necessitated a complete redecoration of the sanctuary. Wight, the architect, who died before the project was completed, had explained his vision: "When one enters the temple of the Living God, he should always be able to walk towards the light." His plans called for light streaming through the Combs Memorial stained glass window on the east wall and a subtle concealed system of lighting throughout.

CHAPTER 8

Objects of Faith: The Visual Expressions of Community and Belief

Members of mainstream Protestant denominations often assume that religious iconography — the material culture of religion — is not a significant element in their spiritual practices and traditions. Yet to sit in the Country Club sanctuary is to be surrounded by the symbols, imagery, and objects of the Christian faith. At the center, literally, is the cross — the focal point for all who worship, and the most readily identified symbol of Christianity throughout the world.

The liturgical furnishings, which had been dedicated and were in place as of May 26, 1946, represent and support the three spiritual functions of a Disciples church: weekly sharing of communion, reading of Scripture, and evangelizing God's word. Dr. Grafton summarized their importance in *The Christian* in October 1948:

> The Communion table ought always to be in plain view of every worshipper so that it stands as a constant reminder of the Master's full giving of Himself for the redemption of the world. The Lectern, which symbolizes the open Bible, should be placed in such a manner as to accent the importance of its symbolism. And the Pulpit, which is one of our basic Protestant and Disciple symbols, representing the preaching of the Gospel, should be

placed in such a way that the importance of this function
of the church is accented."

The white oak furnishings drew on early Christian and Byzantine
design and were carved with a variety of symbols expressing a "language
of ornament" that was widely understood in the Middle Ages. Ivy represented remembrance; five small crosses on the table recalled the stig-
mata, Christ's five wounds; the grape and its vine spoke of the source of
life. The carvings on the pulpit include the pomegranate whose multiple
seeds symbolize eternal life, and five connected motifs on each side of
the front of the pulpit: the thistle — hard and difficult is the way of the
Christian; the oak — courage, strength and dependability; the grape; the
pomegranate; and the laurel — the spirit and the soul. The lectern had
in earlier times been intended to hold music and the church's piece has
been carved with two shafts that represent that purpose. For many years
Country Club's pulpit has had an additional special function; it is the site
of one or more bud vases, heralding the arrival of a child in one of the
church families. The practice was started in February 1954 as a way to
celebrate the family relationships so important to the church.

Disciples celebrate two sacraments: communion and baptism. Martin
Luther had argued that both were unique to Christians and had been instituted by Christ himself. The communion table and the baptistry are the
concrete representations of these sacraments, and both take place in the
sacred setting of the sanctuary. Communion can be served in a variety
of ways, particularly in Protestant churches, and the service pieces have
evolved over time from elaborate hand wrought metals to contemporary
pottery. At its most basic, a communion set will include a chalice, a drink-
ing cup composed of a bowl on a stem with a base, and a paten, the small
circular plate that holds the communion bread. The chalice has taken on
a larger symbolic meaning for Disciples since 1971, when the denomination confirmed a simple representation of a red chalice with a tipped
St. Andrews cross on the bowl as its official logo. In the language of the
Disciples website, "The chalice represents the centrality of communion
to the life of the church. The cross of Saint Andrew is a reminder of the
ministry of each person and importance of evangelism, and recalls the
denomination's Scottish Presbyterian ancestry." [190]

In the early years of the Movement only those who had been baptized
were permitted to take communion and the issue remained contentious
even in the early years of Country Club Christian. Beginning in the early

A carved tapestry: Dr. Warren Grafton preaching from the new pulpit, one of three pieces contributed as memorials to the new chancel.
CCCC Archives

20th century more liberal Disciples, many of whom were associated with the University of Chicago, began advocating for "open communion" — that is, the invitation to take communion is open to all who participate in the worship service, regardless of baptismal status or membership. Open communion is today the policy of the Disciples of Christ.

Disciples practice baptism by immersion. In May 1950, just before Mother's Day, which featured a baby-dedication service, Dr. Grafton devoted an entire discussion in *The Christian* to explaining why immersion is the accepted practice. Infant baptism has no mention in the New Testament, the basis of Disciples of Christ beliefs and traditions. Children are innocent and at all times acceptable to God and in no way are burdened by "original sin" at birth. Baptism is a sign and a seal that the baptized has made a conscious decision to accept Christ through faith and penitence.

A later addition to church artifacts, the "Chest of Joash," first appeared in November of 1960 as part of a new ceremonial presentation of pledges in November. The chest is derived from the Old Testament accounts found in Kings and Chronicles of funding repairs to the temple. Its purpose is to solemnize the giving of gifts through an act of personal dedication as members drop their pledge cards into the chest on Dedication Sunday. The chest that was first used was borrowed from another congregation, but several members designed and built the chest that is now brought out each year.

The four evangelists over the doors on either side of the chancel, a source of interest and attention in the sanctuary, are presented in a linear panel, with each of the evangelists represented by a traditional symbol. Matthew is a winged man, Mark a winged lion, Luke a winged ox, and John an eagle. The symbolism derives from two Biblical visions — one in the Old Testament (Ezekiel, 1 and 10), and one in the New (Book of Revelation, 4:7-8), each of which describes four winged cherubim who resemble a human/angel, ox, eagle, or lion. The assignment of symbol to a particular evangelist is a result of Christian interpretation that developed long after the Gospels were written. The Gospel of Matthew emphasizes Jesus as a human being, complete with human ancestry — hence the winged man or angel. Mark is represented by the kingly lion, while the bull or ox for Luke is an image of sacrifice, and the eagle, thought to be able to look straight into the sun, evokes John's visionary rhetoric.[191]

While perhaps not as obvious as furniture and windows, clerical vestments are also replete with imagery. Following the Protestant Reformation,

Disciples practice full immersion baptism. The baptistry is on the north side of the chancel. *CCCC Archives*

Protestant leaders eschewed the silk and brocades of the Roman Catholic hierarchy. Martin Luther, like many other dissenting clergy who were also university faculty, preferred the simple black robe of a scholar. At the time it was not a particularly distinctive garment, but one that bestowed a recognizable identity on the wearer. Styles, ornamentation, and accessories evolved; there were long periods, as in the early days of the Disciples in America, when ministers simply wore their "Sunday best." Robes, and sometimes formal dress such as a morning coat (Dr. Combs' preference), made a comeback in the early 20th century with liturgical revival and the embracing on the part of some of a more formal approach to worship.

The Four Evangelists, one of two identical panels mounted over the chancel doors. The four figures are Matthew, Mark, Luke, and John in their traditional symbolic representations. *CCCC Archives*

The most common accessory used by many ordained Protestant clerics is the stole, a long thin scarf-like piece of fabric worn over the robe around the neck to a little below the knees and often described as representing the towel Christ used when he washed the Apostles' feet. The dominant color of the stole changes with the church season: purple during times of awaiting the King, and also penitence — Advent and Lent; white for the coming of the Lord — Christmas and Easter; red, the color of flame and blood — Holy Week, and Pentecost; and green for the rest of the Christian year. Black is sometimes used on Good Friday; at Country Club the altar cross is draped in black cloth. These colors also inform decorative cloths and other appointments throughout the sanctuary.

Symbols, images, colors, and objects weave and intersect with one another in a non-verbal tapestry of faith and tradition that is as rich and evocative as the written word. Like language, they convey shared meanings and understandings; they touch our senses and beckon us to respond, alone and in community.

The chalice, signifying the central importance of communion to Disciples, is the denominational logo. The St. Andrews cross recalls the early Scottish origins of the Restoration Movement.

Demolition of the chancel area began on May 8, 1949, and with only a few bumps and delays was ready for dedication on Sunday, November 20th. The schedule of "Duplicate Services" launched on October 5, 1947, had to be temporarily suspended during the construction period in light of the fact that congregants would be gathering in a lower-level room. Described by Dr. Grafton as "one of the most radical steps taken in many years in our church program," the identical services were intended to relieve overcrowding and accommodate those who preferred an earlier worship time. While duplicate services were increasingly common in larger cities, Grafton believed that Country Club was the first major church in Kansas City to institute the practice.

In honor of Dedication Sunday on November 20, 1949, members received a special edition of *The Christian* that provided a detailed history and explanation of all the new fixtures. It remains the single best account of the refurbished sanctuary and the new Memorial Chancel, as well as a clear statement of mid-twentieth century Protestant worship. The writers noted that "the entire treatment of the Chancel does not represent a modernization, but rather a return to the classic expressions of the Gothic. But into this medieval background modern functions have been incorporated … Thus new and old combine … " As planned, the chancel was dedicated to the ten Country Club Christian Church men who died in the war:

> This hallowed place is dedicated to the memory of those
> who gave their most precious possession that their fellow
> men might live in peace and security. That the memory
> of the members of this congregation who laid their lives
> upon the altar of full devotion in World War II might
> ever live, this chancel is dedicated in their honor.

It is not a dead shrine, but a living memorial. It shall ever
be an avenue by which the children of men shall come
into the presence of the Living God. Its constant purpose
shall be to inspire us to live, from day to day in such a
way that these, our honored dead, shall not have died in
vain.

The chancel window was installed and dedicated on January 8th, and
the organ, which had undergone a complete overhaul at the Kilgen Organ
company in St. Louis, was re-installed soon after. Like the other stained-
glass windows in the sanctuary, the chancel window had been designed
by Charles Connick, who used the theme of the Last Supper, drawing
in part on Da Vinci's imagery. Country Club's sanctuary is aligned on
the traditional east-west axis, allowing the morning sun to illuminate the
window's rich coloring.

The centrality of communion in the Disciples church is reaffirmed
by the window, the new chancel furnishings, and the later acquisition
of an extraordinary life-size sculpture of the Last Supper by Domenic
Zappia. He was born in Italy in 1900 and immigrated to this country with
his family when he was very young. He trained as an artist, working in
all media, but he was particularly drawn to wood. In 1925, he moved
to Kansas City where he created works that were commissioned by
churches, theaters, public parks, private collectors and others throughout
the country. The Last Supper, which is directly modeled on the Da Vinci
painting, was originally commissioned by a cemetery in West Virginia,
but that arrangement fell through, and in 1964 it was displayed at the
World's Fair in New York City. Eventually three members of Country
Club, Oscar Nelson, and Don and Lucille Armacost, learned it was available for sale and purchased it as a gift for the church.

In what had become something of a pattern with oversize gifts, there
was no immediate place to situate the sculpture within the church. For
over three decades it was displayed at Unity on the Plaza and then
Rockhurst College (now University) until a major capital campaign
during Dr. Cueni's tenure specifically identified exhibition of the sculpture as a priority. One of the advantages of the many renovations that have
taken place over the years is that often the original stonework was simply
covered up. That was the case with the east wall of the parlor that now
provides a rustic backdrop for Christ and the twelve Disciples gathered
at the table. The room was given in memory of Patricia Woodbury by her

family, and was dedicated on Sunday morning September 10, 2000. As the chair of the Building Committee observed, "This has more religious significance and spirituality than other kinds of things that you do in capital campaigns. This is going to touch people forever."

Another depiction of The Last Supper that followed Da Vinci's painting was presented to the church in 1966 as a memorial gift in honor of Don Robert Bodwell. The relief carved in lindenwood was created in the Oberammergau, Germany, workshop of Hans and Adolf Heinzeller. It was designed to fit in the front of the communion table, and was dedicated at morning services on May 15.

The dramatic life-size sculpture of the Last Supper, now on permanent display in the main parlor of CCCC. *CCCC Archives*

Dr. Grafton had observed that the construction of the chancel had been an unusually smooth and cooperative process. Another project in that same Autumn was anything but. The minutes of the board for September 8, 1949, include the following entry:

> The Chairman spoke on the tremendous amount of
> strength and power in our church membership and
> that some years ago we had started progress in putting
> a Rotating Board into effect. He took it upon himself
> during the summer to write some fifteen representative
> churches who have rotating boards at the present time.

That spare announcement launched one of the livelier, and certainly more contentious episodes in the church's history. The question of board tenure had bedeviled church governance almost from the beginning, and despite several herculean attempts to institute some kind of formula, nothing was ever settled. In the established manner of all boards facing a challenging discussion a committee was duly appointed to consider the matter once again. The committee took its assignment seriously, meeting numerous times during the month. Board members received four notices regarding the October meeting, which the chair opened by announcing that the meeting was very important and the first order of business would be to hear the committee's report on the desirability of a rotating board. To the astonishment of those present, one of the board members pre-empted the committee chair by announcing that he had hired a court reporter from one of the city's respected firms to take minutes. A hasty vote was called, and after approval the reporter was called in from a neighboring room.

Russ Huff, a member of the board at the time, recalled the "long and heated" arguments of that evening. The proposed system for establishing the rotation called for the drawing of names of present members from a container; the order of the draw determined the "class" to which that name was assigned resulting in a one-, two-, or three-year tenure. Those who approved the plan saw an opportunity to bring on fresh voices and expanded opportunities for all (men) in the church; but those who fervently opposed the concept argued that it was engaging in the very ungodly act of throwing dice and would be hurtful to those who had served so long. In Mr. Huff's colorful recollection, "one of the lawyers got up and raising his hand high in the air, said in a voice filled with drama and emotion, 'This is sacrilegious, we are shaking dice at the feet of Christ.'"[192] This prompted Dr. Grafton, who otherwise did not participate in the discussion, to point out that it was not correct that the men at the foot of the cross threw dice for Christ's garments, and furthermore the practice of drawing lots was supported by the story in the Book of Acts recounting that Jesus' followers cast lots to decide on Judas' replacement.

Fifty-one pages and an unreported number of hours later, the vote was taken: 62 for the new plan, 14 against, 2 abstentions. The turning point apparently came well along in the meeting when one of the members stood up and addressed the group:

> I don't think that the only ones who serve their Master are members of this Board. You just have additional responsibilities ... To me it simply means a rotating opportunity, and so I am going to say, knowing that I won't be misunderstood, because I feel as I do, this is what I am doing tonight. I am resigning from the Board tonight effective now. I want to be the first man to come under this and I don't think for a minute that casts me out a black sheep and away from the fellowship of you gentlemen.
>
> Gentlemen, we are talking about progress in the church. There are men eligible and must have an opportunity to enjoy Christian fellowship of this group and the responsibility of it. [193]

He was applauded literally and verbally, and the meeting moved on to the vote to approve the resolution, which was printed in full in *The Christian*, announcing a congregational vote on the matter for Sunday, October 23. The names of the board members had been placed in sealed envelopes and locked in the church's private box at a Westport bank. Despite an effort by those still opposed to table the resolution, it was passed in the congregational meeting and the box was retrieved from the bank for an evening meeting on October 27th, when names were drawn. As a token of goodwill, it was agreed that retiring deacons and elders with significant longevity (unspecified) would be given the honorific of "Emeritus." The rotating system continues today, with the very significant change being the addition of women to the board a few years later.

CHAPTER 9

A Singing Congregation: The Sounds of Worship

Music is the child of prayer,
The companion of religion.
— F. Chateaubriand

"We are a singing church," Dr. Grafton once observed. Whether vocal or instrumental, music has always been a significant part of Country Club's worship and church activities. The appropriate role of music in worship had been a source of disagreement in the early history of the Restoration Movement and was a significant factor in the division that occurred between Disciples and the more conservative Churches of Christ. The latter supported *a cappella* singing, rejecting the use of instruments arguing that they are not mentioned in the New Testament.

One of the driving motivations for reconfiguring the chancel was the dramatic growth of the choirs, to the point that there was no longer adequate seating for the full choir on Sunday mornings, creating an awkward and distracting movement from chancel to sanctuary. Mel Gallagher had assumed the role of the first minister of music after Mrs. Darnall's retirement, and under his leadership the number of choirs and the size of their memberships increased significantly. Accommodating the choir was one issue; placement of the organ was another. The first organ, designed by the Kilgen Company in St. Louis, had been given to the church in honor of Athelia Sweet Berger by her husband Homer in time for the dedication of the new wing in January 1927. The organ was placed in the middle of the choir loft, with the result, as architect Wight later pointed out, that the congregation's attention was directed to the organist's back. When the chancel was rebuilt, choir seating was reconfigured into a traditional split arrangement on either side of the aisle leading to the altar and the completely rebuilt organ was moved to the upper-left (north) side. [194] It was finally replaced by the Schantz organ donated by Mr. and Mrs. Joseph Atha and dedicated in 1971 with a major recital by nationally prominent organist Robert Glasgow. The Schantz Company, located in Orrville, Ohio, employed more than fifty skilled craftsmen to build the instrument, a job that took 27 months to complete. Once again, what began as a fairly straightforward project became much more complex when it was determined that the sanctuary was an acoustically "dead" space that would not enhance the sound of the new organ, the choir, and congregational singing. The resulting rehabilitation of the space produced an appropriate acoustical environment.

The original choir loft in the newly completed sanctuary, emphasizing centrality of the organ and choir seating. *CCCC Archives*

Accomplished musicians have served as choral directors, vocalists, and organists/pianists throughout Country Club's history. Gladys Gwynne, a trained organist, began playing for the church in October 1922, probably initially on a piano. When she married Dr. Combs in 1927, she stepped down, but continued to serve as organist intermittently, often for significant periods of time. She resumed her full-time position shortly after Dr. Combs' death in 1951 and retired in September 1966. When the Schantz organ was installed in 1971, it was dedicated in her honor. Organists continue to be attracted from around the country by the opportunity to perform in recital on the Schantz organ.

In 1970, Dan Smith was hired as organist and choir director, and the dual role was continued by his successor, Dr. David Diebold, who served in that position from 1981 until he retired as minister of music *emeritus* in 2015, creating a music legacy that was recognized throughout the country. Under his leadership, the music program grew to include nine choirs, the creation of a hand bell unit, many special concerts each year, and in 1987 an invitation for the Chancel Choir to perform at the Salzburg Music Festival in Austria in July 1989. In recent years, contemporary worship has also been celebrated with brass, string, and a variety of folk instruments.

Gladys Combs at the organ. She served as the church organist until her marriage to Dr. Combs in 1927. After that, she stepped in as needed, including much of the Second World War, and she resumed her full-time position after Dr. Combs' death until her retirement in 1966. *CCCC Archives*

Music has always served an essential liturgical function in worship. A typical Sunday morning Order of Worship in October 1950 listed twenty-two items, of which thirteen were musical: Prelude, Processional, Gloria Patri, Anthem, Prayer Response, Doxology, Offertory, Communion Hymn (two separate parts), Dedication Hymn, Recessional, Chimes Response to the Benediction, and Postlude. Dr. Diebold provided a regular column to *The Christian* in which he taught and explained the role of music in worship. In February 2009, he provided this description: "In our worship planning, Glen [the Senior Minister] and I pay very close attention to the details of worship: the liturgical designation for the day, the scripture, and the direction of the sermon. Then, we ponder how the music might tie the spoken words together. Every detail is intended to lead us from our arrival in the worship to our exit for service in the world around us."

The number of choirs expanded rapidly to include children, teens and adults as well as specialized groups such as the Men's Glee Club. The latter performed outside the church on numerous occasions as have the regular choirs, and the church in turn has hosted high school and university choirs from across the country. In addition to traditional sacred performances, Country Club choirs put on a number of successful public productions of Broadway, Gilbert and Sullivan, and variety musicals, enriched by lavish costumes and elaborate set designs.

Dr. Grafton announced the acquisition of a new pew hymnal in 1947 with the declaration that "Our Hymnal is Ecumenical." Always the teacher, he explained in a February *Christian* the origins of familiar hymns whose lyricists and composers included Methodists, Quakers, Scotch Presbyterians, Lutherans, Catholics, and a Jew — David the Psalmist. This, he wrote, is a "hymn book of the Church Universal ... If we are so nearly one in the hymns that we sing, why can we not also be one in the name that we bear and the work that we do?" His discussion hearkened back to the early days of the Restoration Movement that argued so strongly for Christian unity, but it also presaged a new post-war era that would promote ecumenism and inter-denominational cooperation.

In 1995, a new hymnal appeared in the pew racks, *The Chalice Hymnal*, the first twentieth century hymnbook to be published exclusively by the Disciples.[195] The hymnal's title is acknowledgement of the significance of communion to Disciples worship and recognition of the denomination's logo. The singing of hymns has always been an essential part of Disciples worship; not surprisingly, Alexander Campbell wrote many hymns of his own and published new hymnbook editions almost yearly between 1828 and 1865. Serious work on *The Chalice Hymnal* began in 1991 with a survey of Disciples congregations in an effort to learn the tastes and preferences of members. From the beginning the committee determined that the celebration of communion should guide the selections, and identified a series of themes that reinforced the practice and the spiritual understanding of the place of communion in worship and its significance to those who shared the bread and wine. In 2003, a smaller collection of more contemporary hymns was published under the title of *Chalice Praise. The Chalice Hymnal* has been very successful and is used by other denominations as well, but in 2019 Chalice Press, the publishers, announced their final printing.

CHAPTER 10

Baby Boom, Cold War, and A Church Crisis

The 1950s have variously been described as a time of bland and mindless conformity, explosive consumerism, the golden era of the American family, and a harrowing period of global tensions. None of those characterizations was universal or experienced in the same way throughout the nation, but they are suggestive of patterns in the nation at large which were reflected in religious institutions and to which those institutions would respond: the post-war population explosion and the consequent building boom in housing, education and religion; movement of large parts of the population throughout the country; widespread affluence; and increasing anxiety about the perceived menace of communism. "All that meant that mainstream Fifties religion was family oriented, very conscious of the cold war, and inwardly traditionalist while trying to adapt institutionally to the needs of a rapidly growing and changing society." [196] In his analysis of American religion in the 1950s, Robert Ellwood dismisses the common argument that the period somehow represented a "normalcy" against which later eras must be measured, concluding that "nothing could be further from the truth." [197]

The pages of *The Christian* provide ample confirmation of the parallels between Country Club Christian Church and society at large. By 1950, church membership was more than 3,000 and the physical accommodations, especially for children, were no longer adequate. Dr. Grafton illustrated the extent of the crowding in one piece in *The Christian* entitled "The Lost Child" — an account of the brief but alarming disappearance of one small nursery participant who was packed into a classroom intended for ten or less, but that Sunday morning was filled with twenty-eight children. The missing child never left the overcrowded room but continued to sit on the floor while all around him stood, obscuring him from view. The 1951 building campaign was dedicated to an expanded educational wing on the north end of the building that would accommodate the growing Sunday school as well as the seven church choirs. The construction of the wing was delayed by the catastrophic Kansas City flood of 1951, but when completed it provided greatly expanded space for its occupants. It was formally dedicated as the Junius B. Irving Memorial, in honor of the man whose generous bequest made it possible.

At the same time that the church committed to the education wing, the board also decided to purchase the land immediately to the north of the church on the other side of 61st Street. Discussions among board members and negotiations with the J. C. Nichols Company and nearby neighbors stretched over many months. The goal for the church was, from the beginning, to move 61st Street to the north end of the lot, creating a single campus that united the original church grounds and the new purchase. That dream was never realized, for many reasons; instead, after nearly a decade the small Gothic chapel that carries George Hamilton Combs' name was built on the new site.

Religiosity and family life, often linked as one entity referred to as the "American Way of Life," were reinforced in the burgeoning popular culture of the era: movies, books, and that newest attraction, television. *Ozzie and Harriet, Leave it to Beaver, Father Knows Best,* and *The Donna Reed Show* provided a celebration of family life, if not exactly an authentic representation. The families in these shows were White, middle to upper-middle class, and lived in comfortably appointed homes where they solved their issues in a well-mannered half hour. Movies such as *The Ten Commandments, Ben Hur*, and *A Man Called Peter* were enormously popular. Religiously themed books appeared regularly on the best seller lists throughout the 1950s. Norman Vincent Peale's *The Power of Positive Thinking*, published in 1952, was on the *New York Times* best-seller list for 186 weeks, 48 of them as number one. While the book was widely popular, it was also criticized by theologians and psychologists for providing a facile approach to addressing life's challenges. Peale was one of several clergymen in the era, along with Catholic Bishop Fulton J. Sheen and the evangelist Billy Graham, who made a smooth transition to public media where they reached large audiences.

Dr. Peale spoke to a sold-out audience of 450 at Country Club Christian on the evening of October 13, 1949, and his writings appeared occasionally in *The Christian*. He, like other popular clergymen, embraced the relatively new field of psychology and psychoanalysis and his influence continued to be felt at Country Club. In the November 20, 1956, board meeting, Board Chairman David Hardy announced "the possible need of studying a counseling service in our church which might further bring about the employment of a person on the staff to handle this service." He went on to say that many churches had considered this as a need and it might be advisable to appoint a committee to study the problem — "such as Norman Vincent Peale conducts at this time."

Not long after, in June 1957, Dr. Wyle, now the minister, spent a week in New York City at the Seminar of the Clinic of Psychiatry and Religion, begun twenty years previously by Peale and his church, until its transfer to the New York City Health Department. He provided a very enthusiastic report to the board, stating that "without question, this is the greatest Counselling Clinic in the world" and that he hoped to use the experience to the benefit of Country Club Christian. In January 1958, the Department of Pastoral Counseling was officially added to the church administrative structure.

Another best seller of a very different sort appeared in the 1950s — *The Revised Standard Version of the Bible*. The RSV was published by the National Council of Churches in its entirety in 1952; the New Testament had been published in 1946. The RSV was considered "authorized" by the Council and became the standard for the majority of Christians, especially Protestants, for many decades. Subsequent corrections and revisions (for example, inclusion of readings from the Dead Sea Scrolls discovered in 1947) by an ecumenical and international Bible Committee have produced several newer editions. In March 1946, *The Christian* noted the RSV's arrival with approval and reported that copies had been made available in the Children's and Youth departments. For many years, Country Club third graders have been presented a Bible, at first the RSV and then the New Revised Standard Version.

In the same issues as announcements of church picnics, news about the thriving Boy Scout troop, and reminders of exciting speakers for the weekly Thursday night dinners (22,000 meals in 1950), *The Christian* reminded church members of deeper, often troubling issues. The church continued to give used clothing in generous quantities to the European camps for displaced persons who were fleeing communist takeover in their countries. Dr. Grafton reflected sadly on the move from "A" to "H" when news of the development of the even more destructive hydrogen bomb was released. An announcement that "The Life you Save May be your Own" urged congregants to attend a Civil Defense presentation at Border Star School, noting that "active community participation is vital to survival in case of atomic warfare."

Thursday night dinners, an essential feature of the yearly schedule, featured major speakers on a wide variety of topics and drew large crowds. *CCCC Archives*

Those anxieties seemed to be confirmed on June 25, 1950, when North Korean troops crossed the 38th Parallel to invade South Korea, and the United States joined the United Nations' "police action" in support of South Korea. Once again, young men were drafted into military service, and once again *The Christian* published the names of church members in uniform. A new vocabulary — Cold War, Iron Curtain, atheistic communism — was in regular usage, and the conflict was the first television war, making nightly appearances in people's homes.

In late 1946, General Douglas MacArthur, serving as essentially the viceroy of occupied Japan, called for at least one thousand Christian missionaries to be sent there as part of his plan to transform the country into a Christian democracy. That plan offers a compelling illustration of the ways religion and international policy were intertwined and influenced one another in the post-war years. MacArthur ordered that Shintoism be abolished as the state religion in December 1945 and soon after Emperor Hirohito issued a proclamation stating that any conception of his being "divine" was false. The General made his views very clear in a letter to a minister: "Democracy and Christianity have much in common, as practice of the former is impossible without giving faithful service to the fundamental concepts underlying the latter."[198] It was a perception shared by many throughout the 1950s.

Country Club Christian Church was one of many American institutions to respond to MacArthur's call. The church's interest in Japan had been strengthened when Margaret Lawrence was transferred there after the Communist takeover in China. The Kansas City connection was further reinforced when she was assigned to the Margaret K. Long School, considered one of the best in Japan, that had been founded in the early 1900s by Kansas Citian R.A. Long. Margaret Lawrence had initiated an exchange of letters and gifts between her students and Country Club's children and youth, and it was Margaret who first conveyed MacArthur's call for missionaries on one of her regular furlough trips to Kansas City in the fall of 1949. As she travelled back to Japan, she composed a long letter to the church describing the Japanese evangelist Toyohiko Kagawa, whose Kingdom of God movement was assuming a prominent role in Protestant evangelism efforts, and who had the endorsement of the American Occupation leadership. Margaret urged that his work be supported by American missionaries, at least 100 of whom should be drawn from the Disciples Brotherhood.

In the February 2, 1950, *Christian*, under the heading "Enlarging our Horizons" Dr. Grafton announced that a member had given $10,000 to support one missionary in Japan for the next three years, and had challenged the congregation to provide support for two more missionaries. The United Christian Missionary Society promised to designate the three missionaries as Living Links for Country Club Christian Church. Dr. Grafton pointed out that there were sufficient funds in the part of the budget dedicated to the Crusade for a Christian World, but that was an "easy" solution. How much more significant it would be to stretch the purse strings by raising the funds above and beyond the budget. Within a few weeks, several substantial gifts, plus a commitment from the board for the remainder, assured the salaries of the additional two missionaries, news that was announced the same Sunday that the president of the

Margaret K. Long School visited the church. Each of the missionaries was introduced to the congregation in special ordination services that affirmed the shared obligations of all to the success of the mission efforts.

The ecumenical and open religious spirit experienced by many who served during the war was to be tested in the post-war years well into the fifties. The Saturday December 4, 1948, edition of *The Kansas City Star* listed the usual religious services scheduled for the next day. Country Club's entry announced that Dr. Grafton "will speak on 'Religious Tolerance' to give his views of the recent Reformation day talk here by Bishop G. Bromley Oxnam of New York." Behind that simple announcement was more than a month of contentious debate in the community and the local news. Bishop Oxnam, a Methodist, was one of the most recognized ministers in America at the time, a man who had recently been featured on the cover of *TIME Magazine* over the caption "Disunity is Denial." He argued passionately for the unification of all (Protestant) Christians, and was in a position to do so as one of the six presidents of the newly organized World Council of Churches. He was a liberal clergyman who opposed communism, but argued that it could only be defeated by "economic justice and racial brotherhood," not by armed conflict. [199] In the eyes of some, these views seemed to align him with groups that were increasingly under observation by, among others, the House Un-American Activities Committee (HUAC), created in 1938. His role as keynote speaker on October 31, 1948, at a major celebration of Reformation Day — the commemoration of Luther's nailing 95 theses to the door of the church in Wittenberg — at Kansas City's Municipal Auditorium was widely anticipated.

There is no extant copy of his remarks, titled "Protestantism and the World Crisis," but noting other similar speeches he presented at the time and the strong reaction in the press, it is clear that he focused on his concerns about Catholicism and what he argued was its overweening influence in American life that threatened the constitutionally protected separation of church and state. The next day, Bishop Edwin V. O'Hara of the Kansas City Catholic diocese responded in a front-page letter to *The Star*, arguing that the "inflammatory address of Bishop Oxnam here yesterday must not be allowed to set Protestants and Catholics at each other's throats in hatred and discord." Noting his friendship with many Protestant clergy, he accepted "with gratitude the friendly and emphatic assurances which have come to me" since the address. Some days later, that letter prompted a rebuttal, this time from the head of the Bible Department at Park College, who stated that "such appeals to personal religion and co-operation evade the issue. The argument is not over piety, but over political philosophy."[200] It was at that point that Dr. Grafton decided on his sermon topic for December 5. It was so well received that it was reprinted for distribution the following week, and the key points were reiterated in the December 9 *Christian*. Arguing that "tolerance is a practical matter" he stated that such tolerance should "grant all the freedoms which are essentially American ... and it should be more than a mere matter of live and let live. It should also be a tolerance that respects the religious views of others." He then outlined three roles of the Catholic church as he perceived them: the teacher of a great religion; a propagator of faith which can make "ruthless" demands such as the expected conversion of a Protestant spouse to Catholicism in a mixed marriage, and the consequent upbringing of their children as Catholics; and finally, the point where, in the eyes of non-Catholics, Catholicism functions as a political entity that infringes upon separation of church and state.

Viewed from today's perspective Protestant/Catholic antipathy is difficult to understand. Cross-faith marriages without sectarian impositions on either partner are commonplace, and ecumenism in general has influenced cultural and religious attitudes. Dr. Grafton was speaking as one pastor in one midwestern church, but his comments reflected broadly held views in the 1950s. The third point in his sermon, addressing the separation of church and state, was the issue that resonated most strongly with mainline Protestants. Articles and announcements in *The Christian* spoke against public funding of parochial schools and the very controversial attempt by President Truman to appoint an official ambassador to the Vatican in 1952. The practice up to that time had been to name a personal envoy who did not receive government funding; after widespread opposition to the appointment Truman resumed the envoy practice that remained in place until 1984 when Ronald Reagan's nominee to the Holy See was officially confirmed as Ambassador. In 1954, Ewart Wyle, Country Club's new minister, asked in an article in *The Christian*, "Is This a Free Country?" There followed an indignant discussion of how both major event venues in Kansas City had been rented to the Catholic Diocese for the same day, after Protestant clergy had tried to book one of the facilities for the annual Reformation Day celebration that, as a consequence, had to be cancelled.

A 1954 entry in *The Christian* announced the forthcoming talk by a former Catholic priest, one of many noted in *The Christian* that was sponsored by an organization calling itself by the unwieldy name of "Protestants and Other Americans United for the Separation of Church and State," more easily referred to as POAU. That organization had been founded by a group of Protestant leaders that included Bishop Oxnam and Charles Clayton Morrison, for thirty-nine years the esteemed editor of *Christian Century* until his retirement in 1947. PAOU was adamantly opposed to public funding of parochial education and throughout the decade engaged in multiple legal actions to advocate for that view. In March 1950 Morrison was the guest speaker at one of the Thursday night church dinners. In its front-page coverage, *The Christian* identified his topic as "Protestantism and the Separation of Church and State," observing that "with all the muddied waters in relation to the federal bill on aid to education, and with the insistence of the Catholic Church that funds be made available to parochial schools, this is one of the liveliest issues of our times."

Stances such as opposition to the Vatican ambassadorship and federal support of parochial schools caused some to argue that organizations such as PAOU were linked to the Communists. The Catholic Church maintained a strong position against communism; thus, the argument went, those opposed to Catholicism must be pro-communist. Bishop Oxnam was indeed called before HUAC (the House Unamerican Activities Committee) in the spring of 1953. He insisted upon a hearing, which was held on July 21, when he defended himself brilliantly until after midnight, resulting in a full exoneration by the somewhat abashed committee. The episode did not end HUAC's relentless pursuit of hidden Communists throughout all levels of American life, but it marked the beginning of the committee's decline. [201]

The crosscurrents of religion, domestic politics, and foreign policy in the 1950s is complex to the point at times of being almost beyond deciphering. There is no way to determine exactly how the members of Country Club Christian Church responded to these influences, either individually or collectively. It is clear, however, that they were receptive to certain points of view that in turn aligned them with a significant portion of the American population. As late as 1961, the same page of *The Christian* had a full column urging members to write to legislators to object to legislation proposing federal aid to parochial schools, and announced the addition of two anti-communist books to the church library. The article, under the heading "S.O.S!!!" noted that Catholic President Kennedy opposed the proposal, but "Protestant churches thus far failed to express themselves in any effective political way." The seeds of dramatic social, cultural and religious change, not yet clearly visible, had been planted and by the end of the decade would herald new directions for institutional religion and spiritual life.

While relations between Protestants and Catholics remained tense throughout much of the fifties, Country Club Disciples maintained warm ties with the Kansas City Jewish community, a relationship grounded in Rabbi Mayerberg's dynamic leadership against the Pendergast Machine and deep friendship with Dr. Combs, whom he remembered as "a spiritual father." Other temple leaders made regular appearances in Country Club's classes and Thursday night dinners, and there were occasional "exchanges" of worshippers between church and temple.

George Hamilton Combs died at home on November 14, 1951, at the age of 87. He had been in poor health, vaguely described as a heart condition, for the preceding year with several hospitalizations. Attesting to his renown and stature, the local paper reported on his condition regularly throughout the year. His funeral on November 17, attended by more than 800 people, was led by Dr. Grafton, Dr. Frank Pippin, pastor of Community Christian Church, and Episcopal Bishop Robert Nelson Spencer, former leader of the West Missouri diocese, who described him as a preacher of preachers.

Administrative management and practices had progressed dramatically from the rather ad hoc operations of early days. There were, however, still bumps characteristic of non-profit organizations run by a mixture of professional staff and volunteers. Most of the issues involved budget and personnel. Board minutes in 1952, for example, recorded yet another reminder that budgeted expenditures could not simply be approved by committee chairmen without following established Finance Committee protocol. Personnel issues could be thornier, arousing strong feelings among many people. In the spring of 1952 the minister of music abruptly resigned, presaging an "unsettled condition" in the church in the coming year that, as the April board minutes noted, was filled with "mistakes, heartaches and misunderstandings." The minutes are discreet and lack some critical details, but at the heart of the resignation was the fact that the minister of music, a highly qualified individual who had succeeded Mel Gallagher, had been summoned a number of times to meetings with the Music Committee, whose members voiced criticisms of his work. None of those meetings apparently had been attended by Dr. Grafton. This was an irregular and inappropriate process that, at the very least, displayed a lack of understanding of lines of authority and staff/board relationships. A special Administrative Review and Recommendation Committee was appointed and held many meetings over the next several months. The committee solicited comments from church members, but only if they were <u>written and signed</u> (no anonymous input!).

The committee issued a comprehensive report, creating the Staff Advisory Committee and outlining a delineation of staff duties and chain of authority. That too caused dissension with numerous amendments being proposed to the Board of Elders. Board members and all committees were held over until the report was issued; the minutes recorded language such as "emergency" and "critical spot" to describe the state of the church. Eventually a new minister of music was hired, but only after several missteps by Music Committee members who didn't follow the approval process. Shortly after the new man joined the staff, the minutes noted that the "Ministry of Music ... was fully reorganized."

It was a very serious episode and one that contributed to Dr. Grafton's decision to resign and accept a call from a church in Detroit. He acknowledged that he did not want to leave Country Club, and the board went on record as "favoring the continuance of Warren Grafton in his ministry at the Country Club Christian Church." But Dr. Grafton concluded it was in the best interests of the church to move on and the Graftons were gone by the end of June 1953. Their departure was accompanied by gracious commentary and letters in *The Christian*, as well as a resolution of reluctant farewell from the board, gifts, and a farewell reception. The paid director of the women's programs also resigned, citing the tensions in the church, and the minister of education left as well, although he did not directly refer to the crisis in his letter. While it is necessary to read between the lines of the multiple records and to infer the issues, it seems clear that at stake was essentially the age-old question of who was in charge. It would be raised again in the years to come.

Grafton's successor, Dr. Ewart Wyle, the senior minister of the First Christian Church of Tyler, Texas, was approved by the congregation on January 3, 1954. Wyle, who had been born in England, came from a generations-long line of pastors. He had served as a chaplain in World War II and he and his wife Ruth had one son who was also training for the ministry. The Wyles were welcomed enthusiastically. His installation service on March 14 was conducted by Reverend A. Dale Fiers, the most prominent leader in the Disciples Brotherhood and at that time the president of the United Christian Missionary Society.

Dr. Ewart Wyle, the third CCCC Senior Minister, 1954-1959. *CCCC Archive*

In his interviews for the pastorate, Dr. Wyle had described his Texas congregation with the puzzling words "a man's church," with the aside that "the women, of course, run things." He outlined his goals for his new church, emphasizing men's ministry, youth, and missions, and to each of these he attached specific initiatives, all of which were enthusiastically launched within the first year of his arrival. He created a Department of Men's Work and within that an organization called the "Men of Country Club." They would undertake a number of ambitious projects including the full sponsorship of a young Japanese couple who would complete their educations in the United States. This, less than a decade after the end of the war, was an ambitious act of reconciliation towards citizens of a former enemy. The group brought in distinguished speakers for dinner programs and were quickly a regular feature in *The Christian*. The organization was part of a larger men's movement within mainstream Christianity at the time, and the "Men of Country Club" participated in meetings in Missouri and throughout the country.

Shortly after Dr. Wyle's arrival, the church hired a new director and associate director of religious education. Both were women, the first to be employed in those positions, and a fact that had prompted discussion among the board at a special meeting. Mr. Bryan, chairman of the Religious Education Committee reported that "a number of our churches have women Directors of Religious Education. The committee started out to find a man and contacted many but all things being equal they would consider a woman." Miss Prudence Harper was twenty-two "with maturity and judgement" and the daughter of a Christian minister in nearby Independence.

There were a number of projects on behalf of youth, but the one closest to Dr. Wyle's enthusiasms was the Junior Board of Deacons, designed to engage high school-age boys once a month as deacons in the Sunday services. By 1957, youth "understudies" were being appointed to shadow individual staff members as a way of introducing young people to church work. The first Youth Sunday was scheduled in 1957, a day when young people assumed entire charge of the service. A new adult Sunday school class was organized in the fall of 1954, designed to attract young marrieds in their twenties. They soon decided on the name of Homesteaders to honor their commitments to family life. And for mission work Wyle proposed a permanent Christian Missionary Foundation to support the work of both domestic and international missions. The church continued to sponsor Living Link missionaries who corresponded and visited regularly. All the new initiatives were readily approved by the board.

Building projects were not as ambitious as in previous years, but there were endless costs for repairs and general upkeep, and in November of 1955 the board approved a plan to enlarge the south portico in an effort to ease congestion between the two services. The plan, providing access to the narthex, included two stairways, one to the balcony and one to the lower level. The portico work was completed in December 1956. Possibly the most appreciated physical improvement was the installation of air conditioning that included noisy window units in the offices. The church year had been defined by the Kansas City climate: formal Sunday School classes ended in the spring and resumed in the fall; all the staff took their vacations in summer; the choir was pared down to a few voices on a rotating schedule; and *The Christian* ceased publication until "Homecoming" Sunday in the fall. Many, but certainly not all, members had summer homes in cooler climes, and the board met only if necessary. Summer in Kansas City was also the polio season, sometimes at epidemic levels as in the summer of 1946 when children's Sunday School classes were cancelled entirely. Unfortunately, the installation of the AC equipment had pre-empted some of the baptistry space that Dr. Wyle pronounced an "embarrassment" as he campaigned for renovation. Changes and expansion of the summer schedule were slow to materialize, but gradually summer ceased to be the "off" time that had been the norm for so many years.

By the beginning of 1958, church membership numbered 3,364. The minutes, and presumably the length of board meetings, grew ever longer until the new chair, John Liesveld, imposed a strict agenda with a precise amount of time allocated to each report. *The Christian*, which had also increased significantly in length, gradually changed in content and style; the news was celebratory with frequent use of superlatives: the finest Easter season ever, the best-attended dinner, and so forth. With the occasional exception of a concerned reference to Communism, there were very few mentions of events and issues in Kansas City and the larger world: the Cold War and intensifying arms race with Russia; Sputnik; Brown vs. the Board of Education, the Montgomery bus boycott, and the expanding Civil Rights movement; and the successful development of a polio vaccine. The church did proudly announce that it had sent 19,000 pounds of clothing for Hungarian relief after the uprising in 1956, and the Christian Women's Fellowship remained active in similar endeavors.

The Christian focused primarily on the events, meetings and activities of the church, and on the members, through profiles and photos, and announcements of special achievements and recognition in the denomination as well as the community. At one point, The Men of Country Club began recognizing a Family of the Year with attendant publicity. By 1958 a more serious and engaged focus returned to *The Christian,* prompted at least in part by a similar stance at the national level of the Brotherhood that highlighted a discussion of Peace and World Order.

Ruth Wyle died on October 9, 1958, of complications associated with diabetes after a long hospitalization at Bethany Hospital. She had been a gentle, well-liked presence in the church. When she was profiled a few years earlier by the local paper she said she preferred to express her voice at home. Her death marked the beginning of a tumultuous period for Dr. Wyle and the church. The associate minister resigned a few months later to accept a call to lead his own church in Springfield, and the choir director resigned to accept an unusual opportunity from the State Department to lead an international chorus to Africa. By February 1959, Reverend William Shoop was installed as the new associate minister; he and his wife, Mary Jean, assumed important roles in the church in the years to come.

At the conclusion of the March 17, 1959, board meeting, the chair of the Board of Elders made a brief announcement: "The Board of Elders met on February 24 which is not any secret to the persons in this room. This meeting was called to consider the voluntary resignation of Miss Prudence Harper, Director of Education, but for the time being this resignation was rejected." The meeting was adjourned without further explanation or discussion. On April 17th at a special meeting of the board attended by 101 elders and deacons, Dr. Wyle made a statement "similar to the one he had made on the previous evening to the Board of Elders." He then read a letter to the board:

> After these many weeks of misunderstanding and many-sided accusations, I have just discovered why so many members of my congregation have been disturbed and even hurt. I have been the cause of this, for I had not realized until now that my casual attitude toward Miss Harper would be completely misunderstood ... Without question we have been careless, for I have enjoyed working with her, and did not think to hide any of our activities. It stands to reason that had there been immoral intent, we would have kept it in complete secrecy.
>
> I am praying with all my heart that you will see fit to forgive my thoughtlessness and that this spirit of Christian forgiveness will pervade this entire congregation."

Dr. Wyle left the room upon finishing the letter. The chair of the Board of Elders said that they had met earlier in the week with Dr. Wyle and Miss Harper, both of whom had submitted their resignations at that time. The Board of Elders had accepted the resignations, whereupon the full board approved that action, as well as the following resolution:

> Be it resolved that the Official Board in accepting the resignation of Dr. Ewart Wyle, gratefully and sincerely acknowledges the remarkable Christian leadership, vision and great capacity for work that he has brought to this church.
>
> All elements of the Church have been blessed by this unique leadership and we feel that their prayers join ours in asking that the Lord bring him great happiness and satisfaction wherever his Christian calling may be.

The Christian, published the previous day, carried Dr. Wyle's final weekly essay with the title "God is Love." It was his farewell, without using that word or alluding to why he was leaving. He concluded by saying that "It will always be my prayer that God's love will guide every heart and that there will be a unity based upon forgiveness and understanding so that the grandeur of God's love may always shine across the pathway of those who form that great company known as the Country Club Christian Church." The essay was reprinted in full in *The Kansas City Star* two weeks later. A lengthy, emotional tribute, titled "Thank You Dr. Wyle," appeared in *The Christian* the week after his resignation, signed simply "Your People."

Dr. Wyle and Prudence Harper were married in June, and not long after moved to La Jolla, California where they began a new Disciples church. The shock these events produced among church members, staff, and the community at large cannot be overestimated. Dr. Wyle was very popular, receiving regular praise and compliments that were at times effusive in *The Christian* and the board minutes. He was welcomed back emotionally by the congregation after each summer's absence. He was the president of the Kansas City-area Ministerial Association, gave multiple public addresses throughout the year in all parts of the country, and was considered a major figure in the Disciples of Christ denomination, holding, among other positions, a seat on the Board of Trustees of National City Christian Church.

In April 1958, the board had created an *ad hoc* Organization Study Committee. The final report, issued in November 1959, explained its purpose:

> Within recent years, it had become apparent to many of those charged with the responsibility of administering Country Club Christian's complex Church program that fast moving changes in the community and in the lives of its large congregation were creating problems with which the Church organization was not ideally suited to cope. This was of real concern to its Ministry and to its lay leaders. [202]

As that comment suggests, concerns pre-dated the formation of the committee. For example, in September 1957, Dr. Wyle, who had been on vacation, submitted a brief statement in lieu of the usual monthly report that was apparently a response to a question that had been directed to him. "Dr. Wyle ... did want the Official Board to know it was the policy of your Minister not to direct any member of his staff as each staff member is an executive in his own right and capable of initiating his own program." He noted the weekly Thursday morning staff meetings as a time of general discussion and conference.

The Organization Study committee had three objectives:
1. To clearly define the basic spiritual, educational, and service mission of the church and each element of the church;
2. To develop recommendations as to the most effective and efficient organization to accomplish the church's mission;
3. To develop recommended modifications or changes in operating procedures which can either increase the effectiveness of the element or increase its efficiency or both.

Throughout the following year, while Dr. Wyle was still there, the minutes would periodically note that the committee was working on the assignment, although its chair acknowledged that they had not met in quite some time at the May meeting after Wyle's resignation. They solicited confidential written statements submitted by a broad range of staff, both present and past, and by lay leaders. The committee held periodic conferences with these individuals to clarify and follow up. In addition, the committee reviewed an extensive collection of materials covering church organization and governance. Dr. Wyle's departure added further motivation and urgency to the process as the report confirmed: "We have been through two hurtful and upsetting experiences within the last five and one-half years. Your Committee believes that some of the weaknesses in our organization contributed to those upheavals." The report was completed by October 1959, and copies distributed to all members of the official board.

The final report was direct, at times blunt, noting that "undoubtedly, there will be ruffled feelings over our report findings. We have not given much space to the complimentary things — and there are many of them ... But we have devoted much space to the findings which are less than complimentary — and there are many of them." The report was divided into three parts: Findings, Recommendations, and Organization. After summarizing the church's strengths, the report addressed the weaknesses of a church:

- That has been weakened by the unhappiness and
  disillusionment caused by the strife and bitterness
  involved in the leaving of two Ministers within the last
  five and one-half years;
- That has been perceived as a "wealthy" church due to
  the size and social standing of its membership, and the
  size of its edifice;
- That seems to have lost some of its leadership as a
  spiritual force in the Community and
  the Brotherhood;
- Whose membership has not grown significantly in
  recent years, has not attracted significant numbers of
  young adults, and has not thoroughly studied the needs
  of the senior members;
- Has not studied the needs of the area it serves now and
  in the future;
- Has not hammered out a statement of its mission or goals;
- Has not solved the problems of integrating the Adult
  Sunday School in the religious and spiritual life of the
  church.

The report went on to specify thirty-two issues that were the consequences of those weaknesses within the ministry, the lay organization,
business affairs, and departmental and committee work. In general, the
issues addressed poor or non-existent channels of communication; lack
of organizational mission; failure to identify responsibility, authority and
duties of staff and lay officials; an excessive number of committees, often
overlapping in function (at the time of Wyle's departure there were thirteen "Departments" overseeing eighty-one sub-committees and groups,
to say nothing of innumerable ad hoc committees); and the ongoing
issue of a static board despite many attempts to establish a regular tenure
system. While praising the dedicated and highly professional work of the
Business Manager, the report expressed concern that only one individual
managed those critically important responsibilities and operations, many
of whose procedures were not written down. And finally, for the first
time, an official church report observed that "no woman is a member of
the Official Board yet the women of our Church are vital to the successful
accomplishment of its mission and have knowledge and a point of view
that can contribute to the wisdom of Board action."

The report is lengthy, detailed and very clear. Some of the key recommendations out of the twenty-six that were provided were to reconfigure the department organization plan into a much smaller group of "Councils" that would oversee functionally related committees and departments, the plan that is essentially in existence to the present day; to have the associate minister assume primary administrative responsibilities; to hire "a competent young man" to be an Assistant to the Administrative Officer; and to recognize the eligibility of women to serve on the official board as already provided for in the bylaws. The bylaws were the "rules" that had been developed in 1956; throughout most of the fifties a copy of the rules/bylaws was included as the opening document in each yearly collection of the board minutes. At the bottom of the first page, the first item in Article III read "Elders and Deacons shall be elected annually by the Congregation. They may be men or women." But policy had never become practice. The committee recognized "that this recommendation represents a radical departure from past practice," and, since the report was being issued so close to nomination and election time, that a plan for inclusion of women be brought before the board no later than October 1, 1960, for implementation in 1961.

At a special called meeting November 24th, the report was approved. A week earlier at the regular monthly meeting, upon recommendation of the Pulpit Committee to the elders, the board had agreed to issue a call to Dr. Lawrence Bash as the fourth Senior Minister of Country Club Christian Church. Dr. Bash was a familiar figure to the members; prior to his move to University Christian Church in Austin, Texas, where the congregation had grown from 60 to 1,000 members, he had led Wyatt Park Christian Church in St. Joseph, Missouri, from 1943-1949. During those six years he had occasionally preached at Country Club services when Dr. Grafton was away. As part of the discussion surrounding Dr. Bash's appointment, Reverend Shoop requested the privilege of addressing the group. He had stated earlier in the search process that he did not want to be considered for the Senior Minister position. His comments further illuminate how serious the events of the past seven months had been.

> On February 1 of this year, I arrived in this church as the Associate Minister. This assignment carried with it certain hopes and aspirations which were soon thwarted by the development of circumstances beyond my control. Since then our membership has been involved in

differences which might have been the sign of healthy concern. The time has come, however, when these differences have led to the kind of controversy in which motives and integrity have been questioned ... We have opened doors looking for skeletons and if there were none there, we created them. One obvious fact to me is that most of you love this church very deeply and want to do the very best for it. As one modern novelist has said, "how often we kill the things we love."

Let us create out of this disorder some peace, unity and goodwill so that we may bring solidarity and strength to our future work together.

CHAPTER 11

Activism: Civil Rights, Vietnam, and Community Engagement

Lawrence Bash assumed the pulpit on Sunday, January 3, 1960, and was formally installed on January 10 when once again Dr. Dale Fiers, president of UCMS, preached the sermon. Dr. Bash was the son of a minister and had been educated at Drake University and Divinity School, and had studied elsewhere including the University of Chicago Divinity School. Prior to beginning his education, he had spent two years in overseas mission work. He had served on a number of denominational committees and boards. His wife, Letha, was active in Disciples mission work and had just been elected chairman of the Board of Managers of the United Christian Missionary Society. She, like her husband, would maintain an active role in community and denominational activities, regularly presenting speeches and leading workshops. An added bonus, as the congregation would come to learn, was that the Bashes were both accomplished pianists who enjoyed playing alone and as a duet. They had one daughter, Jerri, who was a sophomore at Texas Christian University.

In addition to his ministerial work, Dr. Bash had always been very active in civic affairs. From the beginning his focus on church/civic dialogue would inform his sermons and motivate the agenda of his ministry and the church. The theme of the spring series of Thursday night dinners for that winter/spring season was "The Churchman's Obligation to His Community and State" featuring community and governmental leaders. In keeping with the country at large, Country Club continued to express concern and outrage at perceived threats to democratic society. In February 1960, Kansas City's Temple Kelhilath was bombed by several teenage boys claiming support for Nazi ideology. The lengthy and shocked report in the February 3 *Christian* decried the act and said that "we must accept our Christian responsibility and we cannot remain silent when we see injustice being done."

The week before Easter the news came that Warren Grafton had died in Detroit at the age of 58 following major surgery. He was eulogized in *The Christian* in warm terms and recalled as an exceptionally able preacher and administrator, "a creative force." The board sent a representative to his funeral and established a memorial fund in his honor. The response to his death along with Dr. Bash's arrival seemed to herald the beginning of healing within the church. Words such as "reunite" and "moving forward" appear in the minutes of that first year, revealing a sense of relief and new energy, summarized by Reverend Shoop at the conclusion of the February 1960 board meeting: "I look to the happy days ahead in working with Dr. Bash and I see a good feeling of the Church's future with his stabilizing influence and leadership."

The 1959 Organizational plan was quickly put in place with obvious success. The chair of the board, reporting on the Executive Committee that was now meeting twice a month, noted with satisfaction in February 1960 that "the most impressive point to me is that the meetings are held in a quiet church atmosphere with plenty of TIME to think out all sides to a problem … You gentlemen of the Board can be certain that programs presented for your approval at Official Board Meetings have been well thought out and discussed without haste and from all aspects."

The board moved promptly to address the recommendations and initiatives of the Organization Study Report, with particular attention to the Ministry of Religious Education, the Ministry of Pastoral Care, and the role of women in the church. The search for a new minister of religious education had progressed unsteadily, but in September 1960, Reverend Larry Alland was called to that position. The Organization Study Report had stressed that the minister of religious education should be experienced and credentialed in the relevant areas. Alland's wife, Rosemary, also was ordained, with a degree in religious education and a teaching background. Although the official appointment went to Larry, the announcement in *The Christian* made it clear that both would be active in the education ministry.

Church members were not acquainted with the Allands directly, but they were very familiar with the couple's most recent assignment as missionaries to the Congo. Disciples had a long record of missionary work in the Belgian Congo, where Dr. Royal Dye and his wife Eva had served as medical missionaries, making Bolenge "the most widely known mission station in the minds of lay Disciples" in the early 20th century. [203] In recent years Country Club, particularly the women's groups, had been active in supporting current efforts in what was now a time of crisis as the country was engulfed in civil war following independence from Belgium in June 1960. The Congo became yet another pawn in the Cold War conflict between the United States and the USSR, and the vocabulary of faith and foreign policy intersected regularly in reports in *The Christian* that warned that the communists were trying to assume power. Commenting that only seven missionaries remained in the Congo, one article concluded that "This small group was left so as not to create a vacuum into which the communists and others would immediately move." The Allands had been evacuated with their three young children.

The Pastoral Counseling Committee, housed within the Service and Outreach Council, was particularly energetic in developing what was essentially an entirely new area of specialized ministry. Staff ministers had always been expected to counsel parishioners in their pastoral roles, but that was proving increasingly challenging in a church as large as Country Club with its extensive administrative functions. For some years, the church had employed a parish visitor, always a woman, to assist in such matters as hospital visits, shut-in calls and so forth. Since 1958 that position had been held by the very capable and energetic Vivian Boswell. Her annual report at the end of 1960 provides a thorough, and exhausting, inventory of her responsibilities, some of which included: funerals attended, classes taught, committee and circle meetings attended, weekly column for *The Christian,* distribution of flowers and cards, and between 5,000 and 6,000 miles driven to meet her responsibilities. Mrs. Boswell would be instrumental in creating the job description for a full-time pastoral minister.

There was a growing recognition that the exigencies of modern life required expertise and specialized training beyond that of even the most gifted and sensitive of clerics. Although not specifically called for in the report to the board in September 1960, the committee began to actively campaign for a full-time minster of pastoral counseling, stating that they "feel that it is their duty to make known to the congregation the need for professional counseling service within our church." In the meantime, the committee brought in consultants in the field, and hosted regular workshops and institutes, focusing on such issues as alcoholism, family counseling, and juvenile delinquency. In October, the committee assumed responsibility for one of the church night dinners and planned an entire week of meetings around that event that would focus on family life professional counseling. It was very successful and the committee was awarded a modest budget to continue its efforts in that direction.

The recommendation of the Organization Study Report had called for the nomination of women to the board no later than October 1960 in order for them to assume their positions the following year. Two women were elected as "deaconesses," a term that would eventually be replaced by the all-encompassing "deacon." Those women were Elma Hobson and Elizabeth Schmidt. As Mrs. Hobson's son, Dr. Milburn Hobson, wryly observed many years later, "they didn't want to pick out just one woman to make a deacon, so they picked two." Both had been leaders in the church for many years, serving in a broad array of positions. Elma had started the first Sunday school class for business and professional women at Independence Boulevard Church and had continued the class, referred to as the "Hobson Girls" at Country Club after she and her husband transferred in 1936. She was the first woman to preach from the Country Club pulpit; the intriguing title of her sermon was "Choose Your Weapons." Elizabeth Schmidt held a number of denominational as well as church positions, and she would be elected the president of the United Church Women of Kansas City. The president of the Christian Women's Fellowship was also added to the board roster in a non-voting capacity. Women were nominated to the board in regular rotation from then on. It would be several more years, however, before the role of junior deacon was opened to high school girls as well as boys.

Beginning in 1960, *The Christian* presented an occasional series of "profiles" of leading women members in the church — a first for that kind of recognition. However, progress in expanding women's official roles was neither direct nor smooth; old habits and assumptions did not change immediately. The chairman of the board was mortified to learn that a woman who was a member of the Executive Committee and chair of one of the newly established councils had not been invited to the 1961 annual board dinner. She was not a member of the board, still comprised solely of trustees, elders, deacons, and senior staff. The following year, the minutes of the 1962 annual meeting opened with the perfunctory line that

"The annual meeting of the Official Board when the wives are invited to attend was held on Tuesday evening." This after a year of two women sitting on the board. No mention is made of their husbands being invited. And in February 1963, the board minutes noted that daily Easter chapel services would soon begin with a "very good list of speakers which includes some women."

The men were not alone in needing to adjust to the expansion of women's roles in church administration. Articles about women's changing roles started to appear in *The Christian,* such as the piece in March 1960, taken from the Disciples journal *World Call,* that reported on an extensive survey being conducted throughout the denomination to determine women's needs and also more pointedly to ascertain why a significant percentage of members did not participate in activities designed for women in their churches. While in many ways a positive discussion, readers may have paused at the final line that exhorted church leaders to "take seriously the responsibility to minister unto 'the least of these.'" In November 1960, Lois Layman, one of the women leaders in the church as well as the Greater Kansas City Christian Church Commission, provided a column on "Woman's Day" for *The Christian.* This was an annual event in the denomination, during which women assumed responsibility for worship, and the focus was on women's roles in the church. "That role," she observed, "has changed markedly within a comparatively short time." She went on to note that "of significance is the fact that much of our Lord's instructions were first given to women," but she clearly wants to avoid offending when she adds that "There is no place for a competitive spirit in the Lord's mission ... women's work must be done humbly — never militantly — not a 'Carrie Nation' hatchet wielding."

Other, more subtle, changes also signaled evolution away from patriarchy to an equally shared ministry of all members. Traditionally the cover of the Christmas issue of *The Christian* carried a greeting from all the staff that always designated couples as "Dr./Mr. and Mrs. _____. The 1960 issue, the Bashes' first Christmas, followed the holiday message with a list of given names and no titles, e.g. "Lawrence and Letha Bash." For some years, *The Christian* had highlighted news and announcements of The Men of Country Club, the organization created in the mid-1950s, in a boxed presentation headed by a heraldic symbol unlike any other church organization. Under the new council system established in 1960, the group was incorporated as an equal partner with CWF and the separate stylized presentation quietly disappeared. Throughout all the changes, the women of the church continued to engage in active stewardship, prompting Dr. Bash to observe in 1965 in his summary of the annual denominational *Yearbook*, the statistical report of all individual churches, that "our Christian Women's Fellowship led all women's groups [in giving] by a substantial margin as they have for years."

Two major building projects were launched in 1960: the George Hamilton Combs Memorial Chapel, and the Christian Conference Grounds, later re-named Tall Oaks, on a site southwest of Bonner Springs, Kansas, on Highway 32. Both had initially been proposed during Dr. Wyle's tenure. The Conference Center had been conceived as a facility that would serve all Disciples of Christ churches in the greater Kansas City area. Over the years, it has been a place of retreat, hosting not only members of the denomination but other organizations such as summer programs for disabled children. Country Club would be the main source of support as it developed.

Edward S. Tanner, a well-known Kansas City architect, was hired to prepare architectural plans for the Memorial Chapel. Tanner began his career as an employee of J. C. Nichols, and then created his own firm. He designed more than 2,000 homes for the Nichols' developments as well as civic buildings such as the Public Library on 12th Street, and Linda Hall Library on the UMKC campus. As befit a "memorial," the costs were to be met by donations led by the Atha family beyond the regular church budget; already $80,000 had been committed, making it possible to move forward. In November the Memorial Committee gave a detailed report to the board, proposing a budget of $205,000 that did not include the parking lot. The report summarized the many discussions about where the chapel should be located; originally it was planned as an extension to the main building. But the committee unanimously concluded that the chapel should be for spiritual use only — a place apart from other church activities. To encourage interest the committee proposed that ground-breaking be scheduled as part of the 40th anniversary plans in 1961 that occurred in May.

The finished chapel was dedicated the week of May 13, 1962, during which one of six different clergymen spoke each evening. The previous March, the "cornerstone" had been set — actually a large niche, behind which a copper time capsule filled with various historic documents pertaining to the early days and Dr. Combs' ministry, as well as records of present-day activities. In order to accommodate the anticipated number of worshippers, seventy-two chairs were temporarily added to the loft balcony and reservations were required. The balcony was remodeled and fitted with seating in March 1964. At one point, Dr. Bash acknowledged that he had had some concerns about the extent to which the chapel would be used, but those worries were soon dispelled. In addition to weddings and funerals, the chapel had "found its place in the heart of the community for the daily interdenominational prayer services" that in the first year had served over 4,000 persons.

The George Hamilton Combs Chapel, dedicated in 1962 has often been the site of community-wide services and memorials. *CCCC Archive*

The chapel became a center of community and ecumenical engagement, open daily, offering a place for meditation and prayer. It would have a special role in expanding liturgical practices associated with Lent. As Dr. Bash noted on several occasions, "The Lenten season does not have the liturgical significance in the Christian Church that it has in many other denominations." That changed in coming years and the chapel was at the heart of evolving rituals. A Good Friday Vigil of continuous prayer was scheduled even before the formal dedication. Members pledged to be in the chapel for a 30-minute period during the forty-two hour vigil that began at noon on Good Friday and concluded at 6:00 AM Easter Sunday. An organ consisting of 475 pipes was dedicated in the chapel in February 1963. It was donated by Loula Long Combs in honor of her late husband Robert Pryor Combs and his mother, Martha Stapp Combs. It was a family affair; Gladys Combs played the dedication recital.

The church chimes tolled each hour across ten hours on Monday, November 25, 1963, marking the somber beginning of ten one-hour services in the chapel on the National Day of Mourning for President John F. Kennedy, who had been assassinated in Dallas on November 22. "America," said Dr. Bash, "has been brought to her knees," in a distressed column in *The Christian*. He spoke of the riots and church bombing two months previously in Birmingham, and the brutal violence that was engulfing the country. Sunday morning services in the sanctuary, where Dr. Bash's sermon was titled "Absalom My Son — the Therapy of Grief," were followed by a Memorial Service in the afternoon in which all the churches in the Country Club District participated. The service had not been publicly advertised, but the sanctuary was filled. Kansas City Mayor Ilus Davis, a member and deacon of the church, gave the tribute. Monday's services in the chapel were so crowded that some had to be moved to the sanctuary. Speakers included Protestant ministers, a Rabbi, and priests from the Orthodox and Roman Catholic churches. Kennedy's successor, Vice-President Lyndon B. Johnson, was a Disciple who occasionally worshipped at National City Christian Church in Washington, D.C., the site of his funeral in 1973.

~~~~

In an analysis of what he terms the "Spiritual Awakening" of the 1960s, Robert Ellwood describes the early years of that decade as "the repressed fifties." He argues that much of what had shaped spiritual, cultural, social, and political life in America in the 1950s still pertained — but there were fissures and challenges that would soon dramatically disrupt the post-war world. [204] Churches such as Country Club Christian had experienced tremendous growth and were established institutions supported by bureaucracies, hierarchies of professional personnel, and affiliations with a vast array of denominational organizations across the nation. The mainline Protestant denominations collectively represented a Protestant hegemony that, as noted earlier, identified itself with an American "Way of Life": its values, its aspirations, and its view of history, that was captured in *TIME* Magazine's 1960 Easter issue:

> This generally upbeat, laudatory tone, the obvious favor-itism toward Christianity and its American mainline denominations, the unobtrusive but respectable aca-demic scholarship behind its portrayal of the first cen-tury, all make the *Time* article not only a monument to Henry Luce's values, but also a kind of capstone and epitaph for the Fifties-style, public, self-assured, mod-ernist religion, confidently working out of unquestioned great traditions and, like America generally, thought to be doing good on a global scale. [205]

Yet, at the moment of their greatest unified strength and authority, these denominations would be forced to recognize diversity and pluralism.

The most cursory survey of scholarly sources and the internet reveals a religious crisis during the 1960s that was experienced, while not uni-formly, in many parts of the world. The winds of change were broad and diffuse. The influence of Vatican II convened by the immensely popular Pope John XXIII extended far beyond the Roman Catholic Church. John Kennedy had been elected the first Catholic President of the United States and contrary to the fears of many, his religious faith did not influence political or policy decisions. Although some concerns such as Federal support of parochial schools continued, ministers, rabbis, priests, and nuns would soon link arms in protests against racial discrimination and, later, Vietnam, striving for a unity that went beyond sectarian divides. Freedom rides, sit-ins and marches, examples of the non-violent protest championed by Martin Luther King Jr., were signatures of the early years, but assassinations, riots, and war were the hallmarks of a darker time at the end of the decade.

Country Club Christian's reaction to and engagement with the events of the 1960s are the subjects of the following pages. One useful way to consider those events is the evolution of the concept of the "servant church" that emerged in that time and shaped at least some of the response on the part of laity and clergy alike. The dialogue that surrounded the idea of a servant church went in many directions and, in Ellwood's words, sometimes proposed "new ecclesiastical notions [that] quickly burned out or fell to earth on stony ground." [206] But change — sometimes profound change — occurred and he concludes that "all this was in the name of a church that was to be no longer a paternalistic authority figure but a ministering agent of change and hope. This church liked to think of itself as servant rather than magister, not just to the people who comprised it, but through them to the whole community."[207] The writings of Dietrich Bonhoeffer, the German theologian who was hanged by the Nazis near the end of World War II, were especially influential in the early days of the Civil Rights movement, and his works were added to the church library. The servant concept "suggested a revised understanding of how God entered and acted in the world; moving largely outside the church in the secular realm."[208]

For Disciples, the concept, if not the precise term, of a servant church, drew on a long history of engagement in the community at home, and in other lands. Dr. Bash's personal involvement with civic affairs; a church membership that at various times included mayors, a chief of police, city manager, and local and state legislators; and members actively enlisted in the denomination's historic commitment to the poor and marginalized were all significant factors in shaping the church's direction in the years ahead. In a May 1960 report to the board, the chair of the Missions committee, part of the Service and Outreach Council, summarized its purpose succinctly: "We aid in the work of God's Kingdom here in the Kansas City area, in our state, our nation and over the whole world … Our church's growth is measured by our service to others."

In a sermon in April 1962, Dr. Bash proposed a new concept of Christian service that he identified as "time tithing." The Service to Others program would provide opportunities both within the church as well as to some twenty community agencies, each of which would be represented by a church member coordinator. To a greater extent than some other denominations, Disciples had struggled with the conflicting and often ironic commitment to unity while always acknowledging diversity and pluralism. The age-old question of what really constituted "unity" would be asked yet again in the 1960s. In 1957, the renowned Dutch theologian, Dr. Willem A. Visser 't Hooft, the first secretary general of the World Council of Churches, provided a clear statement of the meaning of a servant church in the modern world:

> No faith, no church, no philosophy or ideology has among us such a strong and central position that it can claim to have a monopoly and give shape to the life of

society as a whole. This pluralism, this diversity with regard to our convictions about the meaning of life, has come to stay ... Pluralism means that no church, no philosophy, can run the show. The church is thrown back on its true task. In can only live as a servant church. That does not mean a withdrawal from society, but it means a different form of presence in society. [209]

"A northern city with a southern exposure" is a description that has been applied to Kansas City a number of times over the years, as well as to other former Border State communities such as St. Louis and Cincinnati. Too far north to be part of the Old South, with major railroads, and advantageously situated on large rivers that supported commercial and industrial growth, these cities nevertheless retained the traditions and outlook of their early southern settlers. Missouri and Kentucky were slave states that remained in the Union during the Civil War. Kansas City sat on the border between slave-holding Missouri and free-soil Kansas; its "historical roots on one of the mid-nineteenth century fault lines between slave and free states and Union and Confederate loyalties." [210] By 1921, as Frank Bowen planned a Disciples church in the new Country Club District, Kansas City was a deeply segregated community where Jim Crow shaped policy, law and human relationships.

African-Americans were involved in the Restoration Movement from the earliest days. In the antebellum South it was customary for slaves to accompany their masters' families to church, usually sitting in back pews or the balcony, or listening at windows outside. The often agonized and convoluted discussions of slavery and abolition on the part of Disciples leaders were described in earlier pages. Initially there were few all-Black congregations, but the first one, established in 1838 in Ohio, was a "station" on the Underground Railroad. Following Lincoln's Emancipation Proclamation in 1863, African-American Disciples congregations grew, almost always as separate congregations with their own institutional supporting structures and journals — a "parallel universe" in historian Duane Cummins' words. [211] Not until the denominational restructure in the late 1960s did the two groups become one.

There were several historically African-American Disciples churches in Kansas City. Woodland Avenue Christian Church evolved into West Paseo Christian Church in the late 1930s. Country Club maintained a continuing mission of support to West Paseo, as well as First Christian, sometimes referred to as "Our Church of the Inner City." West Paseo's founding minister, Sere S. Myers, began his Kansas City career at Woodland in 1932, having moved to Kansas City from his birthplace in Mississippi where he was the fourteenth child of former slaves. He was educated at the Southern Christian Institute in Mississippi, a school founded by Disciples after the Civil War to educate recently freed slaves. He retired from West Paseo in 1974, and when he died in 2000 at the age of 102, he was celebrated as a "bridge builder" between the races.[212]

Reverend Myers was also a key leader of the National Christian Missionary Convention, later renamed the National Christian Missionary Convocation, an organization of African-American Disciples that created a partnership with the UCMS. Today the Convocation is part of the Disciples Home Missions, enabling "African-American congregations to receive services through a united structure."[213] The Convocation continued to maintain a distinct if not separate identity. In the summer of 1994, Kansas City hosted a national meeting of the Convocation. Dr. Alvin Jackson, a prominent leader within the Convocation and future moderator of the Disciples, spoke at the Sunday morning services at Country Club and joined 300 conference participants who were bussed to the church for noon dinner.

Civil Rights activism in Kansas City began long before the 1960s. Van Hutchinson traces the origins of the struggles as early as the 1870s as the advances won for African-Americans during the Reconstruction period gave way before harsh Jim Crow practices and laws. He describes the efforts of members of the Black middle class and intelligentsia that included teachers, ministers, and professionals who created clubs and societies and newspapers, including the nationally recognized *Kansas City Call*.[214] Following World War II, in what Hutchinson describes as a turning point, "the emergence of a group of white integrationists" broadened the breadth and intensity of civil rights efforts, but it would be several decades before those efforts moved from their early relatively cautious approach.[215]

In his definitive study of the National Council of Churches (NCC) and the Black Freedom Movement, James Findlay notes there has been relatively little scholarship on "race relations in predominantly white churches in the 1950s and 1960s, a topic recognized but not strongly emphasized in the recent studies of mainstream Protestantism and in the secular histories of the civil rights movement covering much of the same time period."[216] The Disciples of Christ is a member denomination of the

NCC, and Findlay argues that its policies on racial issues usually were representative of the mainline (White) churches. His study, therefore, provides a useful guide to understanding the evolution of Country Club's role and response to race relations in the 1960s. He begins by documenting the "rather tepid efforts in the 1950s of ecumenical church people to deal with racial matters," or, in the somewhat more eloquent words of Liston Pope, Dean of Yale Divinity School, who observed after reviewing responses to a 1956 national survey on religious and civic affairs: "At this time of the greatest need, the influence of religion on human affairs appears to be indirect and, all told, rather minimal"[217]

During the 1950s the NCC sponsored workshops/programs and issued resolutions about race. A survey of the *Kansas City Star* archives for the years 1940 to 1960 reveals similar efforts locally. Articles employing the term "race relations" announced institutes, clinics, and teach-ins promoting education and dialogue with the underlying assumption that positive, or at least improved, relations between the races was morally essential. And almost always, these programs were sponsored by religious (church, temple) or civic (e.g. the Human Relations Commission) organizations. From the 1920s on, the NCC had sponsored "Race Relations Sundays" usually held in the spring. These proved immensely popular, and announcements appeared regularly in the Kansas City papers.

Country Club had an established tradition of supporting the local African-American congregations financially and through charitable efforts, such as clothing drives and volunteer work. By the 1960s there were occasional pulpit exchanges and invitations to one another's services. *The Christian* notes church-sponsored workshops and programs on race relations and includes approving references to Kansas City's Council on Human Relations. But, in general, there is relatively little reference to race as a focus of concern in either theological or civic terms. Not until the early 1960s would a sense of urgency and even crisis be evident.

Racial covenants and red-lining (the systematic denial of financial and other services to potential home buyers based on their color or ethnicity) were not unique to Kansas City real estate practices, but their long-term impact, even after being declared illegal, created a seemingly inexorable racist culture. All examinations of Kansas City's race history are grounded on that premise.[218] Social historian Sherry Schirmer's insightful study, *A City Divided: The Racial Landscape of Kansas City, 1900-1960*, considers race in terms of "geography" — geography as a literal artifact of space, and geography as metaphor. The covenants created rigidly maintained zones by race, long after the 1948 Supreme court ruled such practices illegal. African-Americans denied access to the postwar prosperity and housing boom were increasingly crowded into neighborhoods characterized by derelict housing, poor or non-existent services, and high crime, all of which seemed to confirm negative perceptions Whites held about African-Americans collectively.

These neighborhood conditions had been created and maintained by widely differing approaches to law and civic management. A double standard for law enforcement and judicial process, dating back to the Machine politics days and before, kept the popular bars and jazz clubs (often serving a White only clientele) open in the African-American areas. Black offenders who were charged with crimes against fellow Blacks frequently got off with relatively minor fines or jail time — quite different from when the victims were White. Such practices outraged law abiding African-Americans, who wanted to ensure safe neighborhoods. Schools remained segregated, long after the 1954 Brown vs. the Board of Education decision, because school districts were tied to the "neighborhoods" shaped by the covenants.

It is not possible to consider Country Club's role in race relations and civil rights in isolation, apart from other institutions and other currents in American religious life. The late fifties and sixties were also a time of wide-spread ecumenical efforts that brought together activists, religious institutions, and their leaders in common cause. Many of Country Club's efforts in those years were associated with larger organizations such as the Kansas City Ministerial Alliance, the Disciples denomination, and the National Council of Churches. One example of an attempt on the part of the Ministerial Alliance to effect change in the schools occurred in 1952. The Alliance sent a letter to the Board of Education objecting to the "more than crowded conditions of the Booker T. Washington school and other Negro schools that may be in the same plight." They urged that the Benton elementary school be opened to Black students, arguing that "what little adjustment that will need to be made by the White students in this matter is small compared to the damage that is being done to the Negro students forced to attend school in the conditions such as are present at Booker T. Washington."[219]

This was two years before *Brown vs. the Board of Education*, the Supreme Court case that began in nearby Topeka, Kansas, but housing covenants had already been declared illegal. Benton School was in what had been a predominantly White neighborhood, but after the covenants were outlawed, Black families began to move to the neighborhood as well. Rather than integrate the school, as the Ministerial Alliance had requested, the KCMO School District converted it from a "White" to a "colored" school. White families protested, but the conversion went forward; six days after the school opened in the fall of 1953 a fire destroyed the structure and the students were relegated to split shifts for the entire school year. [220]

By the early sixties, the National Council of Churches was becoming more focused on its efforts and in 1963 established the Commission on Religion and Race. This was a direct consequence of the leadership of the National Council President J. Irwin Miller, the first layman to hold that position. Miller was a Disciple, who was active in the ecumenical and civil rights movements, and the grandson of Z.T. Sweeney, one of the early "dedicators." He came as a guest speaker to Country Club in June 1961. The front-page article announcing his presentation in *The Christian* does not identify the exact subject of his address, but the article focuses on recent charges against the NCC and Christian churches in general that claimed that they were under Communist influence. In March 1960, the Air Force training manual included these charges, informing its users that "Communists and Communist fellow-travelers and sympathizers have successfully infiltrated into our churches ... .it is known that even pastors of certain of our churches are card-carrying communists." [221] The NCC expressed outrage, the Secretary of Defense apologized, and the manual was withdrawn.

The furor reached the larger public and generated support for the NCC. It was, argued Findlay, "the clearest sign for ecumenically inclined church people that the McCarthy era was ending." [222] Dr. Bash joined the fray and addressed the controversy in his regular column in *The Christian*: "The main force of these attacks is coming from the crack-pot fringes of Protestantism, from men who can seldom get along with anyone else and who are making a profitable career of being professional anti-communists. It is really incredible that anyone should seriously believe that Communism has penetrated the leadership of Protestantism."

The Cold War and fear of communism at home and abroad, racial conflict, sectarian disputes — seemingly disparate currents — crossed and re-crossed each other and influenced church dialogue. Responding to these trends was a growing ecumenical movement that brought together a wide array of participants of different skin color, political positions, and religious creeds. *The Christian* provided regular updates and recommendations on civic affairs, and the writers were not reluctant to advocate for certain issues. A piece in March 1962 submitted by the Christian Action and Community Service Committee informed readers that in order to qualify for federal urban renewal funds a community must have a functioning committee on minority housing. Readers were urged to submit their support for the committee to the City Council.

That fall, on November 4, Dr. Martin Luther King addressed 8,000 people at the annual Reformation Day event in downtown Kansas City. Country Club's music director, Hadley Crawford, led the huge interdenominational choir. *The Christian* promoted it in the weeks prior to the gathering; the last announcement included the line that "This is not a service on race relations," a caveat that is puzzling and inaccurate. King's speech, modeled on one of Paul's epistles, was titled "Paul's Letter to the American Christians" and challenged contemporary Christians to be sure "moral progress keeps abreast of technological progress." It was tragic, he declared, that segregation had crept into the door of the church. "All men are one in Christ Jesus," he said, and "it must be realized that segregation is not only politically and economically wrong [because] it substitutes the I-it relationship for the I-thou relationship." [223]

As the decade progressed, attention to race relations evolved beyond occasional speeches and events, as the subject was increasingly incorporated into the everyday rhythms of the church. The visceral shock of President Kennedy's murder presaged a period of mobilized commitment to Civil Rights on the part of mainline churches. The NCC shook off the last vestiges of caution and assumed a leadership role with mainline Protestant churches in a grassroots campaign on behalf of Civil Right legislation. Midwest churches played a particularly effective role: "Belief in equality before the law, awareness of the great gap between ideal and current racial practices, and a sense of moral urgency to correct these injustices, were central concerns of midwestern church people as they wrote to their political leaders in Washington." [224]

Country Club organized an energetic schedule of programming, beginning with an eight-week Symposium on Civil Rights, starting January 30, 1964. Seating was limited to 125 people. The leadoff speaker was Dr. John W. Williams, the African-American pastor of St. Stephen Baptist Church in Kansas City as well as the president of the General Baptist Convention of Missouri and Kansas, and the vice-president of the NCC. Symposium topics included education, police work, housing issues, the Council on Human Relations, and employment. The police focus was handled in two sessions: the first led by Kansas City Police Chief and Country Club member, Clarence Kelley, the second by Earl D. Thomas, member of City Council. Three of the speakers were African-Americans, including the final presenter, Bruce Watkins, a member of the Kansas City Council, who spoke on behalf of the Public Accommodation Ordinance to be voted on April 7.

The Ordinance, which expanded a previous law that had outlawed discrimination in hotels, motels, and restaurants, had been passed by City Council, but 20,000 opponents signed a petition, forcing a referendum. The Ordinance would be the subject of Dr. Bash's sermon on April 5, and it received unequivocal endorsement from the Outreach Council: "This ordinance is right morally. Clergymen of all faiths agree that this ordinance is morally and spiritually right. The brotherhood of man cannot be real with discrimination on all sides." The article went on to note that the vote was being followed by *The New York Times*, CBS-TV with Walter Cronkite, and *Life* Magazine. *The Times* article was detailed, stressing the opposition that included the Kansas City Tavern Owners Association and two "ultra-conservative groups" led by members of the John Birch Society. Opponents to the ordinance drew on familiar language, arguing that its objectives and those "of the Communist Manifesto were identical and 'this Communist conspiracy' should be defeated."[225] The article went on to say those working for passage of the ordinance included "the majority of the city's clergy, the Chamber of Commerce, the League of Women Voters and the Kansas City newspapers."

The Ordinance passed by a narrow margin that was attributed to the aggressive get-out-the-vote campaign in predominantly African-American neighborhoods as well as area churches. *The Kansas City Times* noted the "unusual backing from church and religious organizations, as well as varied and numerous civic groups ... The churches took the most active part in promoting voter approval of the ordinance of any issue within memory of political observers ... Church leaders explained their work on the election by saying that besides being non-political, public accommodation was a moral issue."[226]

Country Club Christian Church received considerable press coverage that spring from national as well as local news. A March issue of *TIME*, discussing the grassroots ecumenical movement, cited Country Club's interdenominational services in the chapel that was quoted in the March 18 *Christian*:

Kansas City's Country Club Christian Church has invited pastors from 31 different denominations to speak from its pulpit. Christian ecumenism also spills over to include Jews: One recent Lenten speaker at the Kansas City church was Rabbi Alexander Graubart of Congregation Beth Shalom.

Ecumenism was further demonstrated in March 1964 by the Holy Week visit of Martin Niemoeller, one of the major clergymen of the 20th century. Niemoeller was a Lutheran pastor from Germany who was the president of the World Council of Churches. He had been imprisoned for seven years in concentration camps for his resistance to Hitler. His experience resulted in a dramatic acknowledgement of his own failure to reject Hitler and Nazism at the deepest level; he had remained an ardent nationalist whose opposition to the Reich was limited to its interference in the church. He spent the rest of his life advocating for pacifism, atonement, and reconciliation.

An ecumenical moment: Dr. Bash, Bishop Helmsing, Dr. Martin Niemoeller at the conclusion of Niemoeller's weeklong sermon series at CCCC during Holy Week 1964. *CCCC Archive*

On the final day of his visit to Country Club, Niemoeller was asked if he would be willing to go to the Social Hall for an informal conversation after the service concluded. Many Protestant ministers were present; what was not expected was the arrival of three Kansas City Roman Catholic leaders: the bishop, chancellor, and vice chancellor of the Diocese. Dr. Niemoeller responded to the moment by talking about the spread of the ecumenical movement among Catholics as well as Protestants. A delighted Dr. Bash wrote in *The Christian* that "It was my pleasure and privilege to introduce a president of the World Council of Churches to a Bishop of the Roman Catholic Church!"

Several weeks later, *The Kansas City Times* published a six-column article on the church under the title "Experimentation Enlivens a Church." Members and staff were gratified by the opening lines that in Dr. Bash's words "were calculated to bring a thrill of pride to each of us":

> With its Gothic-style buildings, its relatively massive plant and its fashionable setting, the Country Club Christian Church hardly seems to be the type of church willing to try out new ideas. And yet, under the guidance of its pastor, the Rev. Lawrence Bash, and many active laymen, Country Club Christian Church has become an experimental congregation. Although the more traditional patterns of pastoral service are not neglected, the church has sought to place more emphasis upon problems which most churches have been forced or have chosen to ignore. [227]

In the article, Dr. Bash pointed out that recent research had shown that adults don't learn very much by being talked to (the usual church format), but gain much more in small groups. "The Country Club Christian Church is not so interested in getting large attendance at Sunday school as in the formation of many small, intimate and involved units."

The article further noted the success of the recent symposium on race that drew in at least 650 persons, who, after listening to a speaker, broke into smaller discussion groups. The profile also highlighted the arrival of a new Minister of Pastoral Care, Dr. Daniel Fielder, who would create a professional counseling ministry providing direct service to people "at all crises of life." Community service in the form of tithing time (four hours per week) was proving very successful. And finally, Dr. Bash outlined the new focus on children, the "forgotten" members of the church, at the 8:30 service. The article was accompanied by a photograph of the Reverend Thomas R. Leavy, Assistant at St. Stephen's Catholic Church, preaching from the Country Club Chapel pulpit, with the caption that his appearance was "probably the first time in the United States that such a program had been held ... The ecumenical initiative shown by the church ... has given the community a leading place in the unity movement."[228]

The church experienced a memorable year in 1964, and, perhaps not surprisingly, one more article in the October issue of the nationally distributed *Reader's Digest* recognized its ecumenical leadership under the title "New Warmth Among Christians":

> The ecumenical spirit extends to relations of Christians with Jews ... Now in many dioceses Catholic priests are encouraged to participate in inter-religious activities, and even bishops are addressing their meetings. At a Lenten service last year at Kansas City's Country Club Christian Church the speaker was Rabbi Alexander Graubart of Congregation Beth Shalom.

Ecumenical exchanges, interfaith meetings, and regular confirmation of the value of faith in its many forms continued into the coming year. The Bashes spent their summer vacation in Europe with the purpose of familiarizing themselves with religious institutions and personalities. One of those personalities was Pope Paul VI; Kansas City Diocese Bishop Helmsing had arranged for an audience.

The 1964 election did not reflect the collegiality and unity of purpose that had seemed to engage religious America. In his October 28th column in *The Christian* Dr. Bash's exasperation was evident. "The happiest thought I have had today is that in one more week the election of 1964 will be over! Not in my lifetime has there been a spectacle which has so depressed me. One wonders how long the free society can endure the degradation of the office of president in campaigns such as this." He focused particular ire on the Republican's distribution of a controversial book, *And None Dare Call It Treason* that re-hashed "the same old discredited charges made in the McCarthy era" and again in the Air Force Manual attacks on the National Council of Churches. Methodist ministers and seminarians had protested against the book by marching in front of the Kansas City headquarters of the Republican party. Acknowledging that it was not his function to tell parishioners how to vote, he did express the hope that there "might be widespread support for the various bond issues being offered Kansas City as these will determine the future direction of our civic life." In his analysis of spiritual life in the 1960s, Ellwood concluded that 1964 was the first year "that many churches, and state and local councils of churches, made ... overt statements of electoral support or opposition."[229]

In the coming years Country Club would continue to offer presentations on race relations by individuals representing diverse organizations and points of view, as well as to publicize comparable programs elsewhere in the city. Community organization, a signature term of the period, was the subject of a two-day seminar in October 1965. Dr. Bash referred to "confusing issues in the world of religion," the "shifting scene of the mid-sixties," and "this troubling age" in his sermons and *Christian* essays and gave a sermon early in 1966 titled "The Christian as Citizen." He drew on Harvey Cox's *The Secular City*, one of the most popular books of the decade. In early 1966, the church hosted a "for members only" meeting on the Fair Housing Campaign, also the subject of Dr. Bash's sermon a few weeks later. The Fair Housing meeting was led by church member Ilus Davis, the mayor of Kansas City.

Country Club's experiences and agendas during this era were clear examples of Robert Ellwood's description of 1964 through 1966 as the "years of secular hope." Theologian Martin Marty observed at the time that "no word seems to turn up more frequently in theology today (or with less precise definition) than 'secular,'" but Ellwood's usage suggests not a rejection of spiritual institutions so much as an embrace of the duty of the spiritual with and within the secular.[230] The Mississippi Freedom Summer, an often violent time of registering Black voters, followed the passage of the sweeping 1964 Civil Rights Act, creating a "fiery anvil on which was forged the Mid-Sixties alliance of the New Left ... and new styles of ministry and consciousness now stirring within the churches."[231] In his role as pastor, Dr. Bash tried to steer a middle course as he viewed with deep concern the dramatic changes and events sweeping across the country.

In October 1966, the church announced the launch of a "massive program" of "Shepherding Groups" intended to include every member that would meet on Sunday evenings for small group discussion of the "ferment in the churches." The meetings were not to be social, and hosts were specifically asked to not serve refreshments. In the same two-week period, the church also announced: a nine week course, to be taught by a University of Kansas professor of religion, using Dietrich Bonhoeffer's *Letters and Papers from Prison*, and Harvey Cox's *Secular City*; a Thursday night dinner speaker, Dr. John W. Williams, an African-American member of the Commission on Religion and Race of the National Council of Churches; and, as the discussion topic for the second session of the Shepherding Groups meetings, a recent conservative article asking the question "Should the Church 'Meddle' in Civil Affairs?" to which the article replied, essentially, "no."

In January 1966, Dr. Bash quoted at length from a recent article by Marty, one of the major scholars of religion in the 20th century. The article carried the intriguing title "Meanwhile Back at the Protestant Ranch," a nod to the significant news coverage of Vatican II, now concluded, and the consequent changes to the Catholic Church. The commentary clearly resonated with Dr. Bash, and it provides a useful portrait of the contemporary mainline Protestant church in general, and certainly of Country Club Christian Church. The current church leadership, Marty argued, was not shaped as its predecessors had been by religious disaffection, depression and war. Rather, it "was shaped during a religious revival, a period of affluence, and a cold war. The civil rights struggles have been the great uniting experience." [232] He went on to ask if the "ease with which the younger clergy united on the racial issue distracted it from other problem areas which are morally ambiguous?" It is a question that would be raised in the coming years as many struggled with the "rightness" of racial equality, and the "wrongness" of violence to achieve that equality. The mid-sixties Protestant church is world oriented, he posited, rather than church oriented, and it is a generation "which has found the city." (The Catholics, Marty acknowledged, got there first.)

One of the points Dr. Bash did not elaborate upon is Marty's recognition of the unease about the middle-class life of people who were "moderately secure and affluent." What, asked Marty, does current Protestant leadership have to say to those people, who, on the one hand "generate the societal and civic religions against which Protestant prophets must preach, [but] they also foot the bills for ongoing prophecy." It was the dilemma that had challenged Country Club Christian Church and generations of the Christian faithful before them: the perception by others of exclusivity and wealth, juxtaposed to the commitment to use that wealth to serve and sustain others. In November 1968, Dr. Bash had commented on the unusually large loss of leadership the past year through death and removal to other cities: "This church has had to contend from the beginning with the myth of affluence — in money, of course; but also in leadership, talent, etc."

On April 4, 1967, Martin Luther King, Jr. delivered a major address at New York's Riverside Church declaring his opposition to the Vietnam War. One year to the day later, he was assassinated in Memphis, Tennessee. The preceding year had been marked by growing militancy within the Civil Rights movement and increasing resistance across the nation to the Vietnam conflict. The war and race relations received attention throughout 1967 from the church in its programs, sermons, and *The Christian*, but there is little sense of impending crisis. Thursday, April 4, 1968, marked the beginning of a new era. Civil disturbances erupted in many American cities in response to King's death. The morning after the shooting, some students in Kansas City, Kansas, walked out of school, announcing that they were going to march downtown. The school superintendent arrived and told the students he would march with them after alerting the Chief of Police and requesting the most senior Black officer to join them in the march, which continued peacefully to the downtown area. Students returned to school and participated in a memorial service that afternoon. Over the Palm Sunday weekend, a large group of priests and parishioners from Grace and Holy Cathedral in Missouri joined up to 15,000 Kansas Citians in a nonviolent march. For a moment that Sunday, it seemed as if Kansas City would avoid the violence of other cities.[233]

The events of the next days during what came to be called the "Holy Week Riot" are chronicled in the aptly titled account "It Finally Happened Here: The 1968 Riot in Kansas City, Missouri."[234] Dr. King's funeral was scheduled for Tuesday, and over the weekend students in the Kansas City, Missouri, school district began to plan a march for that day. Plans were shared with the School Board, who rejected them, saying there would be an in-building service in the schools. Kansas schools did cancel classes for Tuesday. The Kansas City, Missouri, school board decision to remain open was the spark that "provided the precipitating event for the Kansas City riot."[235] On Tuesday, students walked out of the predominantly African-American high schools. At some point what began as a relatively peaceable action escalated into a full confrontation between march participants and law enforcement that would eventually include local police, the National Guard, and the State Highway patrol. Over the next four days looting, vandalism, and physical violence took the lives of six African-Americans, injured hundreds of citizens, and destroyed uncalculated amounts of property.

The two public officials who were most visible during the crisis were Mayor Ilus Davis and Police Chief Clarence Kelley, both of whom were active members of Country Club Christian Church. Davis was praised at the time and in years to come for his leadership and efforts to calm the situation. At one point he had attempted to march with the students, only to be pulled into a squad car by policemen who made it clear that was not going to happen. At his funeral in 1996, Vernon Thompson, the former president of the Kansas City Branch of the NAACP and a participant in the 1968 march, said, "Ilus Davis probably did more than any one single person in Kansas City in the area of civil rights. At the time he did it, it was not popular, but he did in spite of that."[236]

The mayor and the chief of police, Ilus Davis and Clarence Kelley, both members of CCCC, played key roles in the race crisis of 1968. *Missouri Valley Special Collections, Kansas City Public Library, Kansas City, Missouri.*

Assessments of Chief Kelley's actions in 1968 are mixed; the police used Mace and tear gas and were accused of excessive force including the clubbing of an Episcopal priest in clerical garb.[237] Kelley would go on to become the director of the FBI in 1973, and at the end of his life he was recognized for a distinguished career, his integrity, and his capacity to change. Alvin Brooks provided a moving remembrance the day after Kelley died. Brooks has been a leading figure in civil rights activism in Kansas City for decades. He began his career in law and civic life as one of the few African-American police officers in the Kansas City Department and it was in that capacity that he and Chief Kelley had major differences over "promotional opportunities for black officers and how the black community viewed the police." Brooks resigned, but some years later when Kelley, as FBI director, delivered a commencement address at Central Missouri State University, he publicly apologized to Brooks: "I had to go all the way to Washington and then come back before I understood what he was talking about." [238]

Daily services were held throughout the week of the riots in the chapel but attendance dropped after Tuesday and both the Maundy Thursday service and Good Friday Vigil were cancelled due to the citywide curfew. In *The Christian*, Dr. Bash described a "sober Easter Sunday," and gave words of appreciation for both Davis and Kelley as did the board in a formal resolution. The Sunday after Easter he preached a sermon titled "Where Do We Go From Here?" Unknown to him one of the attendees was Kansas City native and well-known columnist for *The New Yorker* magazine, Calvin Trillin. Dr. Bash was surprised, and not entirely pleased to read the account of his sermon in the May 11 issue of the magazine, written in Trillin's signature breezy and sardonic style. [239] Several weeks later, commenting again on that sermon he said "I did not offer a neat solution in my sermon because I did not and do not yet know one."

The civil upheaval that spring galvanized the church and the denomination nationally, but it was not a direct or smooth course to change. In April 2018 on the occasion of the 50th anniversary of Dr. King's death, NPR writer and producer Deborah Begel wrote a painful remembrance of her family's experience in Kansas City. They were members of Country Club Christian, living in Mission Hills. She was a sophomore at nearby University of Kansas, and drove home the day after the assassination. Her mother greeted her with a plan; they would invite the African-American man who had cared for their lawn and his wife to go to church with the Begel family and then come back to their house for brunch. The plan was to attend the other family's church at a later day. "It will be a show of solidarity," her mother announced. Her father would call on Dr. Bash ahead of time to fill him in, but when her father returned from the visit, he was glum, announcing that Dr. Bash was not keen on the idea. But they decided to go ahead with their plan. It was a disaster — in her father's words, "Not one person in the church greeted or welcomed [their guests]. Everyone ignored us. I was ashamed of those people." The family never attended Country Club again. But the experience was not lost on their daughter who wrote: "I was and still am proud of my parents for acting on their principles. Even though the gesture wasn't appreciated by people in that church, my parents made a statement that calls to me today. Reach across the aisle, walk across the street, invite like-minded folks to talk and organize. We can do better." [240]

A few weeks later, the State Assembly of the Christian Church was convened in Kansas City. The assembly created a large list of resolutions, a number of which had been prepared at an earlier meeting in March under the rubric of "A call for the Response of the Christian Churches (Disciples of Christ) to the Urban Crisis." Quoting from the President's National Advisory Commission on Civil Disorders (also referred to as the Kerner Commission Report) which concluded that "our nation is moving toward two societies, one black, one white, separate and unequal … " the Assembly called for "a commitment to national action" that recognized that the crisis was racism. Specific proposals for action followed. The Kansas City Commission of Christian Churches organized a committee of the 74 local congregations and Dr. Bash noted that its "actions may be channeled through existing Negro congregations and other churches in transitional areas."

And then once again, Dr. Bash led his congregation in a service of mourning after Robert Kennedy was murdered on June 6. He quoted psychoanalyst Erich Fromm in a lengthy piece in *The Christian* that linked the nightly broadcasts of the violence in Vietnam to the epidemic of violence in America, creating a "sense of violence as something normal." Moving away from the usual summer slowdown, the final issue of *The Christian* announced a series of Sunday afternoon panels on "The Role of the Church in the Urban Crisis." An intense focus on race and religion continued in the final years of the decade. The CWF dedicated the month of October 1968 to a study of the Mayor's Commission Report on Civil Disorder. Police Chief Clarence Kelley and civil rights activist Alvin Brooks were among the many speakers on race relations and the inner city. Mayor Davis proclaimed February as "Negro History Month" for Kansas City.

The Disciples denomination launched a major "reconciliation" program across the nation and the Kansas City Christian Commission continued to provide support to its inner city and historically African-American congregations. Dr. Bash instituted "Talk Back" sermons on topics such as the Black Power movement and White racism. The latter term had been featured in the Kerner Commission Report issued at the directive of President Lyndon B. Johnson (LBJ) following riots in Detroit and Newark, New Jersey in the summer of 1967. Rather than identify outside agitators and other commonly blamed causes for the disturbances the Report pointed its well-researched finger directly at White racism: "What white Americans have never fully understood but what the Negro can never forget — is that white society is deeply implicated in the ghetto. White institutions created it, white institutions maintain it, and white society condones it." [241]

Many, including LBJ, were displeased by the conclusion, as Dr. Bash observed, "Great numbers of American citizens do not consider themselves to be racist in any sense." Several of the analyses of the 1968 disturbances cited in the previous pages confirm this observation. Hutchinson stated that "for many white observers, the 1968 riot was the first recognition of an 'urban crisis.'" But as he carefully documented, the "crisis" was decades in the making: "the 1968 riot in Kansas City, Missouri, was not the crisis: it was the flashpoint of the explosion of a powder keg that had been packed for years." [242] Alvin Brooks had evoked the same imagery just months before the protests began, warning that "the wrong spark could ignite a situation right here in Kansas City that would cause the same that's occurred around the country." [243] White racism, or Schirmer's more oblique "white mentality" created blinders that permitted the obvious to be obscured.

The people who constituted the community of faith at Country Club Christian Church had worked diligently and at times successfully to meet the crisis — initially in response to events, then more often in a conscious effort to shape them. Their faith was formed by traditions and beliefs that required them to both reach out to others, and to draw them in. Reaching out was long established but drawing in — inclusion — was the greater challenge. But only when movement in both directions drew people truly together could they begin to understand what poet Langston Hughes called their "real stories" — stories that never came out of a book, but out of their own lives. [244]

~~~~~

The Vietnam War, one of the great issues of the 1960s, received little attention in either *The Christian* or board minutes in the early years of the decade. Dr. Bash first spoke of the crisis in a May 2, 1965, sermon titled "The Perils of Power," and had followed that up by writing to the four senators who represented Kansas and Missouri. He shared excerpts of their replies in *The Christian* that, with the exception of Kansas Senator James B. Pearson's lengthy response, were not particularly illuminating but serve as an example of the growing willingness of churches and clergy to declare positions on current events and topics. After 1965, when American combat troops joined the "advisors" who had been there for years, coverage increased. A church committee was once again activated to keep track of members in service, to write letters, and to send *The Christian* and holiday packages.

As in previous conflicts, *The Christian* began identifying members in uniform and publishing their letters and reports. In June 1966, one soldier wrote that "we can win all the battles (and lay the countryside to waste doing it) that we want — and that is what we are here for, that is our job. But it seems to me that if a nation like ours wants to avoid sending future generations back over here, then it's the nation that has to chip in and help out." His article was followed the next week by a notice in *The Christian* that another member had been wounded and had returned to the United States to recover at Great Lakes Naval Training Center outside Chicago. The notice concluded with the comment that the Marine "was one of the wounded men who was denied admittance to the ice show at the Conrad Hilton Hotel because their presence would depress their regular patrons." The fact that the reference gives no other specifics about the incident suggests that it was clearly understood by Country Club's readers. On May 26, the manager of the Conrad Hilton Hotel in a Chicago suburb denied access to the hotel's popular ice show to a group of wounded veterans, stating his concern that their presence would depress the other guests. The predictable outrage was expressed nationally with extended coverage on the front page of *The Kansas City Times*. The church member's mother was interviewed, reporting her son had called her; he and his companions "were all quite shocked about it. I think it is a pretty rotten way to treat boys who are being killed and wounded in Vietnam."[245] It was early days for a war that would last many years, yet already conflicting views and repudiation of those involved were being expressed. *The Christian Century*, the progressive mainstream periodical that would have been read by members of Country Club, moved from an early acceptance of the American presence in Vietnam to strong opposition. [246]

One correspondent to *The Christian* was Lt. William R. Brown, a 1966 graduate of the University of Kansas Medical School. He wrote an extended and moving account of Christmas spent with patients and villagers, accompanied by a 30-inch-tall stuffed Santa sent to him from home. What began as a letter home was also published in *The Kansas City Times*. [247] Carlton Crenshaw, just 22, was injured two weeks after landing in Vietnam in a 72-hour battle in which half the battalion was killed. "His tapes and letters are very articulate and heart-breaking." The notice in the November 1967 *Christian* concludes with the stark line that the battalion was being rebuilt "with new boys from the states."

In addition to letters from those in uniform, *The Christian* had thoughtful pieces that compared differing views of the war (Department of State vs. the National Council of Churches), and theologically and spiritually focused essays pondering the morality of war. Visiting lecturers, most memorably Martin Niemoeller in 1964 when he spoke on "The Vietnamese Situation," added to Dr. Bash's numerous presentations. There is little mention of Vietnam in the board minutes, whether because the conflict was not discussed, or because of the extremely terse and unsigned records that became the norm by the second half of the sixties. The fulsome minutes maintained by Charles Rouse gave way to an economy of information that often makes it difficult to understand the workings and intent of the board. *The Christian*, however, became a forum for discussion and debate. The Service and Outreach Council had regular submissions to the newsletter, and as their chairman stated to the board in late 1962, "We feel the publicity given in *The Christian* has made more people aware of the work of this Council."

The social and political issues of the 1960s dominated the news and provided the focus for church programming. But in the background, attracting less attention, was a significant effort to examine and reorganize the Disciples denomination at the most profound levels. The work continued throughout the 1960s, culminating in approval of "A Provisional Design for the Christian Church (Disciples of Christ)" at the denominational convention in Kansas City in September 1968. As Cummins observed in his detailed description and analysis of the Restructure process, "the Disciples' initiative in restructure did not occur in isolation, but was part of a general religious undertaking" experienced by other denominations as well.[248] A number of issues motivated the Disciples, including a sense that the emphasis on the autonomy and importance of individual congregations had undermined the larger concept of "Church." In the words of A. Dale Fiers, one of the leaders of Restructure, "The local congregation is not the fullest expression of Church. "

Vocabulary was all-important in the Restructure process. By 1965, the term "manifestation" would be employed to designate the various organizational entities within the denomination: national, regional, and congregational. The intent was to eliminate any concept of "levels" with the consequent assigning of rank and the inevitable placement of the congregations, the smallest entity, on the bottom. "Rather, everyone was on an equal playing field, one church without top or bottom."

There was heated opposition to the restructure, particularly by those who feared loss of congregational autonomy. Skillful and sensitive leadership prevailed. One of many positive results, discussed previously, was reconciliation and full inclusion of the formerly separate African-American organizations within the denomination, and the assumption of key leadership roles by African-Americans within a few years. A number of congregations did indeed withdraw from the denomination, but they had been estranged for many years and had not been significant contributors to the ongoing Disciples programs. Their loss, nevertheless, was mourned by the creators of Restructure.

The final and overwhelming vote of approval on the "Provisional Design" at the Kansas City convention has been described as "the most significant organizational action of Disciples in 136 years." Ronald Osborne, the moderator, led the assembled group, 10,000 voices, in singing the doxology. "In the history of the Disciples, this was one of its most storied moments, a stunning improbability, one of the rare triumphs of structural politics."

"Covenant" was another important term to emerge in the process, described by Kenneth Teegarden, a major leader, as "the most significant accomplishment of the restructure." The preamble to the Design, included in *The Chalice Hymnal*, uses the word seven times, affirming the nature of relationships between God and people, and people with one another. Those relationships had priority over any structural design. Teegarden continued:

> [Covenant] is the very beginning of the nature of the church of which we are a part. We are a community bound by covenant ... Our relationships are not hierarchical, they are not constitutional, they are covenantal!

The Design has endured, and has been successfully amended and updated over the succeeding decades. It is a document that affirms continuity and change, tradition and renewal. [249]

The convention was attended by about 10,700 delegates. The importance of the agenda and the fact that the 1968 International Convention Assembly was being hosted in Kansas City by the local Disciples churches ensured regular coverage in *The Christian* and local newspapers. While

R.A. Long had never fulfilled his dream of making Kansas City the official world headquarters for the Disciples, the basis for selecting the city for such an important convention was obvious: in 1968 there were 107 Disciples churches in Kansas City and environs, serving approximately 250,000 members. Four Disciples-affiliated colleges, three homes for the aged, two for children, two seminaries, and an academic Bible Chair all functioned within a 175-mile radius of the city. Dr. Bash devoted several of his columns in *The Christian* urging Country Club's members to attend the convention. Each of the Disciples churches in the city had been assigned a quota of attendees; as the largest congregation Country Club was expected to send 852 registrants. The week of the convention, Dr. Osborne, the convention president, and Dr. George Davis, minister of National City Church in Washington, DC, each took the pulpit at Country Club. Dr. Bash, obviously pleased with the meeting, commented in an October *Christian* that it will "take a little while to assimilate and evaluate all that happened in business session. Since we are now, nationally, The Christian Church (rather than a group of Christian Churches), it might be assumed that some new patterns of doing business will develop."

While coverage in *The Christian* focused almost entirely on the Restructure, local newspapers were at least as interested in the nature of the convention's discussions regarding race, Vietnam, youth, and the urban crisis besetting America. A front-page article in *The Star* opened with the announcement that "There is a new church among churches today in the United States and Canada. It is the Christian Church (Disciples of Christ) ... a single operating structure with shared responsibilities for national, regional and congregational levels."[250] The convention closed with a call for repentance acknowledging the "complicity in the prejudice, the inaction, and the toleration of violence as a solution to social problems, which has created the present urban crisis in our nation."[251]

Civil Rights, Vietnam, social unrest, feminist activism, a growing gay rights movement, and the consequent political upheaval all informed and shaped the sermons, church programs, and the day-to-day lives of those who worshipped at Country Club Christian Church in the 1970s. The church also would focus on matters great and small that defined the existence of a maturing institution: preparation for the 50th anniversary, yet more construction and building renewal, and expansion of the roles of women and young people.

In 1968 the congregation had committed to a $1,000,000 "Golden Anniversary Campaign" to fund significant capital improvements, a new organ, public address system, improved air conditioning, an elevator, and extensive remodeling. Construction was significantly slowed by a major strike of laborers and brick masons in the beginning of April, but good weather and prompt payment of pledges mitigated some of those delays. The most significant addition was the four-story wing to the east of the main building in what had once been a courtyard that was overparked on Sunday mornings.

While construction progress was duly reported in *The Christian*, other matters consumed more and more time and concern. In April 1969, Detroit hosted the National Black Economic Development Conference that had been organized by the Interreligious Foundation for Community Organization, or IFCO. IFCO was a small, inter-faith group begun in New York City in 1967 for the purpose of connecting White religious bodies with Black economic enterprise. It was at heart "an attempt by the mainline churches to continue to influence race relations ... in a time when the great national liberal consensus between blacks and whites was falling apart." Several days into the conference, delegates heard from an energetic Black speaker, James Forman, the former executive secretary of the Student Non-violent Coordinating Committee (SNCC). Forman issued a "Black Manifesto" that expressed more radical ideological views than had previously been espoused in the Civil Rights movement, and presented a series of demands for $500 million in "reparations" from the "white Christian churches and Jewish synagogues."[252]

News accounts of the conference did not immediately generate a strong response, but the actions that the Manifesto set in motion did. On May 4, 1969, Forman interrupted a Sunday morning service at Riverside Church in Morningside Heights in New York City. He read the Manifesto and made a series of demands that included "unrestricted use" of the church radio station and the handing over of "sixty percent of the yearly income from all church stock, property and real estate."[253] Many of the shocked members, along with their minister, walked out, but some remained as Forman read the Manifesto. His encounter at Riverside was followed by many other "visits" to mainstream congregations in the coming months, eliciting a range of responses from rejection to a cautious acceptance of responsibility to address the issues raised by the document. The controversy would play out within the Disciples denomination as a whole, and very actively at Country Club Christian.

The first biennial national convention to be held since Restructure met in August in Seattle, garnering major news coverage across the country as members debated how to respond to the Manifesto. Clarence Kelley spoke in his capacity as a Disciple and the Kansas City Chief of Police. Dr. Bash had a major voice in the proceedings making his strong opposition to the Manifesto very clear. Prior to his appearance at Riverside Church, Forman had approached the National Council of Churches, the large ecumenical organization of more than thirty denominations, seeking support for the Manifesto. It is an important point to remember because the NCC's commitment, one that was often misconstrued, became a central issue in discussions among Disciples, and featured in many of Dr. Bash's comments.

Organizational meetings held before the national convention condemned the language of the Manifesto as "excessive and inflammatory," but also produced suggestions for consideration at the convention that included "expansion of the church's program to meet the urban emergency" and a two-year period (later expanded to four years) of "reconciliation" to raise funds and institute programs on behalf of Black Americans.[254] At the convention, Dr. Bash moved to send the proposal back to committee, saying that "It is highly doubtful that this assembly should give blanket approval of the action of church councils since the National Council of Churches agreed to discuss Mr. (James) Forman's statement (the Black Manifesto). I think the leadership of the National Council of Churches needs to hear from denominational leaders about support for a program that is definitely Marxist." He was challenged by none other than Dr. A. Dale Fiers, who argued that the proposal was not a "blanket endorsement."[255] The heated debate continued at Country Club upon Dr. Bash's return.

The first September issue of *The Christian* after the summer hiatus opened with Dr. Bash's observations about the summer's events:

> We have been involved in the agony of our nation in the time of urban crisis. The Black Manifesto was dealt with twice in sermons, the lengthy Manifesto distributed to those who wished it, as well as the response made to it in the Message of the General Board of the Christian Church. Two of our worship services were held under threat of rumors that they would be disrupted, but there has been no disturbance.

The NCC developed a compromise position in its response to the Manifesto: no NCC funds would be pledged directly to the Black Economic Development Corporation, but member denominations were encouraged to give monies directly as they saw fit. Dr. Bash responded to this bluntly at the end of September: "No funds of the Christian Church (national), nor I am sure of this congregation will go to support the group of 'alienated revolutionaries' who have rallied around the demand for three billion dollars." But, he concluded: "Anyone who supposes that this reflects disinterest in the plight of the poor and the black; or an unwillingness to do our rightful part in measures to ameliorate the misery of inner cities; or a turning from God's call to love our fellow man is as wrong as wrong can be. Let us put it mildly: This is just not our cup of tea."

In October, under the heading "An Alternative to the Black Manifesto," *The Christian* announced a Thursday night dinner presentation about the Kansas City chapter of the Black Economic Union, headlined by one of its founders and Kansas City Chiefs star, Curtis R. McClinton, Jr. He "will be telling us about some direct, positive action being taken on a problem none of us can really afford to ignore." Later that month, the chair of the church board announced in *The Christian* that the board had decided not to include a $450 budget item dedicated to the NCC, a decision based directly on concerns about the Black Manifesto, but one that was "subject to periodic review in the light of future actions taken by the National Council of Churches." The minutes from the relevant board meeting are lengthy and reveal disparate views by the members. In the same issue, Dr. Bash commented further on the meeting, making it clear that he was dissatisfied the debate within the board had even taken place.

The following week in the October 29 issue, Associate Minister Kenneth Rouse, who was the editor of *The Christian,* wrote a front page "editorial" on the matter — a first in the history of the church, significant because in courteous and reasoned language he openly disagreed with those who wanted to remove any contribution to the NCC from the budget. He noted that Dr. Bash had expressed concern that such a move could have a negative impact on ecumenical relationships in general and certainly on NCC programs that the church supported. "One wonders," Rouse asked, "what alternatives we shall propose for the doors we have closed to cooperation with other Christians?" His argument continued:

We have the power to determine that our gift will not be used either directly or indirectly to support a cause of which we disapprove. This fact, apparently, was ignored or considered irrelevant. Why? Can we write off a whole family because we bear a grudge against one of its sons? Can we ignore the needs of a whole nation because we disapprove of one of its leaders? Can we refuse to look at what the Church is doing in the world at large because we dislike so much what happened one day in one place?

Another Missouri delegate to the August convention was the Reverend James Blair, pastor of Central Christian Church in Kansas City. Along with Dr. Bash, he was elected for a term on the board of the national organization. At the meeting he announced the organization of a Black caucus within the denomination "which will try to strategize which way to go as black men in a white church."[256] His use of the term caucus points to the nature of changes in governance that were occurring in Protestant churches. The debate for many African-Americans was whether to establish separate churches or to assume full equality within the established and until that point White churches. The concept of caucus proved a means for achieving the second goal — to speak in a unified voice within the church, a voice that would be recognized and respected by all members. That strategy began with the Disciples at the time of Restructure. In 1971, Blair was the first Black minister to be elected moderator of the state-wide Christian Church (Disciples of Christ) in Missouri in a ceremony at which Dr. Bash was the keynote speaker. That October, Blair was the speaker at the regular Thursday night dinner at Country Club; *The Christian* noted that throughout the mid-1960s in Kansas City, his had been a "tough moderating voice between blacks and whites serving to reconcile and heal."

Underlying at least some of the concerns within the church was anxiety about a possible disruption of services such as had occurred at Riverside Church. The anxiety was heightened when members of the Kansas City chapter of the Black Panthers interrupted a Sunday morning service at Linwood Methodist Church in May 1969. Their leader, Pete O'Neal, took the microphone while a companion tore down the American flag. Police were called. In the ensuing year O'Neal had a number of other encounters with the law. Facing prison, he and his wife fled the country, eventually settling in Tanzania where they continue to live today. In April 1970, the Country Club Board "reactivated" a committee to study the possible action to be take upon interruption of services. Presumably, the original formation of the committee had taken place at the time of the Riverside and Linwood disruptions the previous year. Dr. Bash announced the committee from the pulpit several weeks later, stating that "this fad [service disruption] will surely not persist long since it is clearly 'counterproductive.' On April 12 we had a minor disruption and we congratulate the entire congregation for 'keeping its cool' and not letting the spirit of worship to be destroyed."

Country Club's response to the Black Manifesto was similar to the reaction to discussions about Fair Housing legislation in the mid-1960s. The elders approved a presentation on the Kansas City Fair Housing Campaign in the Social Hall in December 1965, but several months previously had objected to an invitation by the Kansas City Christian Church Commission to Saul Alinsky, a well-known, and controversial community organizer based in Chicago. After considerable discussion the elders concluded that Alinsky's "presence in Kansas City would serve little purpose." The chair of the elders was instructed to inform the Commission that "this Board does not approve of the action of the Christian Church Commission in the Saul Alinsky matter." Alinsky did indeed spend at least eighteen months in Kansas City, working with various groups to provide them with the tools to achieve social change. The church was increasingly invested in Civil Rights throughout the decade but clearly objected to "outside" influences.

With Restructure in 1968, the Disciples of Christ began to put in place concrete measures to fully integrate all members and institutional structures into a unified whole, now referred to as the Convocation. The Disciples, like other mainstream denominations, had a long history of Black membership, generally maintained in a quasi-separate status. The process was sometimes labored as "Black Disciples of Christ found themselves in the hard ball game of ecclesiastical bureaucracies."[257] The centrality of Missouri, and Kansas City in particular, to the denomination meant that the experiences and often tempestuous discussions at Country Club Christian mirrored those of the nation as a whole. By 1971, the church had, as Reverend Rouse urged, made carefully designated contributions through the Outreach budget to programs and institutions that addressed race and poverty. The contributions were generous, more than $16,000 directly to the national reconciliation program and approximately $25,000 budget support to local inner-city churches. What Dr. Bash had aptly referred to as the nation's "agony" was the church's agony as well, resulting in misunderstanding, division, and anger that was not easily resolved.

CHAPTER 12

Century's End:
Affirming the Past,
Envisioning the Future

In the same column in which he announced the "disruption" committee, Dr. Bash also reported that he had changed his sermon topic Friday evening April 17 with the news that the ill-fated Apollo 13 spacecraft had landed safely in the Pacific. National news and issues continued to dominate sermons and columns in *The Christian* throughout the 1970s. The W. Ralph Jones Youth Center on the third floor was dedicated with increasing attention to the needs and concerns of young people. Dr. Bash gave special attention to college students who would be returning in the summer of 1970, not long after the shootings at Kent State and eruptions across college campuses throughout the country. The church was picketed on several Sundays in May by peace advocates, including a group from the University of Kansas who "engaged in many discussions, some of them heated" with worshippers. He urged his congregation to be "open and listening with more patience and tolerance than come naturally in a time of grave crisis." Concerns about drugs and sexuality prompted a shift in engagement with teens and young adults from didactic and unidirectional to a program called Adult-Youth Dialogue introduced in 1972.

When the church celebrated its 50th anniversary in 1971, it counted 3,185 active members. The year would be marked by presentations from prominent speakers such as theologian Elton Trueblood, a dinner to which surviving charter members were invited, the launching of a sanctuary renovation and installation of a new organ dedicated to Gladys Combs, and, of particular note that year, the installation of the first women elders. At the April board meeting, the committee tasked with a study of administrative structure at Country Club gave a report on its conclusions. Part of the study included a questionnaire sent to six Disciples churches around the country as well as three non-Disciple Kansas City churches of comparable size and membership profile. Curiously, one of the questions addressed "whether or not women should serve on the Board of Elders." As the report acknowledged, that question had been decided in the positive more than a decade earlier in the administrative review following Dr. Wyle's departure. Despite that affirmation, it was decided to make a formal motion to the Board of Elders, recommending that women serve as members.

The term deaconess was officially removed; all individuals, male or female, would henceforth be called deacons. A simple enough change, but it had the immediate effect of eliminating the practice of identifying "deacons" and "deaconesses" separately in two alphabetical listings, as well as making the restriction on the number of deaconesses irrelevant. *The Christian* announced the changes with enthusiasm on the front page of the April 18 issue: "For the first time in the history of our Church, we will be voting on the election of two of our women as Elders ... Although the present By-laws state that Elders may be either men or women, it is significant that not until our 50th Anniversary Year, have we considered the election of any of our women to serve as Elders."

The following week, *The Christian* announced the names of the two women, Mrs. Russell V. Baltis, Sr. (Louise), and Mrs. F. Lewell Spies (Ruth), as well as the adoption of the uniform term "deacon." Taut nerves and high expectations for attire (dark) and demeanor (somber) accompanied those early elders, but they performed their roles with grace and joy. "In effect these actions have brought Country Club Christian Church into the twentieth century by recognizing the valid churchmanship of its women that has been effective in our Church from its beginning. These actions not only correspond to our reality, they testify that we are fully one in the Body of Christ." The Board of Elders continued to fret about appearances, reminding serving elders that they were not to "toss" the communion wine back, but sip it discreetly from the rim. Sports jackets, slacks, bright and light-colored dresses, blouses and skirts were "not appropriate" nor were white shoes. In 1972, high school girls were added to the roster of junior deacons that had previously included only boys.

The elders were the moral barometers of the church to which they provided spiritual leadership. In his speech accepting his incoming role as chairman of the Board of Elders, Dr. Milburn Hobson observed that "when we became Elders we agreed to be overseers, teachers, and shepherds ... Let us, as Elders and leaders in His church, feed His sheep."[258] Elders were key to the decisions made at the time of Ewart Wyle's departure, and they have overseen many other less controversial personnel issues, including approval of vacation times and other scheduling adjustments, job descriptions and salaries, and upon occasion providing advice and counsel regarding job performance. They reviewed potential candidates for church positions and made recommendations to the full board. Minutes of the Board of Elders revealed that the group often served as a sounding board for church ministers, providing them confidential space to air concerns, and, when necessary, noting those conversations as confidential or off the record. The elders reviewed all requests for transfer out of membership and issued letters of good standing for departing members to present to their new churches.

As "keepers of the faith," elders still serve as filters for and arbiters of change. In the late 1960s the elders addressed a request from a young adults group for permission to hold an "Experimental Worship Service" or EWS as it was called. The service was to be held at 11 a.m. on Sunday mornings in the Pine Room. Its format was non-traditional and informal, beginning with participants sitting on the floor in a circle and holding hands. After lengthy discussion the elders agreed to approve the service for a probationary period. Some months later, a committee reported on their evaluation of EWS at a special meeting of the elders in a report that was attached to the regular board minutes in April, 1970:

> We would like to stress the deep sincerity which permeates every one actively participating in the experiment. No one of your committee would question the motives, nor the faith of these young people. In most of us older generations, the form of their worship is possibly the most difficult aspect of the entire program to evaluate. To us, nurtured in the traditional church, and accustomed to its form, any change or variation is difficult to accept. However, we are firmly convinced change is the order of the day, and we must listen. Our job is to counsel, guide and direct these proposed changes in channels which

will be to the very best interest of all concerned, and to our church.

The committee made several recommendations, including holding the EWS meetings at a time that did not conflict with morning services and that the group be "accorded counseling by the Senior Minister ... or designate, and duly selected member of the Board of Elders." The alternative meeting time (late Sunday afternoon) did not work out well and the EWS group announced its intention to try to re-schedule the following fall. At that point, they fade from the record. Participants in the EWS class also issued a memorandum of some length which at the time was attached to the minutes, but has since disappeared, making it difficult to describe their goals and aspirations for a meaningful faith experience. Several of the original participants are still members of the church; they remain disappointed in the outcome of the evaluation, questioning the need for "counsel" and what they feel was a lack of understanding on the part of the elders. The tension between supporting the institutional norm and a commitment to change and adaptation would continue in various forms in the years to come.

By the mid-1970s a United States President had resigned, the seemingly endless U.S. presence in Vietnam ended with the fall of Saigon and return of the POWs, and the church sponsored its first Vietnamese refugee family, from among the more than one thousand individuals relocated to the community. The elders and the full board supported the denomination's "Resolution 78" in the fall of 1973, calling for the prosecution of the criminal acts of the Watergate affair. The Resolution was to be sent to President Nixon and all members of the House and Senate. By 1977, Country Club was the largest congregation in the denomination and had assumed a position of leadership in joint ventures with area churches. After fifty years, practices and recurring events had become beloved traditions, uniting members in the routines of a shared faith. Dr. Bash's regular "Sermon on the Steps" with the children started as a cautious experiment but soon grew into an expectation; Family Camp in Colorado (later

(Photos at right) Shared traditions in a community of faith: Dr. Bash with the children listening to his "Sermon on the Steps," Baby Dedication Sunday, Christian Community Camp, *CCCC Archive*

A City Church

renamed Christian Community Camp), today a much-anticipated experience for several generations of church members began in 1974; the Men's Interfaith Dinners, founded by Dr. Bash, were an annual opportunity to bring together Protestants, Catholics, and Jews; 1975 marked the 10th anniversary of the Hanging of the Greens; Baby Dedication Sunday, an occasion with origins in Jewish tradition, was the high point of Mother's Day and Christmas Sundays. Lent, once a minimally observed part of the Disciples calendar, had grown into a liturgically rich season that offered time for reflection and for sharing with fellow Christians in and outside the church.

While all these traditions attest to a vibrant, active church, they essentially name categories but neglect to identify what constitutes those categories: individual members whose actions, motivated by their faith and their engagement in the church, often go unrecorded. The Carswells provide just one of many examples. Dr. and Mrs. Bash were inveterate travelers, and through the years they led a number of tours to various parts of the world. The photos and memories of those trips were the subjects of any number of speaking engagements both in and out of the church. Following a trip to the Holy Land, Dr. Bash was asked by church members, Mr. and Mrs. Frank Carswell, to speak at a special occasion they sponsored yearly, an annual appreciation dinner each spring for the staff of the R. J. DeLano School for Crippled Children in Kansas City. The Carswells were patrons of the school for many years, and Dr. Bash's presentation attracted the attention of the local newspaper. Church members were responsible for countless such acts of quiet discipleship.

Along with increasing attention to youth and young adults, the church also acknowledged the growing cohort of older Americans with their own issues and concerns. Country Club sponsored public meetings, posted regular articles on aging in *The Christian*, and encouraged donations to Foxwood Springs, the denominational residential community for older adults just south of Kansas City in Belton, Missouri, where Margaret Lawrence, the beloved Living Link missionary chose to retire.

Dr. Bash announced his plans for retirement in March 1978. In accordance with church policy, his employment status was formally and enthusiastically "extended" after his 65th birthday in 1975. He would maintain a reduced schedule for about a year and a half and preach his last sermon on Sunday, September 17, 1979, labeled "Dr. Bash Day." He and Mrs. Bash were honored that afternoon at a program keynoted by Clarence Kelley and attended by more than one thousand people. They were presented with a generous love gift and a citation honoring his service, bestow-ing the title of Senior Minister *Emeritus*. His portrait, like Dr. Grafton's, was painted by well-known Kansas City artist Daniel MacMorris, and hangs in the stairwell near the main parlor. It was an emotional occa-sion, prompting Dr. Bash to say that "you did what I thought was utterly impossible. You dissolved me in tears for the first time in my life." [259] The Bashes prepared to retire to Tucson, a favorite location where they owned a home.

His successor was Dr. Eugene Brice, who was called to the Country Club pulpit from his Disciples Church in Tulsa. He was installed as Senior Minister on March 19, 1979. In keeping with past tradition, the installa-tion speaker was a distinguished Disciples clergyman and also close per-sonal friend, Dr. William E. Tucker, the president of Bethany College in West Virginia. Dr. Brice had both an academic and pastoral background, earning degrees from Texas Christian University and his doctorate from Yale. He and his wife and four children moved into the church parsonage at 6420 Ward Parkway. The parsonage had only recently been acquired by the church in 1972 as a gift from Mr. and Mrs. Ray (Mary) Klapmeyer. It was a time when a dedicated pastor's residence was becoming less the norm, especially in urban areas. Ministers wanted the opportunity to

Dr. Eugene Brice, 5th Senior Minister at CCCC, 1979-1991

build up equity with their own homes, and clergy with school-age children had additional concerns about their residential location. The grim tales of tyrannical church committees who oversaw the manse, including everything from décor to dishes, to say nothing of the personal privacy of the occupants, belonged in most cases to an earlier time. But the sense of the house not really belonging to the family that lived there was unappealing to many 20th century clerics. The more typical practice in recent decades has been to provide a housing allowance to ministers who purchase their own homes. The Bashes were the first occupants of the Ward Parkway house. They sold their condominium in Olathe, and Dr. Bash acknowledged that proximity to the church was a welcome change. During Dr. Brice's tenure, the house was used regularly for church meetings and a collective sigh of relief was expressed when a circular driveway was finally installed, making it possible to enter and exit from busy Ward Parkway in one piece.

At the beginning of the new year in 1990, Reverend John Young, minister of education, mused on the character of the decades just past and the potential for the future in a column in *The Christian*. "Some have written that we are leaving the seventies of selfishness and the eighties of unbridled hoarding of things. But wait! There is good news! They also suggest that we are moving into a new decade of concern for the needs of others, and the environment." There are many who would agree with his description of what are sometimes referred to as the "me decades," but as Reverend Young himself acknowledged later in his column, those can also be understood as years when the church placed greater emphasis on the needs of individuals, preparing them in a sense for the new tasks that would be theirs to fulfill in the coming decades.

Sermons, programs, and contributions to *The Christian* continued to mirror and comment on issues and events in the community and world at large: Dr. Brice's anguished reflections on the collapse of the Hyatt skywalk, that trapped at least one Country Club member in 1981; the massacre of Palestinians and Lebanese Shiites by a Christian-affiliated militia in 1982; the long-awaited fall of the Berlin Wall and subsequent breakup of the Soviet empire; a workshop on AIDS as the crisis peaked in 1987. But in the 1980s, there was a perceptible shift in focus from social justice issues at the national level, and political and international events to greater attention to individual spiritual and psychological well-being, including aging, alcoholism, factors influencing and often disrupting family life; the evolving conception of what "family" actually means;

when life begins and how it should end — the latter debated painfully and publicly in the cases of Karen Ann Quinlan and Missouri resident Nancy Cruzan. Speakers and workshop leaders in the early part of the decade tended to represent conservative perspectives including a pro-life advocate, and the James Dobson "Focus on the Family" series, among others. As the decade advanced, programs broadened in viewpoint with greater attention to the internal dynamics of family life, introducing such terms as co-dependency, inner child, the sandwich generation, and blended families. John Bradshaw's "On Family" series was hugely popular and was presented at the church in the late 1980s. Country Club would earn a national reputation in Marriage Enrichment programming with the support of Martha Jane and John Starr and Jerry and Doris Thompson's curriculum, and the later, full scale curriculum development by Reverends Cueni and Aday.

Women's issues were highlighted as part of the larger family framework, but increasingly in recognition of dramatically changing roles and perceptions taking place in much of America. Working mothers, the Feminist Movement, and violence against women and children were all given attention in the form of workshops and sermons, as well as receiving advocacy support from the Outreach Council. Women continued to struggle for an "of course" recognition in their roles in the church; in the early '80s a woman board member was asked to substitute as the chair for the monthly meeting; she was identified as the "first woman to preside at the board," and thanked effusively, if somewhat patronizingly, in two successive monthly minutes.

The Outreach Council budget is one indicator of commitment to a wide range of issues and institutions. In 1988, Dr. Brice announced that Country Club's outreach giving was the highest of any Disciples congregation in the nation. That giving included a donation to a local organization supporting the needs of gay and lesbian individuals, an emphasis that would grow in the subsequent years. Support for racial justice did not fade from the high point of the 1960s; instead it took on a greater local emphasis. A December 1985 column in *The Christian* announced that "For some time there has been a need for a new Black Disciples church in Wyandotte County. And with the support of the Area church and direction by the Committee on Black Church Concerns (David Cole, Minister of Swope Park United Christian Church, Chairperson) much of the ground work has been accomplished ... Watch for further announcements regarding the birth and life of this important Black new church starting in Kansas City."

The announcement underscored the fact that Kansas City remained racially divided, seventeen years after Restructure had sought to eliminate those divisions at least within the denomination. But three and one-half years later in June 1989, under the leadership of Tom Van Dyke, the Social Action Committee of the Outreach Council met with a comparable group from Swope Parkway United Christian Church, a predominantly African-American congregation. In a brainstorming session the sixty participants discussed perceptions of each other's churches and made plans for joint efforts ranging from Bible study, to assistance for runaways, to support for Country Club's Homeless Project. The two churches participated in pulpit and choir exchanges as well, and planned small group inter-church meetings for purposes of using materials from Harmony in a World of Difference, a major Kansas City race relations project.

In 1988, in response to keen interest on the part of members, Country Club began an adult missions work program. The youth program had been successfully in place for a number of years and it was clear the moment had come to expand opportunities. Both programs were under the leadership of Associate Minister Doug Deuel, who explained the new adult program the following year in an October 1989 *Christian*: "Last year as we initiated our adult mission trip program, occasionally I would be asked the question: 'Why would you go to Los Angeles to do a mission project when there are so many needs here in Kansas City?' My response often would be: 'We go to Los Angeles to plant seeds in the lives of our participants. Hopefully, when we return we will be able to find ways to reinvest in our own community.

Not long after the mission trip returned to Kansas City, the church received a letter of thanks from the Los Angeles pastor, saying that "not only did they (the CCCC group) help with physical needs, they have ministered to us in such a way that racial barriers have again been attacked." The subsequent 1989 missions commitment linked the church group with Habitat for Humanity on an in-town project. In 1985 South African Minister Reverend Jacob Alberts spent three months based at Country Club in order to educate the Kansas City community about apartheid and the profound needs of his country. His visit initiated a relationship with South Africa that included several mission trips under Dr. Miles' leadership.

The church committed to another major renovation in 1988, to be funded by a $2.8 million campaign. The renovation greatly expanded classroom space on the third floor, and addressed long-deferred maintenance projects, some quite significant. As Dr. Brice ruefully observed, it was a nine-month project that took nineteen months. At one point recalling Dr. Grafton's admonishment during another renovation forty years earlier to be patient and maintain a "business as usual" attitude with the endless interruptions, he responded simply, "ditto." The expansion came at a time when many churches in all denominations in the country were losing members, but Country Club held steady throughout the 1980s. Management of the membership roster, always outdated, was an onerous process requiring the manual sorting of cards; that finally gave way in 1986 to the purchase of the first, very expensive, in-house computers that in turn required a whole new set of skills of the increasingly specialized staff.

Reverend George Gordon had joined the ministerial staff in 1975, succeeding Dr. Fielder, and beginning a 33-year tenure as the pastoral minister. He earned his doctorate in pastoral counseling in 1980, a relatively new professional vocation within the ministry. Under his direction, services provided by the pastoral ministry would expand dramatically. Confidentiality prevented Dr. Gordon from describing those services in detail, but he periodically provided information in *The Christian* and church meetings to explain his work. The pastoral ministry dealt with issues that paralleled those in society at large: family disruption, drug use, alcoholism, depression and suicide, mental health, aging. Dr. Gordon's own counseling, in individual, marriage, group, and family formats averaged one thousand hours per year and was further supported by part-time staff. As the years went by, his title was changed from minister of pastoral care and counseling to minister of congregational care, representing the increasing participation of lay people in the caring ministries and consequently Dr. Gordon's enhanced role as coach and active trainer as well as a counselor. Reverend Joe Walker serves today as the minister of congregational care.

In 1984, with support from the elders and after several years of planning, the church launched its own program of the Stephen Ministries, a non-profit non-denominational religious and educational organization that trains lay people to be caregivers to individuals in hurting situations. The organization began in St. Louis in 1975, and now includes more than 13,000 member congregations. It is named after the Disciple Stephen, "full of faith and the Holy Spirit," identified in Acts as the one who was chosen to provide caring ministry to those in need. Stephen

Ministers undergo a thorough course of training and are assigned to one care recipient at a time for as long as needed. The work was described in *The Christian* as "applied theology, teaching real skills necessary to help others." The program was accepted enthusiastically at Country Club; in March 1987, Dr. Gordon noted that thirty-five people had gone through the training and continued to meet regularly. He went on to observe that "the Stephen minister finds that it is necessary to give of themselves diligently without the hope of great reward except that of serving the Lord faithfully."

At their January 1988 meeting, the Board of Elders announced approval of a committee for a study of the "singles staff" and to determine the need for a full-time singles staff minister. Single members had received increasing attention in recent years, with the recognition that their spiritual, social, and emotional needs were not being fully addressed. A "Singles Sunday" in October 1985 was organized for the purpose of making the congregation more aware of the church's singles programs as well as to recognize the diversity of the group. Associate Minister Jim Vincent, who was single, wrote in that week's *Christian* that it was possible to feel "a certain sadness, apartness, loneliness, and incompleteness in surroundings which seem to heavily promote partners." At that time, 34 percent of Country Club's adult congregation was single (43 percent of those widowed, 18 percent divorced, and 39 percent never married.)

In March, the board approved a budget line item for the salary of a full time singles minister and the creation of a Singles Council, and by July the appointment of Reverend Carla Aday to that role was approved. She was a recent recipient of a Master of Divinity degree from Yale University, and, like a number of other Country Club clergy, a Texan and a lifelong Disciple. The Singles Ministry flourished from the beginning. Looking back after a year and a half, Reverend Aday could count seven new singles groups, and six events specifically for the purpose of ministering to single adults. *The Christian* carried regular features and announcements about Singles activities. And the Christian Family Camp at Estes Park was renamed, after sixteen years, Christian Community Camp where "everyone is welcome."

The 1980s were a time of institutional and administrative adjustments. The church made a somewhat belated decision to incorporate in line with other congregations of similar size and budget. The denomination moved from an "area" organizational plan to a regional one, resulting in an entity called the Greater Kansas City Region. *The Kansas City Times* noted that the new region was the smallest geographically in the denomination, but its 40,000 members constituted one of the "highest concentrations of Disciples in the country."[260] Dr. Brice, who served as moderator of the Christian Church of Greater Kansas City, was the keynote speaker at the celebration event at the RLDS Auditorium in nearby Independence, and long-time Country Club Parish Visitor Dorothy Blackburn was named the first regional moderator.

The decade had begun with Reverend Young's musings about ways to characterize the 1970s and 1980s and what that could mean for the coming years. Others added their observations about the times; religion was clearly in flux and, to some observers, seemed to be in decline. Many churches experienced reductions in membership, although that was not the case with Country Club. Local news coverage of church activities was dramatically reduced, usually limited to the Sunday services announcements. Some people were drawn to different modes of spiritual expression and movements, both within and outside conventional church structures. The EWS group in the 1960s was one example. The Curcillo movement that began in Spain in the 1940s as a Roman Catholic emphasis on spiritual development expanded in the coming decades and was embraced by Protestants as well, including some members of Country Club.

Reverend Young was not the only Country Club minister to ponder the nature of the congregation he served. Writing in *The Christian* in May 1982, Associate Minister Ervin Crain said "everyone is somewhat reluctant to admit that while the church **should** be big enough to accept people of varying points of view, it doesn't always live up to that ideal." He went on to identify people of differing theological positions who filled the pews on any given Sunday morning: "charismatics, evangelicals, social activists, liberals, fundamentalists, and neo-orthodox ... diversity among Christians is on the increase." What does all this mean to our church, he asked. "To be a vital church in the 1980s it will be essential for all of us — evangelical, liberal, or whatever — to affirm the legitimacy of diversity. Theological variety should not be viewed with alarm because of potential divisiveness, but rather celebrated as a strength within the unity of the whole church." Dr. Brice devoted an entire sermon series "Let's Look at Faith," to the exploration of theological diversity at Country Club in the fall of 1987, noting "the ways in which trends in religion occur simultaneously with trends in politics and culture in general." But the consequence of that diversity, as Dr. Brice pointed out a few years later in 1990, is that it is "extremely difficult for large churches to agree to take stands on social issues ... The larger the church, the greater the diversity of its people. Congregations most vocal in social action have around 100 very homogeneous members, meaning that there is little or no diversity within."

Unity and diversity — the two themes that had dominated Disciples thought and practice since its beginnings — were once again being examined in a 20th century denomination in the heart of the country, sometimes in tension, at other times reinforcing one another. In March 1987, Disciples gathered to consider the denomination's identity and future and, in the words of the conference title, "Reappraise the Disciples Tradition for the 21st Century." The conference itself was productive and concluded that "the Church must be an inclusive community, that we need one another — women and men, lay and ordained, of whatever color or language — in order to be more truly the church God wills." Its real significance, however, is that it recognized the changes, however undefined and confusing, that must be faced. [261]

In January 1991, Dr. Brice announced that he had accepted a call from University Christian Church in Fort Worth, Texas. While the Search committee did its work looking for the next minister, Dr. William Shoop, who had been the associate minister from 1959-1961, agreed to assume the role of Interim pastor during the search for a new Senior Minister. He and his wife, Mary Jean, were well regarded in the church; he had made regular guest appearances through the years and would prove an able leader in the transition period. Once again young church members were in military uniform, this time in the Middle East in the Gulf wars. Their names appeared in *The Christian*, and church members prepared cards, letters, and holiday gifts for mailing, and dedicated the Easter offering to victims of the conflicts. In April, a new carillon was installed, with greatly enhanced capacity, to the delight of David Diebold. There was an increasing emphasis on "small group" ministry — an acknowledgment that individuals could get lost in such a large congregation, and a growing focus on the consequences of an aging church — prompting one sermon to be delivered under the title of the "Geezer Boom." Guest speakers discussed feminist theology; the church hosted a dinner for a large group of homeless individuals.

None of these undertakings was unique to Country Club; they were part of the fabric of other churches as well, representing an evolution from the fires of the 1960s to more measured responses to the needs of the day that recognized the desire for personal spiritual development as well as social justice. In April 1991 Dr. Shoop, writing his regular weekly column for *The Christian*, addressed the need for balance between the two: "One of the most difficult problems facing the Disciples of Christ is whether we can maintain a balance between the concern for social justice and personal righteousness ... Personal transformation and social change are both inherent in the gospel."

Dr. R. Robert Cueni became the sixth Senior Minister in Country Club's seventy-year history in November 1991. The majority of his career had been as a pastoral minister in small and medium-sized congregations in the Midwest. He held a Bachelor's degree in biology from Kent State, a Master's of divinity degree from Christian Theological Seminary, and a doctor of ministry degree from San Francisco Theological Seminary. In the two years prior to the call to Kansas City, he had served an administrative position as the area minister for Trinity-Brazos in Texas. While pastoral work was his true interest, he acknowledged that the administrative experience had been essential for his preparation as the leader of a large urban church and, later, president of a seminary. He and his wife Linda were the last family to move into the parsonage on Ward Parkway, with the welcome assistance of their two adult daughters.

Dr. R. Robert Cueni, the 6th Senior Minister, 1991-2001

The new minister moved quickly to launch initiatives that would address key issues, such as the aging congregation. He recalled that "Prior to coming to the 4Cs I was impressed that the congregation was roughly the same size in 1990 as it had been in 1950. Upon arrival I realized that was misleading. Demographically, this faith community was poised for significant decline. This was primarily due to the fact that the congregation had received 850 fewer new members in the 1980s than in the 1960s. The church had maintained its size by the same people growing older and older." [262] He concluded that "at some point a present generation must be replaced by the next generation," and the goal became to reduce the congregation's average age. That necessitated revision and renewal of the worship services, making them more appealing to younger worshippers. The changes evolved gradually, and not especially dramatically over the next few years. There was some resistance, but younger members were drawn in larger numbers, even to the very formal and traditional 11 a.m. service.

In the early years of his career, Reverend Cueni identified his two ministry passions: writing and a "keen interest in developing healthy marriages." [263] While still in Petoskey, Michigan, he began counseling couples who were about to be married as well as those who were in challenging relationships, a vocation where he enjoyed the work and for which he had an obvious talent. Upon arriving at Country Club, he realized that the church that was performing at least 100-150 weddings yearly was essentially "little more than a wedding mill," providing little, if any, pre-nuptial preparation. Together with Reverend Aday, Country Club launched the GREAT START ministry that was generously funded by the Eli Lilly Foundation and soon gained a national reputation. One of the unexpected and very welcome outcomes of the program was increased young adult membership. GREAT START was followed by an ambitious parenting program, headed by Carla Aday, then the director of the Young Adult Task Force. Again, it was a source of new members with the simple message that "this church cares about you and your children." Together, the wedding, early marriage, and parenting ministries provided what Dr. Cueni termed a "community service niche" that supported families and attracted younger members. [264]

While serving as pastor of Bloomington (Illinois) Christian Church, Dr. Cueni had brought Herb Miller, executive director of the Disciples' National Evangelistic Association, to consult and lead a Parish Enrichment

Conference. It was very successful, producing a report and ninety-one suggestions that became the church's long-range plan, and confirming the importance of engaging a congregation's lay leadership. Within a year of his arrival at Country Club, he had tapped Reverend Miller to lead a Parish Enrichment Conference (PEC) in October 1992. Its purpose was to examine the church's context, where it wanted to be in the future, and how to reach that goal. Country Club had a long tradition of employing consultants. In the early days of the 20th century the consultants had been primarily focused on fundraising and growth. By the last quarter of the century consultants were leading discussions on the character of "membership" (age, gender, socio-economic status, race and ethnicity) and cautioning against growth for growth's sake.

The PEC report lists eight items the church members had identified as strengths, and then offered sixteen items as action steps to build on those strengths. Those items ranged from the practical (needed upgrades to the building) to the spiritual (more opportunities for Bible study and prayer). They would inform and guide church plans and programming for years to come. By 1995, a Future Focus Committee was in place and charged to be "responsible for 1) enabling the catalyst for positive action, and 2) monitoring the congregation's efforts and progress towards long-range goals."

In an early report to the board in 1996, the committee identified the needs of both the aging and young adults as important concerns. Noting that programming for the aging was underway, the report turned to young adults, referring to an earlier consultant's conclusions (Lyle Schaller) during the Brice era.

> [Schaller identified] the barriers to reaching people born after 1955. He stated that the number one barrier can be summarized in one sentence: "IT IS ALMOST CERTAIN THAT NEXT YEAR WILL NOT BE 1957." The X-Generation is different. That's not just because they wear their baseball hats backward and indulge in other idiosyncratic behavior. This post-modern generation represents a paradigm shift and takes a different view of the environment, the workplace and social and religious institutions. [265]

By century's end, the church that had begun in a former cornfield on an unfinished street was confronting the very urban problems of crime and parking. The board met with local police officials, looking for guidance after several successful and attempted robberies. Security guards were increasingly present on Sundays and at times such as the Easter prayer vigil when the chapel was open for extended periods. The days of an open-door church were over, not only at Country Club but elsewhere throughout the country. Unpleasant and even alarming as the crime concerns were, the issue of adequate parking space (a major concern of the PEC report) assumed a dominant and very contentious place in the life of the church. Ward Parkway, which had been a main thoroughfare for years, was the primary locus for parking on Sunday mornings and for weddings and funerals that precipitated large attendance. Irritated motorists who were not coming to church services would race down the one open lane, sometimes oblivious to the young children emerging from their parents' cars and to the fact that the cars on either side were actually parked. Two small houses directly behind and to the east of the church came up for sale and the church purchased them with the intention of tearing them down and providing off-street parking.

The neighbors objected vigorously. They picketed the church and under the aegis of the Homes Association sued to prevent construction of the parking lot. Ultimately, they prevailed; there would be no new parking lot. In the more than twenty years since that divisive time, heated feelings have cooled, but the problem of adequate parking remains. The church has made concerted efforts to be a good neighbor, whether through simple gestures such as water, cookies, and dog treats on Sunday mornings or yuletide caroling through the neighborhood. The circular south driveway with a canopy allows for dry drop offs for services, while expanded handicap parking, and a transportation ministry have all eased some of the problems, but certainly not eliminated them. Sunday morning pew counts have declined, whether from difficulty finding a parking place or larger changes in the religious life of America is still a matter of debate.

Throughout the 1990s, the church maintained a very active outreach and mission program, both international and domestic, from Africa, and Central and Latin America, to Appalachia, Native American reservations, areas ravaged by tornados and hurricanes, urban core neighborhoods, and, of course, the special projects in the immediate Kansas City area. Although the position of Living Link missionary was no longer filled, Country Club had regular short-term mission programs to other countries, such as Dr. Joann Redding's three-month assignment to India in 1995-96. The following year, Reverend Ashok Patek, Dr. Redding's Indian host, and his wife came to Kansas City to acquaint the community with India's culture and needs. As in the past, the church responded to national disasters and tragedies. In 1995, the horrific April 19th bombing of the Murrah Building in Oklahoma City galvanized Disciples across the country when one of the local Disciples churches accommodated the response efforts. *The Christian* ran appeals for much needed financial support. On July 17, 1996, TWA Flight 800 exploded and crashed just twelve minutes after takeoff from JFK International Airport, killing everyone on board. It was a time of international tensions and conspiracy theories about the crash were rife, although the cause was never determined. Kansas City was a TWA hub and was one of the four communities nationally to host memorial services on Sunday the 21st. Country Club Christian Church was the site for the Kansas City service, attended by more than 500 people. Dr. Cueni; Father Thomas Savage, president of Rockhurst College (now University); and Rabbi Joshua Taub of Temple B'nai Jehudah led the service.

Country Club celebrated its 75th anniversary in 1995-96, an occasion that inspired individuals and committees to look back as well as to contemplate the future. Dorothy Blackburn and others brought a more systematic strategy to gathering and organizing historic materials, moving beyond the somewhat ad hoc "let's put the box in that closet" approach to archival management. There were still some charter members willing to share their memories, and many second-generation members who recalled their experiences in the church. "History moments" were scheduled at board meetings, and *The Christian* provided other recollections as well as photos. The Future Focus Committee took on many tasks and agenda items, but perhaps their most significant act was to acknowledge the nature of historic change and evolution that made those tasks essential. Many years before, during Dr. Grafton's ministry, church members had been reminded of the impact World War II had on a new generation and the need to understand that impact moving forward with the work of the church. Now with the approach of the millennium, it was time once again to anticipate the character and needs of the community of faith that would be called to address tasks not yet fully understood.

In November 1997, Dr. Cueni's request for a three-month sabbatical the following summer was approved. His plans followed closely the 75th year focus on the future; he had been awarded a grant from Eli Lilly

Corporation that would support his research of other large congregations in the country that had, like Country Club, sustained themselves for at least fifty years. His project, titled "Vitality in the Tall Steeples," was based on his conviction that while these churches had continued to thrive, there was no guarantee for the future, and it was essential that the church have a plan for moving forward. The announcement of his sabbatical occurred at the same board meeting where board member Wayne Heady reviewed a recent seminar he had attended, led by Lyle Schaller, the nationally prominent church consultant who had worked with Country Club several years previously. His report compared trends in 1983 to those in 1997, and clearly informed Dr. Cueni's plans. There were twenty "trends" — most were directly relevant to Country Club, including the need for ample parking; ecumenical emphasis on "what connects us"; the increasing role of women; more participants in worship instead of spectators; and more team ministry.

Upon his return from sabbatical the following summer, Dr. Cueni reported on his visits to fifty congregations whose criteria would provide meaningful guidelines for Country Club. At the full board meeting in September in an opening time reserved for "Sacred Stories," he observed that each of the churches he visited had its own "sacred story" that leaders must know and renew while also designing the next chapter. It is, he concluded, important to continue what is helpful but to leave behind that which no longer works. As he had observed some years earlier, "Those who rightly interpret the direction of the changes, and who respond to them — such persons in history have mostly flourished. Those who remained the same when the same was no longer fitting — they perished, thinking they were holding to the old virtues, which an irresponsible generation had abandoned. For the most part, they perished because their minds had become like the body of the dinosaur, unfit for the new climate of the world." [266] At his first Executive Committee meeting in August he was presented with plans for a new capital campaign of almost $3 million — the church was moving rapidly toward the new millennia. He undoubtedly had occasion to reflect upon the dinosaur as the planning committee addressed the concerns of those who objected to proposed changes.

CHAPTER 13

To 'Be Church': Planning for the Second Century

"God is our refuge and strength, a very present help in trouble. Therefore, we will not fear, though the earth should change." On the evening of September 11, 2001, Chairman Randy Irey opened the regularly scheduled meeting of the Executive Committee with a reading of Psalm 46. That morning, two planes had slammed into the World Trade Center in New York City, a third had attacked and damaged the Pentagon, and a fourth crashed into a field in Pennsylvania after passengers subdued the al-Qaeda hijackers. Nearly three thousand people were killed outright and more than 25,000 injured — the single deadliest attack on U. S. soil in history, which eventually led to the invasion of Afghanistan by U. S. forces.

The following Sunday's church service was essentially a town hall meeting led by Associate Minister Cliff Jones, who asked those in the pews to report on what they, their families, and friends were experiencing. Church members prepared sandwiches for those stranded at KCI airport after all air traffic was cancelled, and the Chancel Choir scheduled a prayer service for September 13. The church undertook two mission trips to Ground Zero in New York over the next three months, where they worked shifts at St. Paul's Chapel. St. Paul's, located directly across the street from the World Trade Center, became the sanctuary for rescue workers during the massive clean-up and search for bodies. In the years that followed, Country Club would offer programs and workshops on Islam, and on the 10th anniversary of the attacks, September 11, 2011, when he was joined by both an imam and a rabbi in worship, Dr. Miles began a sermon series on forgiveness. In March 2018, the church again provided the location to mourn and to remember, as it had done for city-wide services after the death of President Kennedy and other national events. Funeral services that came to be known as the "FBI Funeral" were conducted for Melissa Morrow, an FBI agent who had been a first responder to the attack on the Pentagon and whose illness was a direct result of her presence on the site. Her eulogy was given by FBI Director Christopher Wray, and the sanctuary was filled with fellow agents, family, and friends.

In the summer of 2001, Dr. Cueni was approached by a search team on behalf of Lexington Theological Seminary in their canvass for a new president. He accepted the position, becoming the 15th president of the Seminary in January 2002, stating that "what we want to do is shape leaders for a post-establishment, post-modern church." Ministers, he argued, must be prepared for "conditions in which the church no longer directs the culture."[267] Dr. Gordon Kingsley, theologian and former president of nearby William Jewell College, stepped in as interim minister while the church searched for its new pastor. Looking back upon that year, he recently recalled "the openness of the congregation, the freedom to prepare and preach as God led, the joy of music and prayers and people on a quest ... "

Dr. R. Glen Miles accepted Country Club's call in the late fall of 2002, moving from his position as senior minister at Sandy Springs Christian Church in Atlanta, Georgia. He had a strong background with urban churches, and held multiple degrees, including a Doctor of Ministry from the School of Theology in Claremont, California, a Master of Divinity from Emmanuel School of Religion in Johnson City, Tennessee, and a Bachelor of Science from Northwest Christian College in Eugene, Oregon. He was installed as minister on February 11, 2003, in a service led by Dr. Richard Wing, senior minister of First Community Church in Columbus, Ohio. He and his wife, Julie, had two school-aged sons and would move into their own home rather than the church parsonage which was sold in October. Proceeds from the parsonage went to the church endowment fund and the earnings are used for mission work in Jackson County.

Several internal steps were finalized in the early months of Dr. Miles' pastorate: plans were completed for a columbarium to be located in the garden of the Combs Chapel, and "The Well," a book/gift shop, opened on the lower level at one end of what had been known as the Colonial Room because of its blue and white decor. The very successful AA and

Al-Anon programs, one of the largest chapters in the city, brought many people into the building throughout the week. The board agreed to participate in the planning stages of More^2 (the Metropolitan Organization for Racial and Economic Equity), a consortium of churches being organized to create a power base for dealing with inequity issues in the metropolitan area. Already in fifty-nine cities, More^2 was scheduled for kickoff in Kansas City on September 19, 2003. The Outreach Council pledged $1,000 to the project. The board voted to participate in the planning stages of More^2 for twelve months and to review its progress periodically throughout the year. At the end of its first year, More^2 was bringing together leaders from synagogue, church, civic and financial (specifically the construction industry) organizations to link youth in poverty to construction jobs.

The Outreach Council's budget totaled approximately a quarter-million dollars in the 2003-04 fiscal year and would remain a priority for church spending. As in the past, outreach targeted both domestic and international projects. At the March 2006 board meeting, the Mission Trip Committee announced its plans to move away from the model of missions that gives a huge volume of goods in one trip to realizing a "more equal partnership between the recipients and trip participants." That goal was especially relevant to the increasing collaborations at the local level with schools and social services, characterizing what Dr. Gordon described as a shift in church-based social activism to an ongoing relationship with those we serve and less like a drop of a parachute team behind enemy lines.

The United States experienced a severe economic recession from 2005 to 2009, with the most impact felt in 2007 and 2008. The board addressed the budget crisis in a variety of ways including budget cuts, but actively encouraged a "culture of stewardship" designed to increase giving. Phrases such as "budget crisis" appeared regularly in *The Christian* and board minutes that revealed another indication of change: lay leaders' voices were present to a greater degree than in the past, providing support to the traditional ministerial exhortations. Upon assuming the chairmanship of the board in June 2009, John Cockle wrote in the June 29 *Christian* that he was in the process of assessing what the church's goals should be for the coming year, but said that effort was overshadowed by the most critical concern: balancing the budget.

During the previous year, the church had operated at a deficit, despite the valiant efforts of church leadership and church staff to increase income and reduce expenses. "Based on the current results of the stewardship campaign, it's clear that we will need to continue to reduce expenses significantly and to seek new income sources," Chairman Cockle wrote. "We are evaluating various options to meet these challenges. It is likely that all areas of the church operation will be affected to some degree, and some of those options may be difficult, but it is critical that we balance the budget while at the same time continuing the important ministries of this church." By the end of the 2010-2011 fiscal year, the financial situation was improving significantly. The difficult decision to close the in-house print shop (ironically created years before as a cost-saving measure) helped to streamline processes, along with eliminating two staff positions. An across-the-board 5 percent compensation reduction (restored the following year), and reduction of program budgets further improved the fiscal outlook.

Dr. Miles clearly noted the challenges before the church in the January 2010 *Christian*, stating: "mainline congregations, like ours, are facing tough times." He drew upon Diane Butler Bass's book, *The Practicing Congregation*, as he described her focus "on how to help great, traditional congregations like ours recover and renew its life ... They are able to do so by being willing to 'retradition.'" In language that is reminiscent of Dr. Cueni's emphasis on telling the story, he went on to explain that retraditioning "implies reaching back to the past, identifying practices that were an important part of the past, and bringing them to the present where they can reshape contemporary life."

The welcome budgetary news made it possible to seriously consider addressing maintenance issues as well as making critical decisions about how to support church programs in the years ahead. At the end of the summer, the Practical Services Council reported extensive damage to the bell tower, and scattered damage to the tiles across the roof. A large sinkhole had appeared in the chapel parking lot, and ongoing masonry issues in the building raised safety concerns. A year later, an article in *The Christian* began with the alarming news that chunks of rock and masonry had fallen from the church's roof. A structural engineer reported that serious damage in a number of parts of the building was due to exposure to excessive moisture and freezing and thawing conditions, requiring major modification of the drainage system. Once again it was time to prepare a strategic plan to address these and other issues.

Several years previously, the Visioning Committee had initiated a collaborative process called "Sacred Conversations," inspired by the book *Holy Conversations* by Gil Rendle and Alice Mann that Dr. Miles had introduced to the church in the spring of 2007. As the committee explained, the process was "quite different from historical approaches to strategic planning at Country Club Christian Church." The committee recognized that its initial approach to planning and change had been very "corporate-like" by increasing tasks, costs, and workloads, but failing to address key spiritual questions, namely: Who are we? What has God called us to do? Who is our neighbor? At the end of October 2010, the Visioning Committee issued a report that provided two key recommendations emphasizing small groups and the development of collective spiritual gifts for service. Together, these would guide the plans for implementing the Strategic Plan in the years ahead.

The sacred conversation format revolved around two broad themes — outreach and inclusion: not new terms, certainly, but subject to ever-broadening interpretation. Outreach and inclusion were increasingly understood to be occupying the ends of the same bridge; one could not truly exist without the other, and they were linked by the term welcome, appearing more and more often in church writing and thought. Outreach had expanded dramatically from a focus in the early days of the church on distant lands and peoples — the "other" not like us — to recognition of our shared humanity and shared human needs. In the past, inclusion was something of a stand-in for ecumenical (we can collaborate and work together). But it demanded an acknowledgement that went far beyond mere tolerance. A decade earlier, while serving as interim minister prior to Dr. Bash's arrival, Dr. Shoop had expressed that sentiment when he wrote in an April 1991 *Christian* that "Staff, lay leadership and the congregation working together make this church a powerful influence for Christ in Kansas City and around the world. In a church of this size it is easy for us to overestimate our sense of self-sufficiency. We are linked to and dependent upon many others in the regional, national and world church ... We are in this struggle together." His comment was prescient, anticipating the conclusions of others in the years to come as they prepared for the church in the 21st century.

As part of the broad-ranging and intense analysis that drove the Visioning process, the Inclusion Study Team, a product of the Visioning Process's Sacred Conversations, reported to the board in September 2009 on its assessment of barriers to inclusiveness at Country Club. Factors included the traditional physical structure, its location on Ward Parkway, the church's name, and current demographics of the congregation: mostly White, middle-to-upper-income residents. The minutes noted a "lively" conversation with "differing viewpoints" about the report, but there was general agreement that it was an important issue that needed further study. The church's image had been a source of concern from the very beginning, addressed by every minister; Dr. Bash had referred to the "curse" of being perceived as a wealthy church. The issue of the name was especially polarizing and would continue to be raised in the coming years.

Inclusion meant sometimes challenging discussions about race, gender, sexual orientation, and age. From the time of his arrival Dr. Miles had stressed both the importance of fully accepting the LGBTQ family into the church, as well as committing to a reassessment of the ministry to youth and children. Those goals came together with the hiring of Justin Ziegler, initially as a student intern, and then in 2008 as the full-time minister to youth. He was the church's first openly gay minister. In 2013, Justin was ordained in the sanctuary. It was not always a smooth or universally accepted process, but the ordination was a time of celebration and reconciliation. It would be several more years before small group gatherings in 2016 affirmed the church's openness to same sex marriage and ordination of LGBTQ individuals — but then pointedly asked, "Does the community at large know this about us?"

That same year, Dr. Miles organized a senior minister's task force on race. These ideas and others, such as broadening worship formats, were brought together in a "Vision of Ministry" that identified specific objectives. The "Vision" was referred to regularly in board reports and elsewhere to assess progress. Outreach had always been central to the mission of the church, even in challenging economic times. Board minutes for March 2015 reported that more than 60 percent of Country Club's attending membership was involved in volunteering with outreach missions of the church, while the national average was just 8 percent, and 20 percent for a "vital" congregation.

Vital congregation is a term that gained usage in the second decade of the 21st century. Country Club was one of twelve churches of similar demographics, but varying denominations, that participated in a study in 2015, the purpose of which was to determine what created a successful, thriving church. Those tasked with conducting the study reported to the board in June that Country Club represented a vital congregation by virtue of a number of key characteristics: communication, outreach and mission, strong staff, small groups, and community interaction/presence.

While community and neighborhood focus expanded, the church continued to address world issues as well. At the end of 2015, the board adapted a lengthier document produced by the national denominational office, and voted to sign, as individual members, a "Statement of Welcome to Refugees" that protested the restriction of admission of refugees of the Syrian war because of their ethnicity and religion.

The first two decades of the new century were a time of change and growth. In 2005, Carla Aday was promoted to Senior Associate Minister assuming many of the administrative duties that had been carried by Dr. Miles. Some years previously, John Young had retired as the long-time minister of education, and in 2008 Dr. Gordon retired. Each of these departures and other personnel changes had significant impact on the programs and organization of the church as a whole, prompting the board in 2011 to bring in consultants to assess the church's administrative structure — something that hadn't been done since 1992. In that time, some job descriptions had become obsolete and the ever-expanding need for data management and vastly enhanced digital and computer capacity ever more insistent.

Dr. Glen Miles, 7th Senior Minister, 2003-2017, at the re-dedication of the church building upon completion of major repairs, October 5, 2014.

Small group discussions identified three major plans to be pursued in the coming years: a physical renovation of the building, a school partnership initiative with the KCMO School District, and a restructuring of the staff in light of the 2011 consultancy. The renovation was initially proposed at a $2 million-plus budget that would be more than doubled as work progressed. A successful capital campaign brought the project to completion in 2014 after two disruptive years of trucks and cranes on the front lawn and loud noises everywhere. Dr. Miles expressed the enthusiasm of all in the September *Christian*: "The building now glistens in the late afternoon sun. The stained glass sparkles, the Schantz organ fills the sanctuary with wonderful music, and the new landscaping creates a welcoming and inviting atmosphere." The jubilant rededication on October 5 celebrated not only the completion of the task but a commitment to the future.

The school partnership proposal emerged from the Inclusion Study Group with several goals: to serve the immediate neighborhood, thereby improving relations, and to assist the struggling KCMO School District. By February 2011, the church had "adopted" nearby Hartman Elementary School at 81st and Oak Streets. The congregation in general supported the plan, but there was also significant support for thinking differently about local outreach. The board appointed a committee to identify an Outreach Partnership Initiative.

Their report in January 2012 explained that "instead of many small projects around the metropolitan area, the work of the Visioning Committee suggested that we join our collective spiritual gifts for service in order both to make a significant impact and to strengthen community ties within our congregation ... the church will need to transition from supporting efforts scattered across the metropolitan area to projects and programs within The Northeast Initiative Partnership when starting new outreach initiatives." The Northeast was an obvious choice: the origins of Country Club Christian were rooted in Independence Boulevard Church which had provided the first pastor and many of the charter members. Ties had remained close through the years; Independence Boulevard remained a strong anchor even as the area surrounding it sank into urban decline, and Country Club had long-standing outreach programs with the parent church and the large number of service organizations that existed in the area.

The Northeast Initiative, as it came to be called, developed over the next several years. In 2013, the committee identified four goals that would guide its plans:

- Develop a relationship with a community of people;
- Improve the quality of life for residents in the Independence Avenue corridor;
- Provide direct and meaningful service opportunities for Country Club members of all ages;
- Provide an additional 100 church members to spend two hours of volunteer time in the Northeast in 2013.

The Northeast was a destination for many incoming immigrants to the city, and volunteers were needed for the expanding ESL programs. Several "Grace at Work" projects (Country Club's long-standing short-term volunteer program) were planned for the Northeast. By 2017, the church's outreach included Della Lamb, Micah Ministries, Grace United, Jerusalem Farms, and Sheffield Place. And, as part of the recognition that support should move in both directions, the Initiative created a marketing campaign that would publicize shops and restaurants in the Northeast to attract patrons from other areas of the city. The recommendation concluded with a warning: "this would be a radical change in how we will 'be Church'!"

In November 2016, Dr. Miles informed the board that he had accepted a call from First Community Church in Columbus, Ohio. His last service at Country Club was February 5, 2017. The Search Committee continued the "conversation" strategy that had prevailed in recent years, asking for input from the entire congregation and staff about what they saw as needed in a new senior minister. Reverend Carla Aday, who most recently had been the executive minister, was called to the pulpit on April 7, the first female Senior Minister in the church's history. The announcement at Sunday's service was greeted with enthusiastic applause. Reverend Aday had spent her entire ministry — twenty-eight years — at Country Club, arriving as the first female minister and first Minister of Singles in 1988 after earning her Divinity degree at Yale. In the ensuing years she had assumed almost every ministerial leadership position in the staff other than Senior Minister. She had been a very active leader in multiple mission programs and had, with Dr. Cueni, developed the nationally distributed Great Start Marriage Enrichment program. She was a well-known figure throughout the community and the denomination. Her installation on September 24 had the spirit of a family affair as she received her robe and commission from former Senior Ministers Brice and Cueni with the assistance of the Regional Disciples Minister Reverend Bill Rose-Heim, and Reverend Gary Walling, who had been the youth pastor in her childhood church in Texas.

One of the first tasks to be identified by Reverend Aday was planning for the Church Centennial in 2021. The Centennial Task Force outlined an ambitious agenda that would honor the past and plan for the future. Board meetings and the agenda of the church in general were guided by the Vision of Ministry that provided direction and goals. It was an orderly, exciting beginning for the new ministry.

Everything changed with the swiftness and ferocity of a Midwest tornado. The worldwide COVID pandemic swept across the country, closing schools and churches, changing work patterns, and disrupting all that had been familiar and usual. Like most of the country, the church initially assumed a shutdown of a few weeks or months, but those months turned into the remainder of the year with little certainty about resuming schedules in the coming year. How would Country Club "be Church"? The question had been posed before, with a clearly different expectation of both its intent and the answers that needed to be found. To "be Church" always had been more than worship services. But to "be Church" was first and foremost grounded in worship and in community. Country Club adapted to streaming services with polished and beautiful programs, and attendance actually increased. Support programs were launched; new strategies for creating community without proximity gradually took hold. At this writing, there are still no ready answers, nor will there be for some time. Along with shock and pain it has also been a time of energy and focus.

More than one hundred years ago, *Collier's Magazine* presented a compelling portrait of Dr. Combs in its series on the ministry that asked the question "Are the Churches Failing?" It is a question that has continued to be posed in the century since, shaping the "quest" that Gordon Kingsley recognized at Country Club all those years ago. As the previous pages attest, the quest has assumed so many forms, usually through a dizzying array of committees, task forces, focus groups, sacred conversations, and other formats that have undoubtedly tested the patience of the most seasoned of organizational veterans. But those seemingly disparate discussions have far more in common than is sometimes readily apparent. They have grown out of the past, rooted in the yearnings and soul searches that shape us as individuals and as a community. More than fifty years ago, a group of church members sought a more intimate, less formal way to worship, and created the Experimental Worship Service. At the time,

Reverend Carla Aday delivers her first benediction as Senior Minister concluding her installation service, September 24, 2017.

they were not well-supported in that effort, but the motivation behind it never faded and in the half century since has found new expression in small groups and worship services such as the 9:01 service launched after Reverend Aday assumed leadership. The Stephen Ministry tapped another dimension of an evolving community of faith — the desire on the part of the laity to assume highly trained and informed roles in church leadership that do not compete with but enhance the work of the clergy. That lay leadership has been critical to the formation of community partnerships that move beyond the concept of a "mission to" to a mutually beneficial "collaboration with."

The last chapter in an account such as this cannot in any way serve as a "conclusion." It is a stopping point, a pause that provides the opportunity to look back and, more speculatively, peer into the future. That pause moved beyond the realm of metaphor with the onset of the pandemic and its strictures that imposed something of a forced march through what it means to "be Church." The past, seemingly locked in the clarity of known people and events, is determined by what has been saved and survived as well as that fragile ephemera we know as human memory. What we understand of the past, however elusive and selective, shapes who and what we are today. We carry that understanding as our baggage, sometimes burdensome, sometimes a rich resource, into the future.

George Hamilton Combs understood well the arc of time and the interplay of what has gone before with the present and future. The tasks of the moment require us to draw upon the past in order to respond in ways that are not always clear but continue to draw upon the story that has shaped and guided us. To do so requires a commitment to that story, but also frees us to meet those tasks in ways that have changed many times in the 100 years that the community of faith called Country Club Christian Church has existed. The walls of the chapel that bears his name hold his words from long ago. They continue to speak today.

What we begin, others who
come after will complete.
The good is like the building of
cathedrals. Only through faith
can those who lay foundation
stones hear bells ringing in
unraised steeples.

ENDNOTES

1   Haynes, Nathaniel Smith. *History of the Disciples of Christ in Illinois, 1819-1914.* Cincinnati: Standard Publishing Company, 1915, 101.

2   Peters, George L. *The Disciples of Christ in Missouri: One Hundred Years of Co-operative Work.* Centennial Commission of the Missouri Convention of the Disciples of Christ. 1937, 173.

3   *The Christian Century,* Vol 35, August 8, 1918, 22.

4   Rains, Paul Boyd. Francis Marion Bains, St. Louis, Christian Board of Publication, 1922,156. eBook: https://www.worldcat.org/title/ francis-marion-rains/oclc/1045624161

5   "Well-Known City Leader Called to Another City," *The Christian Century,* Vol. 28, 6 January 1921, 24.

6   Pearson, Robert, and Brad Pearson. *The J. C. Nichols Chronicle: The Authorized Story of the Man and His Company, 1880-1994.* Country Club Plaza Press, 1994, 20.

7   Worley, William. *J. C. Nichols and the Shaping of Kansas City: Innovation in Planned Residential Communities.* University of Missouri Press, 1990, 70.

8   Morton, LaDene. *The Brookside Story: Shops of Every Necessary Character.* The History Press, 2010, 14.

9   Ibid., 24.

10 Jenkins, Marjorie Cupp. MS, undated, CCCC Church Archives.

11 Robertson and Cupp MS Memoirs, Church Archives; CCCC Board Minutes, n.d.

12 Jenkins.

13 Cummins, D. Duane. *The Disciples: A Struggle for Reformation.* Chalice Press, 2009, ix-x.

14 Garrison, Winfred Ernest, and Alfred E. DeGroot. *The Disciples of Christ: A History.* Bethany Press, 1964, rev. 1969, 127.

15 Ibid., 135-140; and McAllister, Lester G. and William E. Tucker. *Journey in Faith: A History of the Christian Church (Disciples of Christ).* The Bethany Press, 1975, 110.

16 Garrison, Winfred Ernest; *An American Religious Movement: A Brief History of the Disciples of Christ.* Bethany Press, 1945, 67.

17 Weisberger, Bernard A. *They Gathered at the River: The Story of the Great Revivalists and Their Impact Upon American Religion.* Little, Brown, 1958, 41.

18 Smith, Matthew D. "Barton Warren Stone: Revisiting Revival in the Early Republic," *The Register of the Kentucky Historical Society.* No.2, spring 2013, 161-197.

19 Cummins, 67, citing several additional sources.

20 Ibid., 63.

21 Maxwell, William. *Ancestors* Knopf, 1971, recounts the history of his midwestern Disciples family, with an extended description of Stone, who befriended Maxwell's great-great-great grandfather.

22   Quoted in Richardson, Robert. *Memoirs of Alexander Campbell,* Vol.2. 1870, 133.
23   Dains, Mary K. "Alexander Campbell and the Missouri Disciples of Christ," *Missouri Historical Review.* 77, 1982, 13-46.
24   Campbell, Alexander. Talk given at Camden Point Seminary, described in "Notes of Incidents in a Tour," *Millennial Harbinger.* Series IV, Vol. III, No.11, February, 1853, 73. The Bible verse is from Proverbs 31:30.
25   Harrell, David E., Jr. "James Shannon; Preacher, Educator, and Fire Eater," *Missouri Historical Review.* 63:2 Jan. 1969, 135-170.
26   Dains, 42. Quoting the *Millennial Harbinger* article, 134.
27   Trollope, Frances. *Domestic Manners of Americans.* London and New York, 4th ed., 1832, 127.
28   See, for example, Wood, Mitchell. *The Owen-Campbell Debate: Is God Needed for a Perfect Union?* Thesis. SUNY: Empire State College, 2006. Available online through ProQuest.
29   Trollope, 129.
30   Harrell, David Edwin. *Sources of Division in the Disciples of Christ, 1865-1900,* Alabama, 1973, 16.
31   Tuck, Darin. "The Battle Cry of Freedom: The Leadership of the Disciples of Christ Movement During the American Civil War, 1861-1865. MA Thesis, Kansas State University, 2010, 10. The three quotations are from, respectively: Claude E. Spencer, *Periodicals of the Disciples of Christ and Related Religious Groups*; W.T. Moore. *Comprehensive History of the Disciples of Christ*; Winfred E. Garrison. *Religion Follows the Frontier: A History of the Disciples of Christ.* Thesis: https://krex.k-state.edu/dspace/bitstream/handle/2097/4218/DarinTuck2010.pdf?sequence=3&isAllowed=y
32   Campbell, Alexander. *The Millennial Harbinger.* Vol. IV, 34-35 (or 157 for the full volume).
33   Butler, Ovid. "Is Slavery Sinful?" in Jeremiah Smith. *Being Partial Discussions of the Proposition Slavery is Sinful.* Indianapolis. 1868, 124.
34   Austin, Thad S. "A Prelude to Civil War: The Religious Nonprofit Sector as a Civil Means of Debate over Slavery, Christian Higher Education, and Religious Philanthropy in the Stone-Campbell Movement." *Religions* September 8, 2018, 235. *Crossref.* Web. http://dx.doi.org/10.3390/rel9080235
35   Maxwell, William. *Ancestors,* Knopf, 1971.
36   Harrell, David Edwin. *Quest for a Christian America, 1800-1865: A Social History of the Disciples of Christ.* Vol. I, University of Alabama, 1966, 128.
37   Ibid,. 106
38   Lard, Moses. "Can We Divide?" *Lard's Quarterly* 3 (reprint, Kansas City, Mo.: Old Paths Book Club, 1950, 330-36.
39   Garrison, *American Religious Movement,* 116.
40   Webb, Henry E. "The Impact of the Civil War," *"Leaven"* vol.7, 1 Jan 1999, 1.
41   Cummins, 170.
42   This discussion is drawn from Cummins' detailed account of division and restructure in the first part of Ch. VI, particularly 194-204.

43   Harrell, David Edwin, Jr. "The American Myth and the Disciples of Christ in the Nineteenth Century," *Agricultural History* 41:2 April 1967, 181-192.

44   Harrell, *Sources,* 71.

45   Ibid., 73.

46   Conwell, Russell H. *Acres of Diamonds* is widely available, most easily as a Gutenberg EBook at Gutenberg.org. See also "Acres of Diamonds" on the *Material Culture of Religion* website at materialreligion.org.

47   Carnegie, Andrew. *The Gospel of Wealth.* Edited and annotated, online at carnegie.org., 2017.

48   Barton, Bruce. *The Man Nobody Knows: A Discovery of the Real Jesus.* Grosset & Dunlap, 1925, online at archive.org. See an excerpt and interpretation at materialreligion.org

49   Harrel, *Sources*, 88.

50   McAlister and Tucker, p. 287, quoting Garrison, "The Problem of the Unemployed," *Christian Evangelist*, XXXI (June 1894), 386.

51   Harrel, *Sources*, 73.

52   Jenkins, Burris, "The Institutional Church," *The New Christian Quarterly,* IV:4 October, 1895, 73-85.

53   Harrell, *Sources*, 71.

54   *Kansas City Times*, Vol. 83: Issue 311, December 28, 1920, 3.

55   Robertson MS, 1931, 4.

56   Combs, George Hamilton. *I'd Take This Way Again: An Autobiography*, The Bethany Press, 1944, 27.

57   Ibid,. 68.

58   "Are Churches Failing?" *Collier's, The National Weekly.* 49:1 March 21, 1912, 26.

59   Macfarlane, Peter Clark. "George Hamilton Combs," *Collier's, The National Weekly,* 49:4 13 April 1912, 14-15.

60   According to R. E. Robertson, the committee included Frank Gentry, Bert Steeper, Mrs. McDaniel, Mrs. Herschel Caton, Robert Stone, and Robertson. Robertson MS.

61   Combs, 125.

62   Cummins, 160. Long's contributions to the development of the Disciples are noted in a number of places.

63   *The Kansas City Star.* July 10, 1919, 2.

64   Waldron, Charles K. undated MS, Church Archives, Box 14.

65   Woodbury, Sybil Sweet. MS, 1982, Church archives, Box 14.

66   Robertson, 12.

67   Robertson, 14.

68   Combs, 127

69   *The Kansas City Star.* April 16, 1921, 7.

70   Jenkins, MS, 2

71   Morton, LaDene, "Camp Nichols — Soldiers, Sinners and Spies in World War I." KC Backstories.com. April 14, 2017.

72 Combs, 129.

73 "Interchurch World Movement," entry in *Collier's New Encyclopedia. P.F. Collier & Son.* 1921. See also Eldon G. Ernst, "The Interchurch World Movement and the Great Steel Strike of 1919-1920, *Church History*, 39:2, June 1970 212-223.

74 Combs, 103, 105.

75 Davis, Christy. "Almost Famous: The 'Other' Root Brother and His Humble Design." *Kansas Preservation.* Vol 26: No. 1, January-February 2004, 3-5 (see page 5 for a list of his buildings). https://www.kshs.org/resource/ks_preservation/kpjanfeb04.pdf.

76 Cupp Memoirs, MS; and *The Christian*, December 4, 1947, 7.

77 Kilde, Jean Halgren. *When Church Became Theatre: The Transformation of Evangelical Architecture and Worship in Nineteenth Century America.* Oxford University Press, 2002.

78 Ibid., 11.

79 Ibid., 132.

80 There is a vast literature on this topic. Some useful references include Clark, Clifford Edward, Jr. *The American Family Home: 1800-1960*, University of N. Carolina Press, 1986. Harvey Green, *The Light of the Home: an Intimate View of the Lives of Women in Victorian America,* Pantheon, 1983.

81 Kilde, 198.

82 Ibid. 209, drawing on the writing of Richard H. Ritter, *The Arts of the Church.* Pilgrim Press, 1947.

83 Combs, 208-209.

84 See Ogasapian, John, and N. Lee Orr; Chapter 4: "Church Music," in *Music of the Gilded Age*, Greenwood Press, 2007.

85 Stein, Samuel. "The Weekly Duplex Envelope System, The Best," excerpt from *A Guide to Church Finance*, 1920. Online at *The Material History of American Religion Project,* https://www.materialreligion.org/documents; see also James Hudnut-Beumler. "Technique: Every Member Canvasses, Pledge Cards, and the Divided Envelope, 102-110 in *In Pursuit of the Almighty's Dollar: A History of Money and American Protestantism*, University of N. Carolina Press, 2007.

86 "The Duplex Envelope and Weekly Offering," *American Home Missionary*, Vol. XVIII, No. 5, May, 1912, 335.

87 Robertson MS 16-17.

88 Waldron MS.

89 Robertson, MS, 18.

90 Cupp Jenkins MS

91 The Tabernacle Church was replaced in 1942 and renamed First Christian Church. The building was designed by Eliel Saarinen, and the interiors were completed by his son Eero Saarinen and Charles Eames. The building is one of a number of important structures in Columbus, a small town now known internationally for its major 20th century architectural designs.

92 Reeves, Robert Earl. *A Biography of Z.T. Sweeney.* Master's Thesis, Butler University, 1959, 130. https://www.thechristianrepository.com/uploads/8/7/0/0/87007510/robert_e_reeves_-a_biography_of_z_t_sweeney.pdf.

93 Ibid., 93.

94 John Kern, "From Correspondents , 11 *Christian Standard*, 23 December 1871, 407

95 Reeves, 136

96 Haynes, 606.

97 Jenkins

98 Combs, *I'd Take This Way*, 131.

99 Ibid., 131-132.

100 Ibid., 130.

101 Davison, Lisa W. "Educational Ministry," in *The Encyclopedia of the Stone Campbell Movement*. Douglas A. Foster, et. Al. *The encyclopedia of the Stone-Campbell Movement*, Wm.B. Erdmans, 2004, 291-292.

102 *The Kansas City Star*. August 12, 1922, 7.

103 Rains, Paul B. *Francis Marion Rains*. St. Louis: Christian Board of Publication, 1922, 100.

104 For a contemporaneous report see, Cope, Henry F. "Week-day Religious Education: A Survey and Discussion of Activities and Problems." The Religious Education Association. NY: George H. Doran, 1922.

105 Rains, Paul B. "Week Day Schools of Religious Education in Country Club District," printed report, c. 1925, CCCC Archives.

106 Robertson MS

107 Ibid, 128-129.

108 Cruea, Susan. "Changing Ideals of Womanhood During the Nineteenth-Century Woman Movement," *General Studies Writing Faculty Publications*. I. 2005, 190.

109 Wharton, Nettie S. "The Historical Record of the Beginning of the Work of The Country Club Christian Church and of the Organization of The Women's Council." November 21, 1923. MS, CCCC Archives.

110 *The New York Times*, April 16, 1901.

111 Croly, Jennie Cunningham. "Preface," *The History of the Woman's Club Movement in America*, Council of the General Federation of Woman's Clubs of America. 1898.

112 Ibid., 755.

113 Hull, Debra. *Christian Church Women*, Chalice Press. 1994, 4.

114 Errett, Isaac. Quoted in Rains, 155.

115 Rains, 156.

116 Lollis, Lorraine. *The Shape of Adam's Rib,* Bethany Press, 1970, 42

117 Long, Loretta, "Christian Church/Disciples of Christ Tradition and Women" in Rosemary Skinner Keller and Rosemary Radford Ruether, eds., Marie Cantlon, assoc. ed. *Encyclopedia of Women and Religion in North America. 2006,* 302.

118 Peters, 100.

119 Ibid., 102-103.

120 Lester, Hiram J. and Marjorie Lee. *Inasmuch: The Saga of NBA*. NBA, 1987, 21. This is the most complete history of the NBA, available online, https://fliphtml5.com/iqhg/dtcxs.

121 Ibid., 24.

122   Ibid., 31.

123   Lester and Lester, 33.

124   Ibid., 38.

125   Ibid., 40.

126   Ibid., 55.

127   *The Kansas City Star*, 8 April 1910, Vol.73, No.84, 8.

128   Ibid., 7 April, 1910, Vol. 73, #83, 1.

129   *The Philanthropist*, 1917, Vol. 24, 8.

130   *The Philanthropist*, 1917, Vol. 24, 8.

131   *American Home Missionary*

132   Nomination to the National Register of Historic Places, Christian Church Hospital, Kansas City, Missouri, prepared by Mark Miller, 2004 Sec. 8, 8. For a thorough discussion of General Hospital No. 2, see Jason Roe, "As Good as Money Could Buy," Diane Mutti-Burke, Jason Roe, and John Herron, eds. *Wide-Open Town: Kansas City in the Pendergast Era*. University Press of Kansas, 2018, 196-215.

133   *The Christian Philanthropist,* October, 1918, XXV:4, 128.

134   "Hospital's Fate in Doubt," *The Kansas City Star*, February 6, 1926, 1.

135   Foster, 303.

136   Wharton, MS, 3.

137   Carver, Frances Grace, and Cynthia Cornell Novack. "Same Faith, Different Fates: Culturally Defined Answers to the 'Women's Question' in Disciples of Christ and Church of Christ Movements*", Leaven*. 7:4, 2. Online at http://digital commons.pepperdine.edu/leaven

138   Two excellent sources on women's activism in Kansas City in the first half of the 20th century are: Kay Barnes, "Civic Housekeepers: Women's Organizations, Civic Reform, and the 1940 Elections," online at the Kansas City Public Library's site *The Pendergast Years*, https://pendergast.org.; and K. David Hanzlick's chapter, "Morally and Legally Entitled: Women's Political Activism in Kansas City," in Mutti-Burke, Roe, and Herron, eds. *Wide-Open Town,* 157-177.

139   Russ Huff, MS, CCCC Archives, 1.

140   "Congregational Ministries," *The Design for the Christian Church (Disciples of Christ)* Produced by the Office of General Minister and President, Revision Approved by the General Assembly of the Christian Church (Disciples of Christ), July 2017, Section 8. Online at https://disciples.org>our-identity>the-design

141   Paulsell, William O. *The Disciples of Christ and the Great Depression 1929-1936.* Diss. Vanderbilt University, 1965, 170,

142   Merrill, J.L. "The Bible and the American Temperance Movement," *The Harvard Theologica Review.* 81:2 (April 1988) 164, citing Campbell, "Temperance Associations," *Millennial Harbinger*, 6:9, (September 1835), 392.

143   Ibid.

144   Nickelson, Chesla. "Disciples Women: History Nuggets," *Women's Ministries Disciples of Christ;* discipleshomemissions.org.

145   Harrington, Luke T. "How Methodists Invented Your Kid's Grape Juice Sugar High," *Christianity Today*, September 16, 2016.

146   *The Kansas City Star*. July 3, 1923, 2

147   Ibid., September 17, 1923, 1.

148   Ibid., September 19, 1923, 1.

149   *The Kansas City Star*. October 15, 1925, 1.

150   Reddig, William M. *Tom's Town: Kansas City and the Pendergast Legend*. 1947, 121-122. Combs, Jr. did not run for a second term. He moved to New York, where he continued to be active in Democratic politics and had several government appointments under FDR. He was a war correspondent during WWII and continued in a career as a respected news analyst and commentator until 1971. He died in 1977.

151   Pasly, Jeffrey L., "Big Deal in Little Tammany: Kansas City, the Pendergast Machine, and the Liberal Transformation of the Democratic Party," Ch. 2 in Mutti-Burke, et.al.

152   Butler, Jon. "Introduction to a Forum on American Religion and the Great Depression," *Church History*, 80:3 (September 2011), 578.

153   Reddig, 189.

154   *The Kansas City Star,* January 23, 1924, 1.

155   *The Kansas City Journal Post*, February 21, 1938. His column was syndicated and appeared widely throughout the country.

156   "Rabbi Conducting One-Man War on Mighty Pendergast Machine," *The St. Louis Star and Times*, June 6, 1932, 2.

157   Reddig, 189.

158   Mayerberg, Samuel S. *Chronicle of an American Crusader*. 1944, excerpted in Edwin Gaustand and Mark A. Noll, eds. *A Documentary History of American Religion Since 1877*. 3rd ed. 2003, 99.

159   *The St. Louis Star and Times*, June 6, 1932, 2.

160   Combs, 150.

161   Roe, Jason. "Thomas Joseph Pendergast," *The Pendergast Years: Kansas City in the Jazz Age & Great Depression*, https://pendergastkc.org/article/biography/ pendergast-thomas-joseph

162   Handy, Robert. "The American Religious Depression, 1925-1935," *Church History*, 29:1, March, 1960, 2-16.

163   "News of the Churches," *The Christian Century*, XXXVI:12; March 20, 1919, 22.

164   Handy, 7-8.

165   Butler, 577.

166   Handy, 5. Quoting *Home Missions Council Annual Report ... 1928,* 80.

167   This is a very simplified outline of the history of mission organization in the DOC. Many other entities, including the NBA contributed to the evolution of mission practices over the years.

168   Cummins, D. Duane. *A Handbook for Today's Disciples*, Chalice Press, 2010, 52.

169   Harrison, Stephen. *Communism and Christianity: Missionaries and the Communist Seizure of Power in China*. Diss., Vanderbilt University, 2013. Harrison's discussion of missionary activity in the inter-war years is outstanding, particularly the role of women, but unfortunately lacks attention to the presence of the Disciples, which he identifies simply as a "small, liberal denomination." (99)

170 Handy, 4; citing Stanley High, "The Need for Youth," in Leslie B. Moss, ed., *The Foreign Missions Conference of North America, 1929* (New York: Foreign Missions Conference, 1929), 152.

171 Her father was O. W. Lawrence; he was active in several Rock Island County, Illinois churches.

172 A number of accounts including official UCMS reports as well as missionary memoirs document Margaret Lawrence's years in China: Ely, Lois Anna. *Disciples of Christ in China*. Indianapolis, 1948. 43, 46, 52; Gish, Edna Whipple. *My Missionary Life*. c.1987. 15, 20, 25, 28; UCMS. *They Went to China: Biographies of Missionaries of the Disciples of Christ*, 1948. 78, 81-82.

173 Jay Wooldridge "History Moment" description, Minutes of the Board, 14 November 1995, 1.

174 Ellwood, Robert S. *The Fifties Spiritual Marketplace: American Religion in a Decade of Conflict*. Rutgers, 1997, 144.

175 Paulsell, 3

176 Ibid., 4.

177 Ibid., 268

178 Ibid., 296

179 Abrams, Ray H. "The Churches and the Clergy in World War II." *The Annals of the American Academy of Political and Social Science* 256 (1948), 110-119.

180 Hover, Gene and Fran. "The Class Welfare Program." MS, Church Archives, Tri C's box.

181 https://www.weekofcompassion.org/mission.html

182 Madigan, Tim. "Their War Ended 70 Years Ago. Their Trauma Didn't." *Washington Post Opinions*. 9/11/2015; 1; online at https://www.washingtonpost.com>opinions>2015/9/11.

183 Ibid.,6.

184 Ibid., 227, quoting Thomas Childers, *Soldier from the War Returning: The Greatest Generations' Troubled Homecoming from World War II*. Boston: Houghton Mifflin Harcourt, 2009, 5.

185 Country Club Christian Church Elders Notebook, August 15 – December 4, 1949

186 Walters, Kevin L. *Beyond the Battle: Religion and American Troops in World War II*. Diss. University of Kentucky, 2013, Abstract.

187 McAllister, and pp. 411-413, 420.

188 *Biblical Lore in Sun-lit Artistry: The Beautiful Windows of Country Club Christian Church*.1987

189 Roe, Jason. "Wight & Wight Architects," *The Pendergast Years*. The Kansas City Public Library. https://pendergastkc.org/article/buildings-orgs/wight-wight-architects

190 "The Story of the Chalice Logo," https://disciples.org/wp-content/uuploads/2013/06/TheStoryoftheChalice Logo-2015.pdf

191 Taylor, Richard. *How to Read a Church: A Guide to Symbols and Images in Churches and Cathedrals*. Hidden Spring (Paulist Press), 2003, 101-103.

192 Huff, Russ, Typed MS, Church Archives, written in 1992. (While the exact phrasing in the Report is slightly different, the vocabulary and meaning are the same.)

193 "Proceedings", 42.

194 Briggs, Ethel. MS scrapbook and typed history of the choir 1921-1981. CCCC Archives.

195 Turner, Nancy M., "The *Chalice Hymnal*: Broken Bread — One Body," *The Hymn: A Journal of Congregational Song* 48:1, 1997, 33-38. The discussion that follows is drawn from this article.

196 Ellwood, Robert S. *The Fifties Spiritual Marketplace: American Religion in a Decade of Conflict*. Rutgers, 1997, 16.

197 Ibid., vii.

198 Wittner, Lawrence S. "MacArthur and the Missionaries: God and Man in Occupied Japan." *Pacific Historical Review*, Vol. 40, No. 1, February 1971, 80, 82.

199 Leathers, Thomas D. "Unity of Protestant Denominations the Goal of a Dynamic Churchman," *The Kansas City Star*, October 30, 1948, 12.

200 O'Hara's letter is in the *The Kansas City Star*, November 1, 1948. 1. The Park College letter: Woodbridge O. Johnson, Jr, *KC Star*, November 6, 1948, 12.

201 There is an extensive literature on this topic. See for example: Lahr, Angela. "The Censure of a Bishop: Church and State in the McCarthy Era," *Methodist History*, 44:1, October 2005; Sarah Barringer Gordon, "'Free' Religion and 'Captive' Schools: Protestants, Catholics, and Education, 1945-1965," *DePaul Law Review*, 56:4, 2007; Robert Moats Miller, *Bishop B. Bromley Oxnam: Paladin of Liberal Protestantism*, Abingdon Press, 1990.

202 Report of the Organization Study Committee to the Official Board. Country Club Christian Church, November 1959, 1. Unless otherwise noted the following discussion is drawn from this report.

203 Cummins, D. Duane. *Struggle*, 158-159. A lively contemporary account of the Dyes in Bolenge, written in the patronizing language typical of the times: 'Witch Doctor' Will Preach at Christian Church Tonight," *The Morning Press (*Santa Barbara, California) February 4, 1909, can be found online at https://cdnc.ucr.edu/?a=d&d=VPN19430325.2.24&srpos=2&e=-------en--20--1--txt-txIN--------1

204 Ellwood, *Sixties Spiritual Awakening: American Religion Moving from Modern to Postmodern*. Rutgers, 1994.

205 Ibid., 51

206 Ibid., 146

207 Ibid. There is a large literature devoted to examining the history and meaning of the servant church in the '60s. Ellwood's entire book is useful; pages 145-151 focus specifically on the topic. In 1964 *TIME* Magazine's lengthy cover story, "The Servant Church," provides a contemporaneous discussion. Dulles, Avery. *Models of the Church*. Ireland: Image Books, 1987; his six "models" are readily available in online formats. The Anglican priest, Kenneth Leech, who served in the slums of London, used the term regularly in his writings. Several sources on the servant church in Canada are also helpful: Gardner, Philip Alan Tennant, "A Holy or a Broken Hallelujah: The United Church of Canada in the 1960s Decade of Ferment," diss. University of Toronto, 2018; Miedema, Gary. *For Canada's Sake: Public Religion, centennial Celebrations, and the Re-making of Canada in the 1960s*. McGill, 2005.

208 Findlay, James F. Jr. *Church People in the Struggle: The National Council of Churches and the Black Freedome Movement, 1950-1970*. Oxford University Press, 1993, 121.

209 *The Listener* (a radio magazine), BBC, March 20, 1967, as quoted in Gardner.

210 Hutchinson, Van William, *Greater Kansas City and the Urban Crisis*: 1830-1968, Diss. Kansas State University, 2013, Urban Crisis, 331.

211 Cummins, 188

212 "Saluting 100 Years of Bridge Building," *The Kansas City Star*, October 11, 1998, 144; Obituary, *KC Star*, December 17, 2000, 38. Southern Christian Institute became part of Tougaloo, a Historically Black College that exists to this day. West Paseo eventually merged with Swope Park Christian Church.

213 Cummins, 192. See his section on African-American Disciples, 186-193.

214 Hutchinson, 112.

215 Ibid., 224.

216 Findlay, 6.

217 Ibid., 4, 13.

218 Schirmer, Sherry Lamb. *A City Divided: The Racial Landscape of Kansas City, 1900-1960*. University of Missouri Press, 2002. In addition to Hutchinson and Schirmer see also Gotham, Kevin Fox. *Race, Real Estate, and Uneven Development: The Kansas City Experience, 1900-2000*; State University of New York Press, 2002; Owen, Lance. *Beautiful and Damned: Geographies of Interwar Kansas City*. diss. University of California Berkeley, 2016; and Colby, Tanner. Part 2: "Planning for Permanence," in *Some of My Best Friends are Black: The Strange Story of Integration in America*," Penguin, 2012, 73-140.

219 "Ministerial Alliance Urges Lifting Segregation at Benton School," *The Kansas City Star*, November 12, 1952, 3.

220 Hutchinson, 267.

221 "Air Force Training Manual Draws NCC Fire," *Christianity Today*, February 29, 1960, 29. See also *Intermediate Report of the Committee on Government Operations*, Issues 13-24, United States Congress House Committee on Government Operations, U.S. Government Printing Office, 1960, 87-89.

222 Findlay, 28

223 *The Kansas City Times*, "Dr. King Asks Morality Rule," November 5, 1962, 1, 15. Dr. King delivered this address on numerous other occasions; several presentations can be found online on YouTube, as well as in written format.

224 Findlay, 61.

225 "Kansas City Bill on Rights Fought," *The New York Times,* March 22, 1964, 50.

226 "Close Race Bill Victory," *The Kansas City Times,* April 8, 1964, 1, 6.

227 Johnson, James M. "Experimentation Enlivens a Church," *Kansas City Times*, April 16, 1964, 18.

228 Ibid.

229 Ellwood, *Sixties*, 118.

230 Marty, Martin E. "Meanwhile, back at the Protestant Ranch," *National Catholic Reporter*, Vol. 2: No. 10, January 5, 1966, 8.

231 Ellwood, Sixties, 115.

232 Marty. All quotations are taken directly from the original article in *National Catholic Quarterly.*

233 Fly, David K. "Reflections on the Kansas City Riot of 1968," Video Transcript on file at the Missouri State Archives, https://www.sos.mo.gov/archives/presentations/ap_transcripts/kcriot; see also Fly's article "An Episcopal Priest's Reflections on the Kansas City Riot of 1968," *Missouri Historical Review*, 100:2, 103-112.

234 Rhodes, Joel. "It Finally Happened Here: The 1968 Riot in Kansas City, Missouri," *Missouri Historical Review, 91:3, April 1997, 295-315.*

235 Ibid., 298.

236 "Civic Leaders, Friends Honor Ilus Davis," *The Kansas City Star,* September 7, 1996, 27.

237 Fly, (MHR), 110.

238 *The Kansas City Star,* August 6, 1997, 11.

239 Trillin, Calvin. "I Got Nothing Against the Colored," *The New Yorker*, May 11, 1968, 107-114.

240 Begel, Deborah, "A Remembrance — Assassination of Rev. Dr. Martin Luther King," online at https://www.santafenewmexican.com/opinion/my_view/a-remembrance-assassination-rev-dr-martin-luther-king/article_

241 Report of the National Advisory Commission On Civil Disorders. [Washington: United States, Kerner Commission; U.S. G.P.O., 1968. See also a recent and quite useful article: Alice George, "The 1968 Kerner Commission Got It Right," But Nobody Listened, *Smithsonian Magazine*, March 1 2018; online at smithsonianmagazine.com.

242 Hutchinson, 312.

243 Ibid. 315

244 The full poem can be found at: Hughes, Langston. "Aunt Sue's Stories." *The Collected Poems of Langston Hughes,* edited by Arnold Rampersad, Knopf, 2004, 23.

245 *The Kansas City Times*, May 28, 1966, 1.

246 Toulouse, Mark. "Days of Protest: The *Century* and the War in Vietnam," *The Christian Century* 8 November 2000.

247 *The Kansas City Times*, January 6, 1968, 42; *The Christian*, February 7, 1968.

248 Cummins, *Struggle*, 206. His full discussion is covered in pages 204-225. See also McAllister & Tucker, Ch. 18; and Charles M. Bunce, "The 'Christian Churches' Become a 'Church'". *Christian Century*, 13:2, October 25, 1968, 41-45.

249 Cummins, *Struggle* 208, 211, 217, 220, 223.

250 *The Kansas City Star*, September 29, 1968, 38, 45.

251 *The Kansas City Star*, September 30, 1968, 3.

252 Findlay, 188, 189, 202

253 Ibid., 203.

254 *The Kansas City Times*, May 27, 1969, 6.

255 *The Kansas City Star*, August 23, 1969, 3.

256 Ibid.

257 Cardwell and Fox, 126. Cardwell, Brenda M. and William K. Fox. *Journey toward Wholeness: A History of Black Disciples of Christ in the Mission of the Church.* National Convocation of the Christian Church (Disciples of Christ), 1990, 126.

258 Interview with Dr. Milburn Hobson, conducted by Jim Fitzpatrick, November 16, 2019.

259 *The Kansas City Times*, September 18, 1978, 16.

260 *The Kansas City Times*, November 7, 1987, 66.

261 *Mid-Stream: An Ecumenical Journal.* XXVI:3, July 1987, "Working Papers from a Conference on 'Reappraising the Disciples Tradition in the 21st Century,'" Council on Christian Unity.

262 Cueni, R. Robert. *Public Housing Resident to Seminary President.* Lucas Park Books, 2013, 114.

263 Ibid., 60.

264 Ibid., 116-118.

265 "Future Focus Committee Report," May 14, 1996, attached to Board Minutes, May 1996.

266 *The Christian*, December 7, 1994, 3 quoting form an earlier issue, January 17, 1968. The book Dr. Cueni wrote based on his sabbatical research was titled *Dinosaur Heart Transplants: Keys to Renewing a Mainline Church.* Abingdon Press, 2000.

267 "Communication Ministries," January 15, 2002, https://archive.wfn.org/2002/01/msg00077.html

Works Cited

Primary Sources in the Archives or Country Club Christian Church Interviews
Mr. Max Deweese
Mr. Tom Van Dyke
Dr. George Gordon
Dr. Milburn Hobson
Dr. Paul Koontz
Dr. William Shoop
Mrs. Mary Jean Shoop
Tri C's members: Mrs. Carol Duncan, Mrs. Dottie Lambert
Mrs. Cara Louise "Cokie" Stafer
Mrs. Virginia Watson

Memoirs

Jenkins, Marjorie Cupp. Several versions of her memories of growing up and leadership roles in the Church, 1980s. MSs, Archives.
Huff, Russell. Memoir, nd., MS, Archive.
Waldron, Charles. Memoir, nd, Archive.
Wharton, Nettie S. "The Historical Record of the Beginning of the Work of The Country Club Christian Church and of the Organization of The Women's Council." November 21, 1923. MS, CCCC Archives

Records and Documents

Minutes of the Board, 1921-present. Archives
The Christian (newsletter) 1926-present. Archives and on CCCC website.
Miscellaneous Records and Minutes of the Board of Elders, Christian Women's Fellowship (CWF), Women's Circles, Sunday School Classes
Rains, Paul B. "Week Day Schools of Religious Education in Country Club District," printed report, c. 1925, CCCC Archives.

SECONDARY SOURCES: BOOKS, PERIODICALS, CONTEMPORARY NEWSPAPERS

Books

Butler, Ovid. "Is Slavery Sinful?" in Jeremiah Smith. Being Partial Discussions of the Proposition Slavery is Sinful. Indianapolis, 1868.

Cardwell, Brenda M. and William K. Fox. Journey toward Wholeness: A History of Black Disciples of Christ in the Mission of the Church. National Convocation of the Christian Church (Disciples of Christ), 1990.

Combs, George Hamilton. I'd Take This Way Again: An Autobiography. The Bethany Press, 1944.

Croly, Jennie Cunningham. "Preface," The History of the Woman's Club Movement in America. Council of the General Federation of Woman's Clubs of America, 1898.

Cueni, R. Robert. Public Housing Resident to Seminary President. Lucas Park Books, 2013.

Cummins, D. Duane. The Disciples: A Struggle for Reformation. Chalice Press, 2009.

Cummins, D. Duane. A Handbook for Today's Disciples. Chalice Press, 2010.

Ellwood, Robert S. The Fifties Spiritual Marketplace: American Religion in a Decade of Conflict. Rutgers, 1997.

Ellwood, Sixties Spiritual Awakening: American Religion Moving from Modern to Postmodern. Rutgers, 1994.

Findlay, James F. Jr. Church People in the Struggle: The National Council of Churches and the Black Freedom Movement, 1950-1970. Oxford University Press, 1993.

Garrison, Winfred Ernest. An American Religious Movement: A Brief History of the Disciples of Christ. Bethany Press, 1945.

Garrison, Winfred Ernest, and Alfred E. DeGroot. The Disciples of Christ: A History. Bethany Press, 1964, rev. 1969.

Gaustad, Edwin and Mark A. Noll, eds. A Documentary History of American Religion Since 1877. 3rd ed. 2003.

Harrell, David Edwin, Jr. Quest for a Christian America, 1800-1865: A Social History of the Disciples of Christ. Vol. I, University of Alabama, 1966.

Harrell. Sources of Division in the Disciples of Christ, 1865-1900: A Social History of the Disciples of Christ, Vol. II, University of Alabama, 1973.

Haynes, Nathaniel Smith. History of the Disciples of Christ in Illinois, 1819-1914. Standard Publishing Company, 1915.

Hudnut-Beumler, James. "Technique: Every Member Canvasses, Pledge Cards, and the Divided Envelope, pp. 102-10 in In Pursuit of the Almighty's Dollar: A History of Money and American Protestantism. University of N. Carolina Press, 2007.

Hull, Debra. Christian Church Women, Chalice Press. 1994.

Kilde, Jean Halgren. When Church Became Theatre: The Transformation of Evangelical Architecture and Worship in Nineteenth Century America. Oxford University Press, 2002.

Lester, Hiram J. and Marjorie Lee. Inasmuch: The Saga of NBA. NBA, 1987, 21. history.nbacares.org/wp-content/uploads/2017/02/inasmuch-the-saga-of-nba.pdf

Lollis, Lorraine. The Shape of Adam's Rib, Bethany Press, 1970.

The Material History of American Religion Project. materialreligion.org/

Maxwell, William. Ancestors. Knopf, 1971.

McAllister, Lester G. and William E. Tucker. Journey in Faith: A History of the Christian Church (Disciples of Christ). Bethany Press (Chalice Press), 1975.

Morton, LaDene. The Brookside Story: Shops of Every Necessary Character. The History Press, 2010.

Mutti-Burke, Diane, Jason Roe, and John Herron, eds. Wide-Open Town: Kansas City in the Pendergast Era. University Press of Kansas, 2018.

Ogasapian, John, and N. Lee Orr; Chapter 4: "Church Music," in Music of the Gilded Age, Greenwood Press, 2007.

Pearson, Robert, and Brad Pearson. The J. C. Nichols Chronicle: The Authorized Story of the Man and His Company, 1880-1994. Country Club Plaza Press, 1994.

Peters, George L. The Disciples of Christ in Missouri: One Hundred Years of Co-operative Work. Centennial Commission of the Missouri Convention of the Disciples of Christ. 1937.

Rains, Paul Boyd. Francis Marion Bains, St. Louis, Christian Board of Publication, 1922,156. eBook: https://www.worldcat.org/title/francis-marion-rains/ oclc/1045624161

Reddig, William M. Tom's Town: Kansas City and the Pendergast Legend, J. B. Lippincott, 1947.

Richardson, Robert. Memoirs of Alexander Campbell, Vol.2. 1870.

Schirmer, Sherry Lamb. A City Divided: The Racial Landscape of Kansas City, 1900-1960. University of Missouri Press, 2002.

Taylor, Richard. How to Read a Church: A Guide to Symbols and Images in Churches and Cathedrals. Hidden Spring (Paulist Press), 2003.

Trollope, Frances. Domestic Manners of Americans. London and New York, 4th ed., 1832.

Weisberger, Bernard A. They Gathered at the River: The Story of the Great Revivalists and Their Impact Upon American Religion. Little, Brown, 1958.

Worley, William. J. C. Nichols and the Shaping of Kansas City: Innovation in Planned Residential Communities. University of Missouri Press, 1990.

Articles

Abrams, Ray H. "The Churches and the Clergy in World War II." The Annals of the American Academy of Political and Social Science 256 (1948), 110-19.

"Are Churches Failing?" Collier's, The National Weekly. 49:1, March 21, 1912, 26.

Austin, Thad S. "A Prelude to Civil War: The Religious Nonprofit Sector as a Civil Means of Debate over Slavery, Christian Higher Education, and Religious Philanthropy in the Stone-Campbell Movement." Religions September 8, 2018, 235. Crossref. Web. http://dx.doi.org/10.3390/rel9080235

Barnes, Kay "Civic Housekeepers: Women's Organizations, Civic Reform, and the 1940 Elections," https://pendergast.org.

Butler, Jon. "Introduction to a Forum on American Religion and the Great Depression," Special Issue of Church History, vol.80 no.3, September 2011, 575-78.https://doi.org/10.1017/S0009640711000631

Carver, Frances Grace, and Cynthia Cornell Novack. "Same Faith, Different Fates: Culturally Defined Answers to the 'Women's Question' in Disciples of Christ and Church of Christ Movements", Leaven. 7:4, 2. https://digitalcommons.pepperdine.edu/leaven

The Christian Century, Vol 35, August 8, 1918, 22

"Congregational Ministries," The Design for the Christian Church (Disciples of Christ) Produced by the Office of General Minister and President, Revision Approved by the General Assembly of the Christian Church (Disciples of Christ), July 2017, Section 8. https://disciples.org>our-identity>the-design

Cruea, Susan. "Changing Ideals of Womanhood During the Nineteenth-Century Woman Movement," General Studies Writing Faculty Publications. I. 2005. https://scholarworks.bgsu.edu/cgi/viewcontent.cgi?article=1000&context=gsw_pub

Davis, Christy. "Almost Famous: The 'Other' Root Brother and His Humble Design." Kansas Preservation. Vol 26: No. 1, January-February 2004, 3-5 (see page 5 for a list of his buildings). https://www.kshs.org/resource/ks_preservation/kpjanfeb04.pdf

Davison, Lisa W. "Educational Ministry," in The Encyclopedia of the Stone Campbell Movement. Douglas A. Foster, et. Al. The encyclopedia of the Stone-Campbell Movement, Wm.B. Erdmans, 2004, 291-292.

"Well-Known City Leader Called to Another City," The Christian Century, vol.28, no.6 January 1921, 24.

Begel, Deborah, "A Remembrance – Assassination of Rev. Dr. Martin Luther King," April 7, 2018. https://www.santafenewmexican.com/opinion/my_view/a-remembrance-assassination-of-rev-dr-martin-luther-king/article_90fb694c-e1c5-5b8c-b2e5-e7bc024607e4.html

"Notes of Incidents in a Tour," Millennial Harbinger. Series IV, Vol. III, No.11, February 1853, 73.

Campbell, Alexander. The Millennial Harbinger. Vol. IV, pp. 34-5 (or 157 for the full volume).

Dains, Mary K. "Alexander Campbell and the Missouri Disciples of Christ," Missouri Historical Review. 77, 1982, 13-46.

Ernst, Eldon G. "The Interchurch World Movement and the Great Steel Strike of 1919-1920, Church History, vol.39, no.2, June 1970, 212-23.

Fly, David K. "Reflections on the Kansas City Riot of 1968," Video Transcript on file at the Missouri State Archives, https://www.sos.mo.gov/archives/presentations/ap_transcripts/kcriot.

Fly, David K. "An Episcopal Priest's Reflections on the Kansas City Riot of 1968," Missouri Historical Review, 100:2, 103-12.

Handy, Robert. "The American Religious Depression, 1925-1935," Church History, vol. 29, no.1, March 1960, 2-16.

Harrell, David Edwin, Jr. "The American Myth and the Disciples of Christ in the Nineteenth Century," Agricultural History, vol.41, no.2, April, 1967, 181-192.

Harrell, David Edwin, Jr. "James Shannon; Preacher, Educator, and Fire Eater," Missouri Historical Review. Vol.63, np. 2 Jan. 1969, 135-70.

Harrington, Luke T. "How Methodists Invented Your Kid's Grape Juice Sugar High," Christianity Today, September 16, 2016.

Hughes, Langston. "Aunt Sue's Stories." The Collected Poems of Langston Hughes, edited by Arnold Rampersad, Knopf, 2004.

"Interchurch World Movement," entry in Collier's New Encyclopedia. P.F. Collier & Son. 1921.

Jenkins, Burris, "The Institutional Church," The New Christian Quarterly, vol. IV no.4, October 1895, 73-85.

Kern, John. "From Correspondents, 11 Christian Standard, December 23, 1871, p. 407.

Lard, Moses. "Can We Divide?" Lard's Quarterly 3 (reprint, Kansas City, Mo.: Old Paths Book Club, 1950, 330-36.

Long, Loretta, "Christian Church/Disciples of Christ Tradition and Women" in Rosemary Skinner Keller and Rosemary Radford Ruether, eds., Marie Cantlon, assoc. ed. Encyclopedia of Women and Religion in North America, Indiana University Press, 2006.

Macfarlane, Peter Clark. "George Hamilton Combs," Collier's, The National Weekly, vol.49 no.4, April 13, 1912, pp.14-15.

Madigan, Tim. "Their War Ended 70 Years Ago. Their Trauma Didn't." Washington Post Opinions. 9/11/2015; 1. https://www.washingtonpost.com>opinions>2015/9/11

Marty, Martin E. "Meanwhile, back at the Protestant Ranch," National Catholic Reporter, Vol. 2: No. 10, January 5, 1966

Merrill, J.L. "The Bible and the American Temperance Movement," The Harvard Theologica Review. Vol 81, no. 2, April 1988.

Morton, LaDene, "Camp Nichols – Soldiers, Sinners and Spies in World War I." KC Backstories.com. April 14, 2017.

Nickelson, Chesla. "Disciples Women: History Nuggets," Women's Ministries Disciples of Christ. discipleshomemissions.org

Rhodes, Joel. "It Finally Happened Here: The 1968 Riot in Kansas City, Missouri," Missouri Historical Review, vol.91, no.33, April 1997, 295-315.

Roe, Jason. "Wight& Wight Architects," The Pendergast Years. The Kansas City Public Library. https://pendergastkc.org/article/buildings-orgs/wight-wight-architects

Smith, Matthew D. "Barton Warren Stone: Revisiting Revival in the Early Republic," The Register of the Kentucky Historical Society. No.2, Spring 2013, 161-97.

Toulouse, Mark. "Days of Protest: The Century and the War in Vietnam," The Christian Century vol. 117, no. 31, November 8, 2000.

Trillin, Calvin. "I Got Nothing Against the Colored," The New Yorker, May 11, 1968, p. 107+

Turner, Nancy M., "The Chalice Hymnal: Broken Bread – One Body," The Hymn: A Journal of Congregational Song 48:1, 1997, pp. 33-38.

Webb, Henry E. "The Impact of the Civil War," "Leaven" vol.7, January 1, 1999, https://digitalcommons.pepperdine.edu/cgi/viewcontent. cgi?article=1623&context=leaven

Wittner, Lawrence S. "MacArthur and the Missionaries: God and Man in Occupied Japan." Pacific Historical Review, Vol. 40, No. 1, February 1971.

"Working Papers from a Conference on Reappraising the Disciples Tradition in the 21st Century" Mid-Stream: An Ecumenical Journal. Vol.XXVI:, no.3, July 1987, Council on Christian Unity.

Theses and Dissertations

Harrison, Stephen. Communism and Christianity: Missionaries and the Communist Seizure of Power in China. PhD. Dissertation, Vanderbilt University, 2013. https://ir.vanderbilt.edu/bitstream/handle/1803/14457/Harrison.pdf?sequence=1

Hutchinson, Van William, Greater Kansas City and the Urban Crisis: 1830-1968, PhD. Dissertation, Kansas State University, 2013. https://core.ac.uk/download/pdf/18529337.pdf

Paulsell, William O. The Disciples of Christ and the Great Depression 1929-1936, PhD. Dissertation, Vanderbilt University, 1965.

Reeves, Robert Earl. A Biography of Z.T. Sweeney. Master's Thesis, Butler University, 1959. https://www.thechristianrepository.com/uploads/8/7/0/0/87007510/robert_e_reeves_-a_biography_of_z_t_sweeney.pdf

Tuck, Darin. "The Battle Cry of Freedom: The Leadership of the Disciples of Christ Movement During the American Civil War, 1861-1865. MA Thesis, Kansas State University, 2010. https://krex.k-state.edu/dspace/bitstream/handle/2097/4218/DarinTuck2010.pdf?sequence=3&isAllowed=y

Newspapers

The Kansas City Journal Post
The Kansas City Star
The Kansas City Times
The New York Times
The St. Louis Star and Times

Index

Aday, Carla, 204, 215
    contributions to the text, viii
    forward, xiii–xiv
    with Marriage Enrichment program, 197
    with Singles Ministry, 200
    as Senior Minister, 217–18
African-American Churches in Kansas City, 65, 162–63, 167, 186
    Woodland Avenue Christian Church, 106, 162
    Swope Parkway United Christian Church, 198
Bacon, Langston, xix, 23–27, 30, 36, 40, 44–45, 66, 93
Bader, Jesse, 46–47
Bash, Lawrence, 150, 152–53, 156-59, 161, 166, 168–73
Bethany College, 7, 10–12, 195
Black Manifesto, 183–87
Blair, James, 186
Bowen, Frank, xv–xx 1, 16, 20, 26–27, 32, 66, 78, 83–84, 94, 105, 162
Bowen, Mary, xvii, 1
Brice, Eugene, 195–97, 199, 201–2, 205
Brooks, Alvin, 175, 177–78
Brookside Community Hall, xviii–xxi, 20, 57
Brookside Hotel, xix, 40, 68
Brookside Shopping Center, xviii, 221n8
Butler University (North West Christian University), 10–11, 43, 101
Campbell, Alexander, 2–5, 7–13, 47, 59, 74, 83, 131–32, 222n24,
Campbell, Thomas, 2–5, 9
Cane Ridge Revival, 4, 11
Chalice (symbol), 118, 123, 228n190
Chancel Renovation, 123–25, 128–29
Christian Church Hospital, 63–68,
Christian Women Board of Missions (CWBM), 59–61
Civil Rights, 145, 161–167, 230n208. *See also* Black Manifesto, African-American
    Churches in Kansas City, Civil War
Civil War, 10, 12-13, 16, 21, 28, 33-34, 57–59, 89, 162–63
Colorado Christian Camp, 200
Combs
Chapel, 157–59, 210
George Hamilton, xiii, 16–18, 20–27, 29–32, 36, 39, 42–47, 50–52, 54–56, 67–72,
    75–78, 80–82, 86, 90–95, 98–101, 105, 108, 115–16, 129–30, 141, 218, 220,
    223n56
George Hamilton JR., 76
Gladys Gwynne, 130, 159, 190

Martha Stapp, 64, 159

Robert Pryor, 159

Communion

  open and closed, 118

  token, 3

Communism, response to, 74–75

Connick, Charles T., 106, 114, 124

Country Club Plaza, xvi, 19, 26–27

COVID Pandemic, 218

Cueni, Robert R., xiii, 124, 197

Davis, Ilus, 79, 159, 172, 175–77

Declaration and address of the Christian Association of Washington, 2–4, 6

Ecumenism, 14, 47, 113, 131, 139, 158, 165–66, 168–71, 208

Experimental Worship Service (EWS) Class, 191–92, 218–20

Gothic Style (architecture), 33–36, 123, 170

Grafton, Warren, 35, 40, 101–8, 113, 117, 119–20, 123

Great Depression, 70–71, 73, 77–83, 87–88, 90–98, 227n152

GREAT START marriage program, 204, 217

Holy Week Protests, 169

Independence Boulevard Church, xix, 18, 20, 22–26, 34, 65, 82, 94, 115, 216

Institutional church, 17, 19

Irving, Junius, 32, 48–49, 106, 134

Jenkins, Marjorie Cupp, xix–xx, 28, 45–46, 54

Jenkins, Burris, 17–18, 45, 98

Kelley, Clarence, 168, 175–77, 184, 194

Last Supper Statue. *See* Zappia Sculpture

Lawrence, Margaret, 85–86, 89, 100, 137, 194

Liturgical Movement, 35–36

Long, R. A., 63–67, 97, 137, 182

Mayerberg, Samuel, 78–81, 141

Miles, R. Glen, 198, 209–17

The Millennial Harbinger, 7, 10, 12

Missions, 37–39, 59–62, 82–83, 97, 143–44. *See also* Christian Women Board of Missions

  domestic, 101, 161, 163

  international, 84–86, 95, 112–13

Modernism, 14

National Benevolent Association (NBA), 61–64

National Council of Churches, 135, 163–66, 171, 173, 180, 184–85

Nichols, J.C., xvii–xviii, xx, 27–32, 40, 134, 157, 221n6

Niemoeller, Martin, 169–70, 180

Organization Study Committee, 147–48, 153, 155

Organ (instrument), 60, 124, 128–30, 139, 190, 216

The Outreach Council, 154, 161, 168, 180, 187, 197–98

Owen-Campbell Debate, 8–9

Parking dispute and lawsuit, 206
Pastoral Counseling, 135, 154, 199
Pendergast, "Boss" Thomas, 70, 75–82, 141, 227n150, 227n151, 227n161
Race relations in Kansas City, vii, 163–167, 172–174, 183, 198. *See also* Black
    Manifesto, African-American Churches in Kansas City, Civil Rights
Rains, Francis Marion, xvi, 51, 60, 221n4
Rains, Paul, 50–52, 54, 90, 221n4
Red-lining and racial covenants, 164–66, 230n218
Restoration Movement, xvi, 1-4, 7, 12–13, 128, 131, 162
Restructure of the Disciples of Christ, 180–84, 186–87, 198
Scott, Walter, 2, 5
Servant Church, 160–62, 230n207,
Seven C's, 108–10
Shannon, James, 7
Slavery. *See* Civil War; African-American Churches in Kansas City
Snively, George, 44–46, 48, 51, 63
Social Gospel, 74, 93, 17–19, 62
Stained-glass windows, 35, 106, 114–16, 124, 216, 222n188
Stone, Barton, 2, 4–6, 11, 13, 71
Sweeney, Z.T., 42–44, 46, 48, 166
Tanner, Edward, 157
Tall Oaks Conference Center, 157
Temperance, 58, 62, 73–74
The Last Will and Testament of the Springfield Presbytery, 6
Tri C's (Country Club Couples), 104, 110, 112
Trollope, Frances, 8–9, 222n27
Vietnam, 106, 174, 177–80, 182, 192
Welch's Grape Juice, 74, 226n145
Wight & Wight architects, 115–16, 228n189
Women joining the Board, 56–62, 68–72, 149, 190
Women's Clubs in Kansas City, 59, 225n111
World Trade Center Attacks (9/11), 209
World War I, 20, 34, 59, 98, 110
World War II, 100, 123, 142, 161, 163, 228n179
Wyle, Ewart, 135, 139, 142–49, 157, 190–91
Zappia Sculpture, 124–25

About the Author

Dr. Linna Place is an American social and cultural historian. In her more than forty years of teaching at the University of Missouri-Kansas City she introduced courses on using material culture to understand and interpret the past that included a popular living history course taught at several of the important historic sites in the greater Kansas City area. She earned her Master's Degree in American folklife and material culture from the Cooperstown Graduate programs, and her doctorate in American Studies from the University of Kansas. Her research on religion in the 19th and early 20th century, women's history, and American folk art focuses on the intersection of social institutions with the social, cultural and economic events and issues of the time. She has lectured and consulted with numerous museums and cultural agencies throughout the region. Linna and her husband Craig and their three children are long-time members of Country Club Christian Church.

For more information about Country Club Christian Church visit us in person or on the web:

6101 Ward Parkway
Kansas City, MO 64113
816-333-4917
www.cccckc.org